Mediating Child Custody Disputes

A Systematic Guide
for Family Therapists,
Court Counselors,
Attorneys, and Judges

Donald T. Saposnek

Mediating
Child Custody Disputes

Jossey-Bass Publishers
San Francisco • Washington • London • 1983

MEDIATING CHILD CUSTODY DISPUTES
A Systematic Guide for Family Therapists, Court Counselors, Attorneys, and Judges
by Donald T. Saposnek

Library of Congress Cataloging in Publication Data

Saposnek, Donald T.
Mediating child custody disputes.

(The Jossey-Bass social and behavioral science series)
Bibliography: p. 313
Includes index.
1. Custody of children—United States. 2. Joint custody of children—United States. 3. Divorce mediation—United States. I. Title. II. Series.
[DNLM: 1. Child welfare. 2. Divorce. 3. Parent-child relations. WA 320 S241m]
KF547.S26 1983 346.7301′7 83-48163
ISBN 0-87589-582-4 347.30617

Manufactured in the United States of America

The paper in this book meets the guidelines for permanence and durabiluty of the Committee on Production Guidelines for Book Longevity of the Council on Library Resources.

JACKET DESIGN BY WILLI BAUM

FIRST EDITION

Code 8329

The Jossey-Bass
Social and Behavioral Science Series

For Donna and Sativa

Preface

This book was written to serve as a practical guide for professionals who want to learn to resolve custody disputes efficiently and effectively. The perspectives and techniques described here are useful to a wide range of practitioners who work with custody or visitation matters, including psychologists; social workers; marriage, family, and child counselors; child and family psychiatrists; family therapists and divorce counselors of every discipline; attorneys who practice family law and/or mediation; family and conciliation court counselors; and judges who deal with family law matters. This book will be of benefit to mediators specializing in financial aspects of divorce settlements as well as to those who deal only with custody and visitation matters. Much of the focus of this book is on the more difficult challenges encountered in mediation. It is my contention that when mediators are fully knowledgeable about, and have grappled with, the more difficult cases first, then they will be more comfortably prepared to undertake the easier ones.

Testifying in court as an expert witness in many custody battles during the years of my practice as a clinical-child psychologist has contributed to my increasing disenchantment with the adversarial approach to custody and visitation disputes. From the family systems point of view, which I espouse, it made little sense to justify to the court why one parent was better for the children than the other parent. The task seemed similar to arguing that the length of a rectangle was more important than the width in determining its area. Clearly, children need to experience *both* their parents as adequate rather than be confronted with critical evaluations of their parents' worthiness. Moreover, the inevitably bitter and stressful interactions among spouses, their attorneys, and their expert witnesses in the courtroom left me feeling increasingly frustrated and dissatisfied.

When longitudinal research studies of children of divorce (see summaries by Wallerstein and Kelly, 1980; Hetherington, 1981) demonstrated consistently that among the best predictors of good outcomes for children were regular and continuing contact with *both* parents and reduced interparental acrimony, I was one of many mental health professionals who became convinced that another approach to custody and visitation determinations was in order. What was needed was exactly the opposite of the adversarial approach. Consequently, in 1978 several colleagues and I began working informally with a small network of local attorneys to develop a mediation approach for resolving these disputes outside court. Within a year, the network had expanded to include a considerable number of interested attorneys in our community. Coincidentally, on January 1, 1981, three years after we independently developed and implemented an effective model, the "mandatory mediation law" went into effect in the state of California. This law requires mediation by either private or court-appointed mediators before any contested custody or visitation dispute comes before a judge. A number of other states have begun to develop custody and visitation mediation programs (Brown, 1982), and several states soon will be following California's lead in establishing mandatory mediation. Recognition of this powerful alternative to the traditional adversarial approach has indeed spread rapidly.

Nationally, during the past several years, awareness of the benefits of using mediation in divorce settlements has increased.

The mediators typically are therapists or lawyers who work alone or in therapist/lawyer teams to resolve every aspect of a divorce, including custody issues, spousal and child support issues, property settlement, and related tax issues. Because of the relatively recent development of divorce mediation, controversy reigns over a number of issues in this field. One particular question concerns the qualifications of lawyers versus therapists to handle divorce mediation work and whether this work demands the developed skills of *both* professions, necessitating mediation teams. At present, numerous short-term training workshops have been devised to meet the needs of professionals entering the mediation field, but there is pressing need for new academic programs that will offer extensive training and lead to certification in divorce and family mediation (see Brown, 1982). Certainly, given the complexities of financial issues in many divorce settlements, mediators need training to achieve expertise in legal and financial matters if they are to do justice to any couples they advise. Because even *lawyers* who are not specifically trained or experienced in family law may have difficulty dealing with legal and financial aspects of divorce settlements, formal training for mediators is strongly advocated. Moreover, nonlegal professionals who mediate the financial aspects of a divorce settlement may in fact be engaging in the unauthorized practice of law. In order to protect themselves against such allegations, most mediators, whether or not they are lawyers, request divorcing spouses to have their agreements reviewed by their respective attorneys before considering them final.

While these controversies continue, several books on divorce mediation have been published (for example, Coogler, 1978; Irving, 1980; Haynes, 1981). These books focus primarily on the financial and legal aspects of divorce settlement but are sparse in their treatment of custody and visitation issues. This book, however, presents a comprehensive and detailed model for custody and visitation mediation. Because of the complexities of such issues, as much expertise and skill are required in mediating custody and visitation matters as in mediating financial issues. Hence, the in-depth approach, perspectives, and techniques for successful custody mediation provided here will be of significant value to therapists, lawyers, and judges involved in this extremely sensitive, difficult process.

Chapter One presents an historic overview of the ways child custody and custody disputes have been conceptualized and dealt with in Western society. It is noteworthy that the need for changes in the traditional and legal approaches to custody determinations has arisen as a result of the relatively recent exponential increase in divorces, with the attendant increase in custody disputes. Such increases have revealed and highlighted the inadequacies of adversarial treatment of these issues. Chapter One also contains a review of literature concerning the needs of children and concludes with a comparison of the adversarial and mediational approaches to addressing these needs.

The difficulties and challenges of mediation work are examined in Chapter Two. Beginning and experienced mediators alike will no doubt recognize many of the dilemmas presented in this chapter. In addition to identifying the elements of mediation that are stressful for the mediator, Chapter Two describes attitudes and approaches that mediators can employ to cope effectively with the pressures inherent in this kind of work.

Because setting the context is of primary importance, all of Chapter Three is devoted to detailing how to prepare the spouses for the mediation process. After discussing how many, how long, and how often sessions are scheduled, how fees are set, and how relationships with attorneys are handled, this chapter tells how to explain the mediator's role and then presents a prescriptive, verbatim monologue for explaining to the spouses the benefits of mediation. A prescriptive monologue with commentary is then presented, detailing the explicit assumptions and ground rules that the mediator tells the spouses in beginning the mediation process. These explicit assumptions serve to pre-empt much of the spouses' resistance to the mediation process.

Chapter Four presents the three phases of mediation in detail. Specific guidance is given for gathering essential information both on the phone and in the first session, in the beginning phase of mediation. Then, details of the various co-parenting options available are presented for the middle phase of mediation. Included with this information are cautions for the mediator in developing co-parenting plans, suggestions for utilizing new language in discussing new co-parenting proposals, and an extensive section on when and how to interview children within the mediation process. Specific techniques are offered for structuring these interviews, building rapport, and utilizing the children's input. Finally, strategic ways for requesting proposals from the spouses are presented. For the ending phase of mediation, specific guidance is offered for strategically shaping the proposal, maintaining balance, and eliciting agreements. An examination is made of the "last issue"—that is, a typically trivial but symbolically important issue that occasionally deadlocks the negotiation process and frustrates the mediator.

Chapter Five concerns the construction of the final mediation agreement. The various sources of referral and the ways in which they determine the specific structure and formats of the agreement are detailed in this chapter. The specific content of the agreement includes the designation of legal custody, the regular time-sharing plan, the plan for sharing holidays and special days, the adjunct clauses for facilitating cooperative time sharing, and the plans for future modifications of the agreement. Finally, a discussion is presented of how financial issues may be linked with time-sharing plans.

Chapters Six through Nine elaborate the various strategies that participants use to maneuver each other through the custody dispute and mediation process. My basic premise is that people's attempts to influence each other are rooted in certain needs. Rather than try to determine *why* people have these needs (as the traditional psychotherapist is likely to do), the mediator observes *how* participants attempt to meet their needs and then initiates interventions designed to address those needs without obstructing mediation. The mediator may be able to help participants partially or wholly satisfy their needs; redirect them into therapy, where resolution may more appropriately take place; or encapsulate them enough to allow parenting negotiations to proceed to agreement without disruption. Very often obstructive needs can be set aside, if not satisfied, once a structured parenting agreement is developed.

The concept of strategies, as it is used here, derives from family systems theory, which has been developing in the field of family therapy over the past ten to fifteen years. According to this view, the family is conceptualized as a cybernetic system in which the actions of each member influence the actions of each other member reciprocally. This view has gradually replaced the traditional linear view of causality, and it is the conceptual basis for the mediation approach presented in this book.

Chapter Six elucidates nine strategies that children employ in their attempts to cope with their parents' divorce. One example is their use of *reuniting strategies,* which are innocent attempts to appeal to each parent to be drawn by need or attraction to the other and to reunite. Through such efforts, the child often becomes what I have called an *innocent but functional contributor* to the spousal conflict, since parents' frequent misinterpretations of their child's strategies regularly result in needless escalations of their custody battle. Among the factors motivating children's strategies are the need to reduce the distress of separation, to reduce tension in the family unit, and to protect their own and their parents' self-esteem.

Chapter Seven provides insights into thirty-one specific strategies that spouses use before, during, and sometimes even after mediation. These interactional maneuvers, regularly seen in mediation, usually take the form of indirect resistance, undertaken to satisfy a hidden personal agenda, often under the guise of "seeking what is in the best interests of the children." Among the many reasons spouses may employ maneuvering tactics are the needs or desires to reunite the family, to disengage emotionally, to ease feelings of distress over the family's breakup, to protect their financial status, and to assert power or seek revenge or retaliation. On occasion, strategies employed by one spouse may be complementary to strategies utilized by the other—all of which leads to very difficult challenges for the mediator and requires effective tools to facilitate the difficult negotiations that result.

Chapters Eight and Nine present twenty specific mediator interventions for facilitating the mediation process to a successful conclusion. Chapter Eight is devoted entirely to showing the mediator how to elicit cooperation between the spouses and how to reduce resistance to compromising and reaching agreements. The specific strategies presented are grounded solidly in the techniques of brief strategic therapy, which have proven extremely effective in reducing therapy clients' resistance to change. In Chapter Nine a wide array of specific interventions for dealing with conflict are examined. After a discussion of general aspects of conflict management, strategies to reduce or divert conflict and to break impasses are presented. These interventions are arranged sequentially, from the less potent to the maximally potent techniques. They derive both from brief strategic therapy methods and from insights this author has gained over a number of years of guiding couples through the mine fields of hostility toward compromise and agreement.

An analysis of the elements that contribute to the success or failure of mediation is presented in Chapters Ten and Eleven, along with five representative successful case studies and five representative unsuccessful ones. These are exemplary composite cases in which names, places, and identifying data were changed to protect the privacy of the clients. They range from relatively easy to extremely difficult cases and cover the wide gamut of variables that typically confront mediators. The unsuccessful cases are particularly illustrative of the limitations of mediation and are, consequently, quite humbling. In each case the reader is guided through detailed descriptions and analyses of the strategies used by each of the participants and the specific interventions used by the mediator to facilitate progress toward agreement, thus integrating and applying in a graphic manner the information presented in the earlier chapters. Moreover, each case study concludes with a one-year postmediation follow-up and mediator commentary about the case.

Chapter Twelve examines many of the special issues that arise in mediation. These include disputes exclusively over visitation, mediating custody when one parent moves far away, and the role of stepparents and grandparents in the mediation process. Also included are discussions of changing attitudes toward parents' sexual mores and behavior, including homosexuality; drug abuse; alcoholism; and domestic violence. Helpful perspectives and specific guidance are offered for appropriate mediator response to these diverse issues.

Chapter Thirteen presents various ethical and moral issues and values conflicts that regularly confront mediators. Included among these are the problem of mediator bias, issues of quality of parenting that arise when one or both parents manifest inadequate parenting abilities, the dilemmas of balancing fairness against feasibility in agreements, parents' rights versus children's rights and needs, individual parental "freedom" versus maintenance of family integrity, as well as other challenging family and social values conflicts. This chapter poses more questions than answers and, it is hoped, will help provoke critical thinking so necessary in new areas of social intervention.

A summary of this book's focus is presented in Chapter Fourteen. It highlights the ideal spirit of custody mediation and offers specific recommendations to mediators, attorneys, and judges for continued development of mediation work as a positive and effective alternative to adversarial approaches.

Finally, Appendixes A, B, and C provide the reader with the texts of California's statutes regarding joint custody, mandatory mediation, and family conciliation courts, respectively. Appendix D contains sample confidentiality forms for private and court-related mediation, and Appendix E offers four sample mediation agreements, which present a representative range of length, detail, and content typically developed in mediation.

Acknowledgments

I would like to express my deepest gratitude to my colleague Claire Delano, who originally prompted me to consider mediation as a rational alternative to court battles and who gave me the impetus to arrange the early meetings with attorneys to consider the mediation alternative. It is with her creative facilitation and continued support that our mediation work in the Family Mediation Service of Santa Cruz has blossomed as it has.

Special thanks go to Marsha Fox and Isidro Quiroga for their stimulating contributions to the early stages of this book's evolution and to Hila Michaelsen and Joanna Hamburg, who have been rich sources of ideas for the later formulations of this book.

I would also like to extend my respectful appreciation to the Santa Cruz County Superior Court judges Chris Cottle, Rollie Hall, and Donald May for their dedicated support of the family mediation program. I am especially indebted to Judge Harry Brauer of the Santa Cruz County Superior Court, for providing his support and his challenging legal perspectives that led to the clarification of many difficult issues involved in implementing our Family Mediation Service program. To the many attorneys of Santa Cruz County who have been willing to take a chance on a new approach, I extend sincere thanks.

My appreciation is extended to the Faculty Research Committee of the University of California at Santa Cruz, who offered support through a faculty research grant for compiling the contents of this book.

Finally, I am warmly grateful to my wife, Donna, for her insightful advice, extensive editorial help, and patient support throughout the writing of this book.

Santa Cruz, California
September 1983

Donald T. Saposnek

Contents

The Author

Donald T. Saposnek is a clinical-child psychologist and cofounder of the Family Mediation Service of Santa Cruz, California. He currently divides his professional time between child custody mediation and research, private practice of family therapy, and teaching in the psychology department of the University of California at Santa Cruz.

Saposnek received the B.A. degree in psychology from the University of California at Los Angeles (1966), the M.A. degree in psychology from the California State University at San Jose (1967), and the Ph.D. degree in clinical-child and developmental psychology from The Ohio State University (1971). After completing a clinical internship at the Institute for Juvenile Research in Chicago, he spent the next several years in New Jersey at the Children's Psychiatric Center in the practice of clinical-child psychology and community consultation, and in university teaching and clinical research. Saposnek undertook custody mediation, in addition to his other professional activities, in 1978, four years after moving to California.

Saposnek's publications include an article titled "Aikido:

A Model for Brief Strategic Therapy," published in *Family Process* (1980), and a chapter titled "Short-Term Psychotherapy," for *Personality and the Behavioral Disorder,* 2nd edition, edited by N. Endler and J. McV. Hunt (Wiley, in press). Saposnek is currently engaged in research on outcomes of mandatory mediation, with the aim of developing new procedures and social policies for dealing more effectively with custody and visitation disputes.

Mediating Child Custody Disputes

A Systematic Guide
for Family Therapists,
Court Counselors,
Attorneys, and Judges

1

Mediation as a Cooperative Problem-Solving Approach

And the king said, Bring me a sword. And they brought a sword before the king. And the king said, Divide the living child in two, and give half to the one, and half to the other. Then spake the woman whose the living child was *unto the king, for her bowels yearned upon her son, and she said, O my lord, give her the living child, and in no wise slay it. But the other said, Let it be neither mine nor thine,* but *divide* it. *Then the king answered and said, Give her the living child, and in no wise slay it: she* is *the mother thereof.* [I Kings 3:24–27]

All too often, modern arbiters of child custody do not encounter parents of such self-sacrificing conscience, and must resort to and rely on the procedures of legal justice. However, our procedures of *legal* justice have, for the most part, not blended well with our contemporary understanding of *psychological* justice in child custody disputes. We all too frequently summon the sword and sacrifice the child in the name of legal justice for the parents, rather than support and encourage conciliatory efforts between the parents in the name of psychological justice for the child.

Child custody mediation is an alternative approach for resolving custody disputes in a way that is most congruent with our current knowledge of the needs and development of children of divorce. When applied skillfully, and supported by a network of legal and mental health professionals, the methods of mediation can provide a truly sensible and psychologically sound alternative to adversarial methods. In order to gain a perspective on the issue of child custody disputes and resolution by mediation, let us first briefly explore the historical roots, the contemporary research on children of divorce, and the different approaches to dealing with custody disputes.

Historical Perspectives

It is known that some 2,000 years ago fathers had complete and absolute control over their children and over their wives and property as well. Under Roman law, fathers could sell their children or condemn them to death with impunity. In those times, children were viewed as unimportant creatures that needed only physical care until the age of seven, at which time they were treated, and expected to act, as servants to their masters (Aries, 1962).

English common law condoned fathers' absolute rights over their children, a condition that extended into the last century. As their fathers' property, children were considered valuable as income-producing workers in factories and mines during the Industrial Revolution. The exploitation and abuse of children was extraordinary during this period. Children as young as four or five were put to work in the mines, and seven-year-olds would not infrequently be worked fourteen to sixteen hours a day (Leve, 1980).

During the first part of the nineteenth century, the courts of England began to recognize that parenthood involved not only rights and privileges, but also responsibilities for the welfare of children. The development of the doctrine of *parens patriae* gave courts jurisdiction over the welfare of children. This doctrine was formally enacted in 1839 in what was known as Talfourd's Act, which empowered the court to determine custody of children under the age of seven. Soon thereafter, English mothers' rights to custody gradually increased until in 1925, the Guardianship of Infants Act was passed. This gave mothers and fathers equal chances of receiving custody (Derdeyn, 1977).

In the United States, custody decisions reflected English law. In various court decisions, fathers' superior rights to custody were justified by their control over family money and resources. An 1826 text contains the observation that "in consequence of the obligation of the father to provide for the maintenance of his infant children . . . he is entitled to the custody of their persons, and to the value of their labor and services" (Kent, 1826, quoted in Derdeyn, 1977, pp. 162–163).

Toward the middle of the nineteenth century, the status of women began to change. Women entered the work force and obtained the vote and the right to own property of their own. Child welfare took on a new light as reformers urging child labor laws influenced public opinion. As interest in child development increased, the importance of maternal care was emphasized. King (1979, p. 156) notes that "after centuries of legal bias in favor of the father, a number of states enacted statutes creating a legal presumption that the mother should be given the custody of a child of tender years." Moreover, at the turn of the century, even when custody was awarded to the mothers, fathers still were considered to be financially responsible for their children. This made awards of custody to mothers easier, since the previous linkage between fathers' custody and financial support was broken.

The "tender years" presumption grew in strength quite rapidly, as numerous awards of custody were made to mothers. This was soon followed by court decisions based upon a "best interests of the child" standard. Derdeyn (1977) points out that it was the frequent use of the "tender years" and the "best interests of the child" standards that eventually resulted in the mothers' superior right to custody. Moreover, where fathers' rights to custody had been based upon financial advantage and the tradition of English law, mothers' rights to custody were based upon a moral assumption that mothers were better caregivers for children (Oster, 1965).

The moral presumption that mothers should be favored in custody disputes made functional sense in American society in the early 1900s. As Roman and Haddad (1978) noted, "Industrialization, which divides the wage labor of men from the private labor of women, is behind the exaltation of motherhood and the *invention* of maternal instinct. That is, maternal instinct came along precisely when it was required, making a virtue out of what seemed to be a necessity. Its enshrinement parallels the development of a new, not god-given, family form which we have come to call the nuclear family, a refuge from the world and the social—but not economic—center of personal life. As our culture became both urban and industrialized, the father worked away from the house and left the raising of children, for all practical purposes, in the hands of the mother" (pp. 36-37). However, these authors add that even today in agrarian communities farm labor is still divided between husband and wife, and there is no inequality of importance in parenting. Mother and father work in the fields together and take care of the children together.

Because we are no longer in the midst of the Industrial Revolution, and because the nuclear family is changing in organization and function (Toffler, 1980), we need to revise our ways of conceptualizing the custody of children. Indeed, recent legal moves have reflected society's changing views and changing values. In 1970, under the Family Law Act, California modified Section 138 of the 1931 Civil Code, which incorporated the "tender years" presumption. This section (now 4600) was amended "so that the mother no longer automatically receives legal preference over the father as to the custody of a child of tender years" (King, 1979, p. 156). The change addressed the sex discrimination problem that was implicit in the "tender years" presumption, and it enabled the court to focus on using the "best interests of the child" standard.

Part of the intent of the "best interests of the child" standard was to counter the historical trend of deciding such issues on the basis of parental culpability. With the concomitant predominance of no-fault divorces, courts have been trying to separate out issues of *moral* unfitness–which may include adultery, other sexual misconduct, substance abuse, and unpopular religious, political, or social beliefs–from behaviors that clearly would interfere with the parents' ability to give adequate care to a child. Moreover, courts have tried not to punish parents for what may be considered immoral behavior by depriving them of or restricting contact with their children. Apparently, however, this tendency is difficult to abandon, as the practice still continues. Under the guise that it is in the best interests of the child to deny custody to a parent who may be viewed as immoral or at fault, the courts perpetuate the practice. As Derdeyn (1977) aptly noted, "The human penchant for obscuring difficult decisions with a moralistic overlay of right and wrong or reward and punishment can be relied on to maintain culpability as an externally important issue" (p. 724).

The trend toward equality of rights for both parents was given a large boost when the California Legislature enacted Civil Code Sections 4600 and 4600.5, the so-called joint custody statutes. Section 4600 begins: "The Legislature finds and declares that it is the public policy of this state to assure minor children of frequent and continuing contact with both parents after the parents have separated or dissolved their marriage, and to encourage parents to share the rights and responsibilities of child rearing in order to effect such policy." Section 4600.5(a) begins: "There shall be a presumption, affecting the burden of proof, that joint custody is in the best interests of a minor child where the parents have agreed to an award of joint custody or so agree in open court at a hearing for the purpose of determining the custody of the minor child or children of the marriage."

In the event that joint custody is not awarded, Section 4600(b, 1) states: "In making an order for custody to either parent, the court shall consider, among other factors, which parent is more likely to allow the child or children frequent and continuing contact with the noncustodial parent, and shall not prefer a parent as custodian because of that parent's sex." (See Appendix A for California statutes regarding joint custody.)

With the designation of equal parental rights, the decreasing use of parent-oriented fault-finding presumptions, and the increased awareness of the importance of determining the child's emotional and developmental needs, judges must exercise ever-increasing discretion in each custody decision. This points the courts in a more humanistic direction, but leaves the judges with the onerous task of deciding what, indeed, *is* in the best interests of a child (Derdeyn, 1977).

The Needs of Children of Divorce

As an attempt to aid judges in making custody decisions, Goldstein, Freud, and Solnit published their book *Beyond the Best Interests of the Child* in 1973. They proposed that custody be awarded to a single "psychological parent," with whom the child will maintain a continuous, day-to-day relationship and emotional bond, and that the noncustodial parent be stripped of his or her legal rights to parent the child: "Once it is determined who will be the custodial parent, it is that parent, not the court, who must decide under what conditions he or she wishes to raise the child. Thus, the noncustodial parent should have no legally enforceable right to visit the child, and the custodial parent should have the right to decide whether it is desirable for the child to have such visits" (Goldstein, Freud, and Solnit, 1973, p. 38).

Presumably, the findings of such an influential book should be based on authoritative understanding of the needs of children. However, as Roman and Haddad (1978) noted: "The authors do not cite, nor does there exist, any social science data to support the proposition that a single official parent is preferable to two" (p. 109). Indeed, the work of Goldstein, Freud, and Solnit is based almost exclusively on psychoanalytic speculations, and it ignores the more empirically based literature of developmental psychology.

Curiously enough, the research that has been done on the issue of children's needs after divorce consistently points to conclusions that are diametrically opposed to those recommended by these three authors. Specifically, it has been demonstrated that children need continuous and regular contact with *both* parents and that they need a reduction or cessation of interparental conflict following a divorce. If we were to follow the proposal of Goldstein, Freud, and Solnit, the first of these needs would be frustrated by the tenuousness and insignificance of the child's relationship with the noncustodial parent, and the second would be frustrated by the escalating power struggles that would doubtless characterize many, if not most, of the interparental relationships. Such conflicts would ensue as a direct result of the severe imbalance in parental control over the child's relationships with the parents.

Evidence in support of children's need for a continuous and conflict-free relationship with both parents is plentiful. Some of this evidence is from studies of the effects of the father's absence on child development, and some is from studies of the ways in which children cope with a variety of postseparation parenting arrangements.

Children's experience of divorce is almost always traumatic, confusing, and painful. Even when the parents and children know ahead of time that the divorce will very likely be a constructive change for all concerned, children still experience considerable emotional distress. Moreover, Wallerstein and Kelly (1980) found that even when children (of all ages) acknowledged the destructive, neglectful, and unhappy quality of their parents' marriage, very few wanted their parents to divorce. The overwhelming majority seemed to prefer the unhappy marriage to the divorce. "Many of the children, despite the unhappiness of their parents, were in fact relatively happy and considered their situation neither better nor worse than that of other families around them. They would, in fact, have been content to hobble along. The divorce was a bolt of lightning that struck them when they had not even been aware of the existence of a storm" (p. 11).

These initial reactions are quite understandable, considering the major impact that divorce has on children's lives. The basic security provided by the nuclear family unit is shattered, the children's trust in their parents' love for them comes into question, and the children develop deep worries about whether they will continue to be cared for or even wanted. Moreover, they experience the loss of one of their parents and, frequently, the personal decompensation, deterioration of parental functioning, and reduced availability of the other. While children generally can handle a single such crisis with no significant psychological risk, Rutter (1978) alerts us to the finding that children who have been exposed to chronic stress or several concurrent stresses and then have to deal with major family disruptions suffer adverse effects that are compounded exponentially. Thus, children who have already experienced earlier stressors in their lives are at high psychiatric risk when faced with the additional consequences of the divorce. Such consequences may include geographical uprooting, economic deprivation, increased use of child care, changes in intrafamilial relationships, and changes in support systems outside the nuclear family (Kurdek, 1981; Hetherington, 1981).

For children, one of the most frightening aspects of such changes is their own sense of a loss of control over what is happening. At each stage in a child's (as in an adult's) development, it is the sense of being in control of one's world that gives the confidence to attempt mastery of each new developmental task. Without this sense of control, children and adults are prone to feelings of helplessness and depression. And, indeed, in their longitudinal study of children of divorce, Wallerstein and Kelly (1980) found that a full 37 percent of the children were psychologically troubled and manifested moderate to severe clinical depression *five years* after the divorce. The children experienced rejection and neglect by one or the other parent and repeated disappointment in the unreliability of the "visiting" parent. While older adolescent children were able to turn to others for support, younger children were literally at the mercy of their poorly functioning parents, with no sense of being able to do anything about their circumstances. Moreover, it was found that children who did turn to others for support could also turn to their parents, while the ones who could not count on their parents for support also could not turn to others. Over time, this tendency resulted in the better-adjusted youngsters getting better and the more poorly adjusted ones getting worse.

Probably the most salient aspect of the divorce experience for children is the sudden loss of a parent from the home.

Wallerstein and Kelly (1980) point out that, contrary to the belief of many clinicians, children tend not to have foreknowledge of their parents' imminent divorce. Even when divorce plans are discussed ahead of time, this knowledge does not help the children to accept or deal with the divorce any more skillfully. Moreover, 80 percent of the preschool children Wallerstein and Kelly studied were not given an adequate explanation of the divorce or assurance of continued care. "In effect, they awoke one morning to find one parent gone. Among this relatively educated and concerned group of parents, the hesitancy in explaining their divorce reflected a high level of anxiety and discomfort about discussing the family breakup with their young children" (p. 39).

Particular responses to the sudden disappearance of one parent are closely linked to the child's developmental stage. Because younger children are less able to understand the meaning of the separation and are cognitively egocentric, they blame themselves, expect reconciliation, and fear abandonment. Neal (1982) points out that preschool children tend to explain such situations in terms of their personal subsystem; that is, although they often accurately perceive an event, they interpret it in a way that causes excessive personal distress. He writes, "Children at this level understand parental divorce as one parent moving away from the child—an accurate perception—and assume that they must have done something bad in order to cause this distance to occur. The syllogistic quality of this inference is that: A person who does not like someone else moves physically farther away from them; Daddy moved physically away from me; Daddy does not like me" (p. 13).

Older children tend to respond to the absence of a parent less egocentrically, but still in a cognitively restricted manner. Five- to eight-year-olds can attend to triadic behavioral sequences and often believe that they caused a fight between their mother and father that led to the divorce. Nine- to twelve-year-olds, by contrast, can understand how one parent may feel upset at another parent, irrespective of the child's behavior. But these children are still restricted to believing that one parent can feel negatively toward the other parent only in response to that other parent's behavior. They cannot yet appreciate parental feelings changing independently of the people or situations that evoke them. Adolescents can view adult feelings as independent of the social context, but they cannot make sense of why good intentions on the part of adults do not guarantee positive responses from others. Hence, adolescents believe that if parents really *wanted* to try, they could make their marriage work. Consequently, teenagers frequently blame their parents for the divorce (Neal, 1982).

The absence of a parent following a divorce has an even more serious impact on children than the divorce itself. Because only 10 percent of single parents are fathers, most research in this area has focused on the influence of father absence. Contrary to the belief that other people (relatives, siblings, friends, neighbors, daycare centers, and so on) can replace the functions of a father, Hetherington (1981) and Pederson, Rubenstein, and Yarrow (1979) assert that fathers make a unique contribution to the functioning of the family and the development of the child. This contribution is both direct and indirect. The father may play an active, direct role in shaping the child's behavior by providing discipline, offering guidance, and acting as a model. When the father is absent, there is only one parent to carry out the functions of both parents. The single parent, or even two adults of the same sex, offers the child a more restricted assortment of positive characteristics to model than do a mother and a father (Hetherington, 1981).

Indirectly, the father can support the mother in her parenting role in three ways: with monetary aid; with assistance with childcare and childrearing tasks; and with emotional support, encouragement, and validation of her functions as a mother. Moreover, as Hetherington, Cox, and Cox (1978) point out, when the mother feels valued and cherished in her role, her self-esteem, happiness, and competence are increased, which in turn influences her relationship with her children. A father can also serve as a buffer between the children and an emotionally unstable mother. In this way he can help to counteract any deleterious effects the custodial parent's behavior might have on the children. His complete absence, of course, would prevent this buffering function (Hetherington, Cox, and Cox, 1979). One can speculate that the same findings would also hold true in reverse, when the father is the primary custodial parent.

Children deprived of frequent access to their fathers show diminished self-esteem lasting as long as five years after the divorce (Wallerstein and Kelly, 1980). Moreover, when left in the exclusive care of a distressed and inconsistent mother they show a disruption of cognitive skills, social behavior, and self-control (Hetherington, 1979). The children who were most stressed were those who had had close and affectionate relationships with their father during the marriage and who experienced a disruption in this relationship after the divorce. Hetherington (1981) notes that with the exception of a poorly adjusted or immature father, frequent availability of the father is associated with positive adjustment and positive social relationships, especially in boys. Moreover, a continued and mutually supportive relationship between father and child is also the most effective support system for divorced women in their parenting role. "The recommendation that has been made [by Goldstein, Freud, and Solnit] that the custodial parent have the right to eliminate visitation by the noncustodial parent if he or she views it as adverse to the child's well-being is one that seems likely to discourage parents from working through their differences and that runs counter to the available research findings" (Hetherington, 1981, p. 50). Wallerstein and Kelly (1980, p. 239) further note, "Some of these visiting relationships could even be considered detrimental to development, because they infantilized the child or hurt his feelings or exploited the relationship to help the adult. Nevertheless, they played a significant role in protecting the child against the pain of loss and the psychological impact of that loss. Even in these poor relationships the father's presence kept the child from worrying about abandonment and total rejection and the nagging self-doubts which followed . . . . The maintenance of some continuity in the father-child relationship, unless the relationship was psychologically or physically destructive of the child's well-being, appeared preferable to complete loss of contact, even though the relationship may have been impoverished from its conception or gradually deteriorated during the years."

Next to the cessation of an ongoing relationship with a parent, the most destructive consequence of a divorce for children is continued bitterness and conflict between the parents. While varying degrees of parental discord are expected during the first year following the separation, discord that continues longer than one year has serious negative effects on children. One distressed twelve-year-old boy, whose divorced parents had been arguing and battling in court over custody for the previous ten years, told a mediator that he wanted to teach first or sixth graders when he grew up. When asked why he wanted to teach those particular grades, he replied, eloquently, "'Cause they don't argue so much in those grades . . . but in all the other grades they argue a lot; . . . I hate arguing!"

Wallerstein and Kelly (1980) found that a central cause of children's poor adjustment at five years after the divorce was the failure of the divorce to provide its intended relief. When parents continued fighting after the divorce, and especially when the postdivorce conflict exceeded the marital conflict, the children had a great deal of difficulty accepting and integrating the divorce. Moreover, children frequently are coerced or persuaded into taking sides in parental battles, which creates a terrible conflict in them over divided loyalties. Such a tug of war greatly compounds the children's difficulties. When the mother is hostile to and critical of the father, the child begins to denounce the father as an acceptable role model. For young boys, this results in a disruption of sex typing (Hetherington, Cox, and Cox, 1979), and for girls it can be associated with disruptions in heterosexual relations at adolescence (Hetherington, 1972).

To date, the research has consistently shown that children in single-parent families function better than children in conflict-ridden nuclear families. However, when the conflict persists and escalates after divorce, the children of single-parent families show more problems than do children in discordant nuclear families (Hetherington, Cox, and Cox, 1979). Hence, it is essential to make every effort to minimize conflict between parents after a divorce.

The Adversarial Approach

Although only 10 percent of all custody decisions are contested (Foster and Freed, 1980), these cases present some of the most volatile, hostile, and destructive transactions seen between two humans in a court of law. And, until recently, these contested cases have been dealt with exclusively by an adversarial process. For the most part, the adversarial process has proved itself to be a just and effective approach for discovering the facts and critical issues in criminal and other matters, so that decisions could be made to attribute blame and responsibility or to resolve disputes. However, this same adversarial process, when applied to domestic conflicts, tends to do more harm than good. As Coogler (1978, p. 8) noted, "Whatever may be said in support of the adversarial process for resolving other kinds of controversies, in marital disputes this competitive struggle is frequently more damaging for the marriage partners and their children than everything else that preceded it."

Because divorces and custody decisions were, in the recent past, made on the basis of finding one person at fault, and/or unfit, the adversarial process seemed fully appropriate as the most efficient method for arriving at such decisions. In each such contest there were a winner and a loser, and the courts assumed that, once the decisions were made, the matter was settled. While the matters of property and the legal dissolution of the marriage were indeed settled, the matters of custody and visitation were very often far from settled. In reaction to the humiliation of defeat, the losing spouse would frequently try to get back at the winning spouse by gathering damaging evidence regarding the unfitness of the other spouse, the quality of care given the children, and/or the immoral acts of the spouse, and by filing an Order to Show Cause (OSC) petition to reverse the custody decision. Such relitigation frequently continued for years following an initial decision. As Wright (1981, p. 5) observed, "When the triumph of victory and the humiliation of defeat were the only outcomes likely in the traditional custody battle, many couples would throw their energies into this very dramatic, win-or-lose conflict."

The recent trends toward no-fault divorces and custody decisions based on the best interests of the child rather than on the fitness of the parent have been attempts to reduce the acrimonious nature of such domestic conflicts. Yet the adversarial process by which these new standards are applied inherently breeds acrimony. Moreover, when children are involved in the process, they typically become repeat victims. This victimization can be obvious and publicly painful, as when a child must betray one parent by testifying in court on behalf of the other. Or, it can be more subtle and insidious, as when a parent or lawyer solicits an "evaluation" of, or "treatment" for, the youngster by a child psychologist or psychiatrist as a tactic to help achieve the goal of obtaining custody.

Without doubt, many parents (and attorneys) who seek a therapist for help with the child's distress do so out of a genuine concern for the emotional well-being of the child, in spite of the fact that the parents are in the midst of a custody or visitation dispute. Indeed, when the child's distress is evident, such professional support may be quite advisable. However, when such an action has a primarily tactical intent, it can be problematic for the child. Typically, in such cases, the parent who is about to launch a bid for custody of a child seeks a therapist to help the child deal with the emotional upset manifested in the aftermath of the divorce. However, what that parent often does not tell the therapist until later is that the parent was sent there by the attorney in hopes of documenting some harm that has occurred or will occur to the child as a result of being in the custody of the other parent. Or, if there is no chance of finding harm, the attorney may hope that the therapist, by seeing the one parent and child together, can be seduced into writing a report and perhaps even testifying to the effect that a "strong bond of attachment clearly exists between this parent and the child." Frequently, if the therapist calls the attorney on being informed of the referral, he or she will be told that the attorney simply wanted a skilled professional to help the child with his or her emotional problems. However, on completion of the assessment sessions, the therapist not infrequently is requested, or subpoenaed, by the attorney to testify on behalf of his or her client.

Regardless of whether the request to evaluate the child or child-parent relationship is presented in a straightforward or in an indirect manner, the experience of the child will be nearly the same. The child will be led to consider and/or express a preference for a custodial parent and will be coerced in various ways to participate in discussions that frequently will result in the betrayal of one parent. Moreover, when evidence of harm to the child is sought or suspected, the child will feel the intensity of focused probing for pathology. This can cause considerable discomfort in the child and lead to the development of a self-fulfilling prophecy, in that the child will begin to manifest what is being looked for, in hopes of pleasing the probing adults.

Evaluations and therapy are never neutral events for children, who frequently feel scared, guilty, and/or resentful at having to participate. They may be well aware of the intent of the sessions or, what is often worse, they may have their own distorted understanding of that intent. As we well know, children's personal, uninformed explanations of events frequently are far more frightening than any reality could be. Moreover, any evaluative data that come out of such a one-sided, restricted context are guaranteed to be biased. For one thing, there is a tendency for individually oriented therapists (in contrast to family systems-oriented therapists) to attribute children's problems either to internalized conflicts or, in the broadest perspective, to a dyadic parent-child interaction rather than to the triadic parent-parent-child interactions inherent in custody disputes. For another, the demand characteristics of the soliciting parent's reports and the attorney's implicit or explicit appeal can strongly bias the therapist into attributing cause and blame to the other parent. This is particularly easy to do when the therapist conceptualizes from an individual or dyadic model of problem formation and when the therapist receives no contrary data from the other parent, by virtue of having no contact with that parent.

It is also noteworthy that children who participate in such evaluations occasionally feel betrayed when they later find out that a judge made the custody decision based upon what they told the therapist. For in spite of what they may be told to the contrary, they often believe that their conversations will be confidential. Moreover, they not infrequently tell the therapist what they think he or she wants to hear, rather than what they really feel, especially if the therapist subtly puts pressure on the children to support the soliciting parent's position. The children may also feel betrayed if they find that the therapist's promise to help them obtain what would be best for them is not fulfilled. For example, although the therapist may believe that placement away from the least adequate parent would be best, what the children may actually need is for their parents to stop fighting and share parenting. However, because acrimony is often increased rather than decreased after a sole custody win, the therapist's one-sided participation in the adversarial struggle does, functionally, betray the children. Such experiences can cause children to lose trust in any help that mental health professionals might offer in the future.

While the adjustment problems that children have following a divorce are commonly attributed by each parent to the quality of caregiving by the other parent (see Chapter Six), Wallerstein and Kelly (1980) have documented that they are due more to postdivorce time-sharing arrangements and interparental conflict than to the style of parenting. It has also been found that the adversarial approach exacerbates the effects of these factors. In their study on the outcome of relitigation, Ilfeld, Ilfeld, and Alexander (1982, p. 65) concluded "that relitigation over a custody issue represents moderate to severe parental conflict that adversely affects the children."

The Committee on the Family of the Group for the Advancement of Psychiatry (1980) points out that the major defect of the adversarial process is that it "accentuates differences rather than diminishes them" (p. 122). The committee cites one of the most eloquent critics of this process, Judge Byron F. Lindsley: "The adversary process, historically effective in resolving disputes between litigants where evidentiary facts have probative significance, is not properly suited to the resolution of most family relations problems . . . . [Where] there are children and the parties cannot or will not recognize the impact of the disintegration of the marriage upon the children, where they fail to perceive their primary responsibilities as parents—that is, custody and visitation—we make it possible for parents to carry out that struggle by the old, adversary, fault-finding, condemnation approach . . . . This kind of battle is destructive to the welfare, best interests, and emotional health of their children" (Committee on the Family, 1980, p. 122).

Indeed, the adversarial process trains parents, through discussions and modeling, to fight even more effectively, using slander, accusation, defamation, and any other weapons available. Yet such contests are construed as a proper means of achieving the best interests of the child. By any standard of common sense, as well as the accumulated research data showing that children need co-parenting and a cessation of interparental conflict, the adversarial process must rank very low as a method of making satisfactory and lasting postdivorce parenting arrangements.

The Mediation Alternative

Short of parents amicably agreeing between themselves, mediation is the ideal approach for making postdivorce co-parenting arrangements. There are a number of reasons for this. In contrast to the adversarial approach, mediation is a cooperative problem-solving method. Instead of pitting one parent against the other, both parents are encouraged to solve their mutual problem, which is how to optimize the time their children share with each of them. The essential differences between a cooperative and a competitive or adversarial process were eloquently outlined by Deutsch:

> 1. Communication
>
> (a) A cooperative process is characterized by open and honest communication of relevant information between the participants. Each is interested in informing, and being informed by, the other.

(b) A competitive process is characterized by either lack of communication or misleading communication. It also gives rise to espionage or other techniques of obtaining information about the other that the other is unwilling to communicate. In addition to obtaining such information, each party is interested in providing discouraging or misleading information to the other.

2. Perception

(a) A cooperative process tends to increase sensitivity to similarities and common interests while minimizing the salience of differences. It stimulates a convergence and conformity of beliefs and values.

(b) A competitive process tends to increase sensitivity to differences and threats while minimizing the awareness of similarities. It stimulates the sense of complete oppositeness: "You are bad; I am good." It seems likely that competition produces a stronger bias toward misperceiving the other's neutral or conciliatory actions as malevolently motivated than the bias induced by cooperation to see the other's actions as benevolently intended.

3. Attitudes toward one another

(a) A cooperative process leads to a trusting, friendly attitude, and it increases the willingness to respond helpfully to the other's needs and requests.

(b) A competitive process leads to a suspicious, hostile attitude, and it increases the readiness to exploit the other's needs and respond negatively to the other's requests.

4. Task orientation

(a) A cooperative process enables the participants to approach the mutually acknowledged problem in a way that utilizes their special talents and enables them to substitute for one another in their joint work, so that duplication of effort is reduced. The enhancement of mutual power and resources becomes an objective. It leads to the defining of conflicting interests as a mutual problem to be solved by collaborative effort. It facilitates the recognition of the legitimacy of each other's interests and of the necessity of searching for a solution that is responsive to the needs of all. It tends to limit rather than expand the scope of conflicting

> interests. Attempts to influence the other tend to be limited to processes of persuasion.
>
> (b) A competitive process stimulates the view that the solution of a conflict can only be one that is imposed by one side on the other. The enhancement of one's own power and the minimization of the legitimacy of the other side's interests in the situation become objectives. It fosters the expansion of the scope of the issues in conflict so that the conflict becomes a matter of general principle and is no longer confined to a particular issue at a given time and place. The escalation of the conflict increases its motivational significance to the participants and intensifies their emotional involvement in it; these factors, in turn, may make a limited defeat less acceptable or more humiliating than mutual disaster might be. Duplication of effort, so that the competitors become mirror-images of one another, is more likely than division of effort. Coercive processes tend to be employed in the attempt to influence the other [1973, pp. 29-30].

Although Deutsch was writing about the general nature of interpersonal conflicts, the relevance to custody disputes is striking. Resolving custody disputes by a cooperative approach has qualitative benefits for children that cannot be achieved through competitive procedures. Such benefits include increased chances for continued cooperation and communication between the parents, reduction of ongoing conflict as a result of both parents perceiving themselves to be on the same side, and an attitude of mutual flexibility in problem solving. While mediation certainly does not always elicit all these benefits, it does achieve a level of cooperation that is basically unattainable in an adversarial context.

In addition to providing a constructive context within which specific negotiations can take place, mediation greatly expands the variety of possible resolutions to the custody dispute. While it is rare for judges to award physical custody using any formula other than the traditional one—residence with one parent and alternate weekend visitation with the other—mediation offers broader possibilities. The importance of having more choice is supported by Wallerstein and Kelly (1980), who found that children tended not to like visiting their noncustodial parent just every other weekend, but wanted more time with that parent. In fact, children who already were spending frequent periods with the visiting parent still wanted increased time. "The intense longing for greater contact persisted undiminished over many years, long after the divorce was accepted as an unalterable fact of life" (p. 134). Moreover, the authors add, "It has been, in fact, strikingly apparent through the years that whether or not the children maintained frequent or infrequent contact with the non-custodial parent the children would have considered the term *one-parent family* a misnomer. Their self-images were firmly tied to their relationship with both parents and they thought of themselves as children with two parents who had elected to go their separate ways" (p. 307). The flexibility of mediation allows parents to satisfy this need by arranging a co-parenting situation that provides significantly greater access to both parents than that typically attainable by a court-rendered decision. Moreover, it helps children to feel safer and more loved to know that the decisions about postdivorce parenting arrangements were made by their parents rather than a judge who is a total stranger to the children. Furthermore, future research may possibly reveal that children for whom judges make undesired custody decisions develop resistance to the judicial and legal system as they grow older.

The rapid increase in legislation dealing with joint custody has certain implications for mediation. As of this writing, over half of the states across the nation expressly provide for and authorize joint custody as a legal option for resolving custody disputes, and five states have a preference or presumption of joint custody (Folberg, 1982). While few individuals would disagree with the awarding of joint custody in cases where both parents agree, awards of joint custody in cases where one or both parents do not desire it stir controversy. Some feel that it should not be imposed upon unwilling parents (Committee on the Family, 1980); some are ambivalent about imposing it, at least until further research is done (Nehls and Morgenbesser, 1980; Wallerstein and Kelly, 1980; Clingempeel and Reppucci,

1982); and some feel that, together with a structure such as mediation for working out the details, joint custody should be strongly preferred (Roman and Haddad, 1978; Poll, 1981; Wright, 1981; Ilfeld, Ilfeld, and Alexander, 1982).

Whether joint custody is imposed or mutually agreed upon by a couple who are in a custody dispute, the details for making the arrangement work effectively need to be negotiated. Mediation is the ideal format for such negotiations, since it rests on the principle of cooperative sharing. Although California is the only state that has a mandatory mediation law at this time, other states have already begun to develop mediation methods as a way of implementing the rapidly increasing numbers of joint custody decisions.

Mediation can be voluntary or involuntary. Unless a particular jurisdiction implements a mandatory mediation program (as is true only in California as of this writing), most mediation is voluntary, engaged in by couples who seek it on their own or at the urging of their attorneys. While it appears that couples who choose a mediation approach tend to be less adversarial and irrational and more willing to compromise than those couples ordered by a court to mediation, research is needed to delineate the differences between these two populations.

Several other benefits of mediation have been suggested by Ilfeld, Ilfeld, and Alexander (1982), who revealed that the relitigation rate in cases where couples shared joint custody was one half that of cases where one parent had sole custody. These authors concluded that joint custody arrangements reduced parental conflict and hypothesized that joint custody families would do even better if they agreed to (or had mandated by the court) a process of mediation and/or arbitration of major decisions on which they could not agree. (In arbitration a third person is chosen to hear both sides and then decide the matters for the parents, whereas in mediation the decisions rest with the parents.) Indeed, evidence for this hypothesis was offered by Milne (1978), Bahr (1981), and Pearson and Thoennes (1982b), whose data suggested that successful mediation clients relitigated less often than those using adversarial approaches.

Mediation also can result in considerable monetary savings to both the clients and the public (Bahr, 1981). Pearson and Thoennes (1982b) found modest savings in private attorneys' fees among successful mediation clients who were diverted to private mediation before the issuing of temporary orders. More impressively, McIsaac (1981) documented that mediation administered through a conciliation court as part of California's mandatory mediation process cost only *one fourth* as much as a trial would for resolving custody and visitation issues. He points out that this significant savings of public funds was the most persuasive argument presented in getting California's mandatory mediation law passed. A difficulty that had to be overcome was for the governor to be able to justify increasing the divorce filing fee, the marriage license fee, and the cost of filing any motion to modify or enforce a custody or visitation order. Once the bigger picture of overall financial savings was documented, the legislation was promptly signed. Looking to the future, Folberg (1981) cites evidence that "181.7 million dollars per year could be saved in the U.S. if all child custody cases were mediated" (p. 4).

Over and above the savings in time, effort, money, and emotional stress offered by mediation, the participants experience a shift in consciousness about the nature of conflict resolution. The conceptual framework of mediation requires the participants, who are generally used to adversarial thinking, to shift attitudes, beliefs, feelings, and behavior. This shift in consciousness can snowball and diffuse its effects throughout a community. It is perhaps too idealistic to hope that a society as complex as ours could resolve most of its conflicts through cooperative rather than competitive approaches. However, it clearly makes much sense to eliminate or reduce competition in those areas of dispute resolution where competition is more destructive than constructive. In particular, it does not seem too much to ask that we at least spare children the wrath of their competing parents after a divorce. Through the cooperative process of mediation, parents can retain control over decisions affecting their children and work together to make the most appropriate plans for them.

2

Attitudes and Skills Needed for Effective Mediation

Typically, spouses begin mediation at their psychological worst, struggling for their very self-esteem and self-worth as human beings. As Felder (1971) notes, "People going to a divorce lawyer are mostly bitter and revengeful, . . . reduced to a basic level, filled with greed, vengeance, pettiness; . . . adults fighting over the most trivial things, women hurting men even when they can gain nothing by doing so, people ready to sacrifice their children as tools against the other spouse . . . . In matrimonial cases, everything goes, there is no limit to the hurt people will inflict on one another . . . . There are few conditions of stress so protracted and so personal and incapable of being shared with other people. It seems to get worse and worse as the litigation drags on. Friends are ripped apart, the whole fabric of life is torn. It is unlike any other stress situation" (pp. 227–228). Many couples find that mediation exacerbates the animosity in their relationship. In addition to the typical marital issues, with all the paradoxical and convoluted patterns of interaction, another problematic element is present: a survival threat. Each spouse's self-concept, lifestyle, moral values, competence as a parent, worth as a human being, and feelings of being lovable are threatened. Moreover, each spouse's capacity for flexible compromise, for empathy, and for dealing with often overwhelming feelings of anger, grief, jealousy, resentment, and revenge is also challenged.

Both spouses have much to protect. They must each protect their own relationship with their children, their finances (often from threat by the other spouse), their integrity, and their sense of personal worth. They may feel subject to explicit and implicit criticism by their former spouse, by their children, by the judge, and even by the mediator. Each may put up a childlike resistance, for each will feel that his or her own inner child's emotional survival and autonomy are at stake. It is ironic that in this struggle, each spouse perceives himself or herself as powerless and the other spouse as powerful. The result is like a tug-of-war, with each spouse feeling overpowered by the other although in fact neither has moved an inch. It is the task of the mediator to help the couple to develop an awareness of the futility of this struggle and to create some slack in the rope so that they can direct their energies to more productive purposes.

A primary task of the mediator is to get the spouses apart when they feel stuck together. The mediator has to get the couple to work together just enough to cooperate in sharing the children, while keeping them enough apart that their conflictual patterns are not triggered off into self-perpetuating vicious circles. In carrying out this task, the mediator often finds himself or herself in what can only be called a double bind situation (Bateson, Jackson, Haley, and Weakland, 1956), in that the mediator is expected to respond in one of two ways, for both of which he or she will be punished. Negotiations often reach such an impasse that they seem unsolvable. If the mediator expresses pessimism, one of the spouses may well pull out of mediation, saying things like "This is hopeless; he obviously has not changed and this is a waste of time; I'd rather go to court." Then as soon as one spouse pulls out, the other defends by throwing an accusation back, and the hostility escalates once again. If, however, at some other point when the negotiations appear to be going very well, the mediator says, "The situation seems very hopeful; I know you can do it," then one of the spouses may well resist such optimism by triggering off resistance in the other spouse, with accusations or innuendos. Or the spouse may suddenly throw out a radical, poorly timed proposal in an attempt to resolve the whole situation too soon, throwing the other on the defensive. Then the one spouse quickly pounces on the other for being resistant.

Because the stakes are so high, the tactical struggles between spouses will be numerous. The mediator must be alert if he or she is to stave off the destructive effects of these struggles. There is no time for passive observation, since the couple's interactions rarely calm down. Moreover, at some point during the process, their interactions almost always reach a point of tension that threatens to terminate the mediation process abruptly and prematurely.

The mediator must constantly be thinking many moves ahead. The only possible resting spot is a mutually agreeable resolution to the custody issue, with built-in steps for preventing or settling future disputes. Hence, the mediator must continuously assess each spouse's emotional state, perceptions of the other spouse, possible next moves (such as voicing proposals, accusations, criticisms, or support), feelings about the mediator, and understanding of the mediation process itself. In addition, the mediator must assess each spouse's needs regarding the children, what it means for the children to be with each spouse, and what "giving them up" might mean to each spouse. He or she must assess the ambivalent feelings each spouse has for the other, the degree of their remaining attachment, the degree to which their comments reflect genuine concern for the welfare of the children, and so forth.

The mediator must pay exactly equal attention to the concerns of each spouse. From the mediator's point of view, the balance point between them is the only workable leverage spot. As in political campaigns, each spouse may persistently try to convince the mediator, lawyers, friends, relatives, personal therapist, and judge of the virtue of his or her side and the villainy of the other side. Often, each will tell convincing and self-righteous stories that reveal the other spouse to be an uncooperative, immature, unjust fool. Moreover, the emotional impact of such an appeal within a context involving children is tremendous. Even therapists and lawyers who can remain impartial in other contexts will often get swallowed up in the perspective of only one side of the dispute. The mediator must make every effort to resist such tactics and remain neutral.

It is not uncommon for the mediator to receive calls from a therapist (or even a lawyer) who is aghast at hearing (from the mother) that the mediator is even considering helping a "bad" father continue contact with the "victimized" child. The mediator then has an even more complex problem: he or she must deal not only with the feuding couple but also with those other persons who are imbalancing the interactional system by giving too much support to one side. Haley (1976) points out that when the therapist is intervening from a systems point of view—which assumes that all members reciprocally affect one another—every person who is significant within that system automatically becomes part of the "problem." For the mediator, other persons who assert one-sided positions hamper the mediation process. The mediator must deal understandingly with those persons and their concerns but must not be swayed. It is only by adhering to the systems point of view, in which there is typically neither individual truth nor objective reality but only degrees of descriptive accuracy about the system itself, that the mediator can succeed in resolving the dispute. (See Chapter Six for further discussion of the systems perspective.)

Just as Haley (1976) includes the marital therapist as part of the marital problem, so is the mediator necessarily part of the mediation problem. He or she will often be disliked by at least one, if not both, of the spouses, and at one point or another may be viewed as uncompassionate, naive, incompetent, unhelpful, destructive, or just plain mean. Whichever spouse loses the leverage typically will try to cast the mediator in the role of troublemaker or incompetent. Often, one spouse will express this negative feeling to some other significant person, such as a lawyer or new spouse: "My mediator doesn't really understand my side, or he wouldn't have been taken in by those lies from my ex-spouse."

Because the mediator receives very little information ahead of time and must work within a time limitation, the task can feel quite difficult at the outset. The issues are obscured and the spouses typically very well defended. This situation can be characterized as the mediator stepping lightly across a mine field. If he accidentally steps in the wrong place, the entire process can blow up in his face. Moreover, the wrong place may be one that appears neutral to the mediator (for example, talking about the benefits of joint legal custody) but to one of the spouses (who desires sole custody) appears as if the mediator is taking sides with the other spouse. Often that spouse does not speak up about this perceived bias at the beginning of mediation but later suddenly challenges the mediator's position. In response, the mediator may well reflexively defend his position and before realizing it is backed into a corner of partiality. Such an event may abruptly terminate the mediation process or create within the affected spouse an unsurmountable degree of resistance to any compromises.

For the mediator, this is very similar to the courtroom experience of an expert witness who, as the court's representative, attempts to remain neutral. Through cross-examination, the witness is forced to state a position and, by defending it, loses the original position of neutrality. Hence, it is essential that the mediator remain aware of potentially explosive issues.

Perhaps the most challenging aspect of the entire mediation process is the unpredictability of the outcome until the very end. The mediator never knows from moment to moment in the negotiations whether a couple will suddenly escalate their hostilities to the point of stalemate, or proceed to resolve the issues peacefully. This unpredictability is seen at various levels of the mediation process.

At one level, it is manifested in the unexpected behavior of a couple within a given session. Spouses will often enter the first mediation session in a very hostile mood. Throughout the mediator's introductory statements they may sit and glare. As they are encouraged to speak, they may begin by blurting out accusations, prophecies of disaster, statements of hopelessness about the mediation process, and refusals to compromise. Then, just as the mediator proceeds in spite of the ominous discouragement, something unexpected often happens that gets the couple unstuck from these stances and ready to consider compromises. The something unexpected may include the resolution of a particularly emotional issue, the couple's acceptance of a suggestion by the mediator, an emphatic comment made by one of the parties to the other, or any of a number of unforeseeable factors.

Other spouses enter mediation appearing friendly, lighthearted, and cooperative. Occasionally, spouses may even touch affectionately. (On at least two occasions, spouses I worked with even held hands.) This cooperative demeanor may persist for some time into the session. Experience has shown, however, that it is a dangerous mistake to assume that it will necessarily continue throughout the negotiations. Often the spouses will suddenly and unexpectedly turn on each other. Coming as it does out of the blue, this reaction will throw even experienced mediators off balance. Seasoned mediators learn to be cautious with apparently cooperative couples. If the spouses were really all that cooperative with each other, they would not need to seek mediation. Truly friendly couples work out custody and visitation issues before consulting lawyers, judges, and mediators. Although it can be very appealing to listen to a couple talk in a friendly, respectful, or even loving manner about their early marriage and about each other, a mediator working with such a couple should be prepared for the hostility that often erupts during the actual discussion of custody, or it may come as a disheartening shock. The mediator must be prepared to remain skeptical throughout the session and even to expect the worst while working toward the best outcome. This attitude is a necessary survival tool if the mediator is to cope with unpredictability within a session.

Unpredictability is also a problem *between* sessions. A couple may leave a session angrily, showing resistance to compromise and pessimism about the mediation process. Although the mediator may feel that the negotiations are guaranteed to fail, he or she schedules the next appointment anyway. At the next session, the spouses come in acting friendly and cooperative and inform the mediator that they have "worked it out." Once again, the mediator may feel puzzled, even though delighted with the surprise.

Another possibility is that spouses may leave a constructive session joking, talking affectionately, and even hugging and kissing in the parking lot. Then, an hour before the next session, one spouse calls the mediator to cancel the session because the couple has decided to go to court, having just had a major fight. Such sudden decisions occur for a variety of reasons, almost all of which are unpredictable. The mediator who expects a linear, logical process may be quite demoralized by such vagaries. Once again, expecting the unexpected is the safest policy.

Perhaps most frustrating of all for the mediator are the unpredictable moves that occur just before signing the final mediation agreement. At this final point, one of the spouses may suddenly refuse to go along with the agreement, even though he or she helped to design it. That spouse may be taking the last opportunity to make a power play, to express fears about letting go, or to get back at the other spouse one last time. Such a move is also a challenge to the mediator who finds the proverbial rug suddenly pulled out from under him or her after spending hours helping to lay the groundwork of trust. Often, after further negotiations, the agreements can be revised and accepted. Some, however, remain unresolvable and must return to court for adjudication.

Occasionally, it happens that one spouse calls the mediator the day after signing the agreement and informs her that the agreement is off. The spouse explains that after thinking it over, he is not satisfied with the agreement and will not abide by it. Such occurrences, fortunately, are rare, and because the spouse who reneged is usually unwilling to return to mediation, the case is best referred back to the lawyers.

The context of mediation is a central factor contributing to the variety of unpredictable behaviors shown by couples undergoing this process. Mediation takes place in a time-limited and highly structured context, deals with emotionally charged content, and concerns itself with participants who frequently are both angry and mistrustful. Moreover, both spouses feel the pressure of the mediator's explicit expectation that they will cooperate and compromise with each other, even though they may feel very little mutual trust. Furthermore, small crises are often catalyzed in the mediator's efforts to restructure the marital system. The resulting potential for unpredictable behavior is clearly very large.

Mediation offers some spouses a controlled and efficient setting in which to vent anger and express hurt over specific issues, after which they often can cooperate with each other enough to reach resolutions within a session. Other spouses may remain angry with each other in the office and feel inhibited by the presence of the mediator but be able to reach agreement on their own after the session. In both cases, the mere opportunity to talk with each other away from the adversarial context can rapidly yield cooperation out of hostility.

Another variable that contributes to unpredictable behavior is the natural emotional ambivalence that exists between two divorced spouses. An emotional divorce often does not occur at the same time as a legal divorce. Strong feelings that bind (for example, love, dependence, fear) can alternate rapidly with strong feelings that divide (for example, anger, hatred, resentment, revenge). One spouse, for example, called me before our first session, demanding assurance that she would be permitted to enter the mediation office before her former husband arrived so that she would not have to be together with him in the parking lot, since, she said, he was "violent and assaultive" and she feared for her life. Then she arrived for the first session in a car driven by her ex-husband, held hands with him in the parking lot before the session, and spent a good part of the session, as well as later on the phone with me, praising him for his kindness. They reached an amicable settlement in the next session. Such ambivalence is not unheard of by marital therapists, who may spend six months supporting a woman's decision to leave a "cruel and inconsiderate" husband, only to have her cancel the next appointment because she has reunited with him. However, when such a move occurs within a week of hearing what might be considered life-threatening concerns, the contrast can be disorienting to the mediator.

The transactions that take place between each spouse and his or her children, new spouse, parents, and friends between mediation sessions may also contribute to unpredictable behavior. For example, one man who had filed for sole custody of both his children, and insisted in the first mediation session that he would settle for nothing less, then came into the second session offering sole custody to his ex-wife. Although he gave a variety of inconsistent reasons for this action, it turned out that during the interim week one of his children had unexpectedly (and for equally inconsistent reasons) told him that he wanted to live with his mother. These words hurt the father deeply, so he reversed his position, and tried to save face by offering pseudo-reasons for his action. In essence, he attempted to deal with his hurt feelings by depriving himself of his desired choice.

In another case, a father had agreed to a very reasonable and workable shared custody plan, only to arrive at the next session insisting on sole custody. During the interim week, his new wife had informed him that his ex-wife was taking advantage of him and that he had better go for sole custody to prove that he would not be pushed around. Such transactions are clearly beyond the control of the mediator but can result in puzzling sudden moves that hamper the mediation process.

Further contributing to unpredictability is the occasional poorly timed legal maneuver occuring right in the middle of the mediation process. For example, one man who had come to many constructive agreements with his ex-wife in the first mediation session refused to return for the next session. It turned out that during the interim week he had received a subpoena for a court hearing on the custody issue. The secretary of his wife's lawyer, not knowing that mediation efforts were in progress, had mistakenly sent a subpoena to the husband as a matter of standard legal procedure. However, the husband interpreted this as power escalation by his wife, and he refused to cooperate any further in mediation. Even though he was given an adequate explanation, his trust had been irretrievably damaged. Such mischances are not uncommon among courts and law offices during the mediation process. They often function as "disinformation" (Watzlawick, 1976), in that the perceived validity of certain information is determined by a particular context, making later evidence of its invalidity very difficult to accept.

The unpredictability of a couple in mediation often leaves the mediator wishing that he or she could exert more control over the situation. A helpful axiom for mediators to follow is this: Never expect a couple to be cooperative or uncooperative until the final agreement is fully signed. Even then, of course, there is no certainty of a predictable follow-through. The mediator really has no choice but to accept such unpredictability as the grandest challenge of the process.

Because of the many special difficulties that arise in mediation work, it is necessary to bring certain attitudes and skills to the process. These contribute both to the effectiveness of mediation and to the survival of the mediator.

An effective mediator's style might best be characterized as active, assertive, goal-oriented, and businesslike. He or she must utilize the skills of brief behaviorally oriented family therapy, crisis intervention, negotiation, organizational development, and child development counseling, coupled with a sensitivity to the emotional and psychological aspects of the mediation process. The mediator must deal with the emotional aspects of the process without allowing them to disrupt the problem solving. Too tight control restricts the complexity of the emotional issues that need to be assessed, while too loose control allows the emotional charge to overwhelm the rational structure needed to reach resolution. There is a thin line between these extremes that the skilled mediator learns to walk.

The mediator must truly enjoy skilled, controlled problem solving. Because of the unpredictable and sudden moves often made by the couple in mediation, the mediator must constantly be prepared to respond appropriately and instantaneously to each crisis as it arises. Since there is so much at stake at each crisis point, there is little room for error on the part of the mediator. Each intervention must be at once well thought-out, accurately timed, and rapidly implemented. These requirements necessitate that the mediator possess both the professional skills and the emotional stability demanded of a psychotherapist. The mediator must be capable of leading a hostile couple away from antagonism and into cooperative areas of negotiation. Mediators who cannot tolerate open and intense conflict will burn out quickly and, moreover, may cause irreparable damage to the couple's potential for future negotiation. While we are just beginning to understand the negative effects that psychotherapy may have on clients (Strupp and others, 1977), the negative effects of mediation on couples are as yet unknown. However, we can speculate that if negative effects experienced by a client in psychotherapy can weaken or destroy the client's confidence in the possibility of obtaining future help (as most therapists have discovered to be the case), then negative effects from a mediation experience may be even greater, considering the intensity of emotions involved, the enormous personal significance of the issues at stake, and the extraordinary necessity—and difficulty—of the mediator's maintaining a balance between the couple at every point throughout the mediation process. Hence, it is incumbent on the mediator to maximize the probability of a satisfying resolution to the mediated issues by being properly prepared. It should, however, be remembered that successful resolution is at times well out of the control of even the most skillful mediator.

The mediator needs to maintain a functional perspective in dealing with the interactional dynamics that are the grist of the mediation process. A functional perspective deals with the effect that a particular behavioral sequence has on interpersonal interactions. For example, suppose that a father insists on having the children live with him exactly 50 percent of every week, is unwilling to compromise, and is willing to go to court to fight for this plan, even though such a schedule of time-sharing would be inconvenient for all the parties involved, including himself. Regardless of his real motives (which might be based on power assertion and/or revenge and retaliation strategies—see Chapter Seven), his behavior has the effect of scaring the mother into protecting her own relationship with the children. She may then come back with an insistence on sole custody (which might be based on an emotional survival strategy—see Chapter Seven). Her behavior is likely to escalate the conflict, which could have the effect of scaring the children into defusing the tension between their parents through the use of a tension detonating strategy (see Chapter Six). The children's behavior might have the effect of further polarizing their parents' positions, since the parents might each interpret the children's behavior as evidence for the validity of their own positions.

Throughout, each member's behavior can be viewed simply in terms of its functional effect on the other members. Such a perspective circumvents the moot theoretical questions of whether a particular behavior is conscious or unconscious, intentional or impulsive, normal or psychopathological. When the tactics that children and spouses employ are described functionally, they can be used by the mediator to form specific intervention strategies of his or her own that serve to direct the course of mediation more sensitively. Such a functional perspective helps the mediator to maintain objectivity, since particular strategies are intrinsically neither good nor bad, honest nor dishonest, right nor wrong, but merely serve to influence the thoughts, feelings, and/or behavior of other persons. Working from this perspective, the mediator does not feel so inclined to judge the participants, which would risk bias and the loss of neutrality. By understanding the participants' strategies, the mediator can plan counter-strategies to facilitate a constructive outcome.

It is very important that the mediator maintain a nonjudgmental attitude. Each spouse frequently attempts to tell the mediator negative things about the other spouse, implicitly and explicitly trying to sway the mediator's sympathies. In order not to succumb, the mediator needs to understand fully the dynamics of marital and family interactions so that when empathy is elicited within the mediator, it can be put into a helpful systems perspective. If the mediator becomes overtly critical of one of the spouses, the impartiality necessary for a successful resolution will be lost. Clearly, no intervenor is devoid of personal reactions and values, yet the necessity for keeping them out of the mediation process is paramount.

The ability to remain nonjudgmental also requires that the mediator be aware of, and reasonably resolved about, his or her own familial issues and personal values, which might be aroused in the course of mediation. Issues arise in custody disputes that touch every person on some level. The mediator is confronted with a broad range of emotional triggers—from the overt pain of children and parents going through divorce to the mediator's covert personal response to allegations of child neglect or molestation, alcoholism, or drug abuse. Moreover, it may be difficult for the mediator to deal fairly with spouses who have authoritarian child-rearing practices, religious beliefs that seem extreme or destructive to healthy child development, or vengeful motives for spending time with their child. These issues can elicit what psychoanalytic theory refers to as countertransference reactions and lead a mediator away from the task of fair management of the dispute. Keeping such reactions in check is especially important in mediation work because, unlike psychotherapy, there is little or no time to digest or even dissipate such reactions. They must be dealt with immediately and thoroughly by the mediator, since the expression of such reactions has no useful place in the mediation process. Allowing a personal reaction such as anger to intrude into the mediation process can unnecessarily prolong it, complicate it, or cause it to fail—ultimately, in most cases, at greater cost to the children involved. Hence, although there are strategic ways to ensure greater degrees of physical and emotional protection for the children within the final settlement (see Chapter Four), the mediator must be able to accept a wide variety of life-styles and child-rearing practices and not feel that the only good ones are those valued by the mediator himself.

The mediator must function as a diplomat, allowing each family member equal protection for his or her vulnerability throughout the mediation process. Each member must be given the maximum opportunity to save face in the midst of the threats and accusations that are frequently thrown about. A successful resolution can best come about when both the spouses and the children feel reasonably secure and esteemed. The message "You are not lovable" often rings through the house of the divorcing family. Each spouse may offer proof of this statement, and the children may absorb it as an assumption about themselves as a natural outcome of the divorce itself.

Hence, the mediator must work diplomatically to minimize any judgments and criticisms proffered about the spouse by the person who knows all of his or her faults better than anyone else—the ex-spouse.

It should be noted that, in general, there are differences between the approach of spouses who attend mediation voluntarily and the approach of those for whom mediation is mandated. Couples who attend mediation voluntarily may manifest fewer and less intense struggles, which makes the mediator's job significantly easier. However, research has yet to determine whether the outcomes of mandatory mediation differ significantly from the outcomes of voluntary mediation. It appears that the issues presented and the strategies utilized by voluntary participants in mediation are not much different from those of involuntary participants, in spite of any differences in the intensity of expression. Moreover, when a mediator grapples with the most difficult cases first, then the easier cases can be surprisingly enjoyable. It is with such a belief that this book is focused on the more difficult challenges presented in mediation, so that the reader may be comfortably prepared to deal with the easier ones.

The most effective way to ensure objectivity in the mediation process is to adopt a sensitive scientific approach to the task. Each session of the mediation process can be viewed as a mini-experiment. Each case begins against a backdrop of previously known patterns to mediated settlements of custody disputes. And each case also begins with a set of new data that are unique to the particular family involved. The initial data collected before mediation begins generate hypotheses that are then tested in mediation, and the feedback that is obtained is used to generate new hypotheses about each family member's strategies, real needs, and likely acceptable outcomes. When the mediator has clear evidence that he or she has generated enough useful hypotheses, then negotiations are begun for the creation of the final product—a balanced, workable settlement. This scientific, methodical attitude helps the mediator to stay objective, to calculate each next move carefully, and to remain skeptical of the validity of any sudden changes in a family member's position until he or she is satisfied that the new data are indeed valid and not just artifacts of a temporary emotional state.

Although the scientific aspect of this attitude is essential, it must always be complemented by sensitivity. Support for and understanding of the psychological and emotional state in which each spouse appears to be, and sensitivity to the pace needed for the process to unfold properly may be key factors in the long-term stability of any final decisions made by the couple. Whereas a mechanically scientific approach can result in further alienation of the couple, a sensitive scientific approach will maximize efficient human contact throughout the mediation process.

It is also important for the mediator to acknowledge the uniqueness of the content of child custody mediation. Some freelance mediators—working in such areas as tenant-landlord disputes, small-claims disputes, consumer-seller disputes, and collective bargaining disputes—believe that the skills they utilize in their work are sufficient for child custody mediation. While it may be true that such general mediation skills are necessary for child custody mediation work, they clearly are not sufficient. Wallerstein (1981) points out that child custody mediation is a very special type of mediation. The mediator must be competent to give valid, current, and helpful information about child development, about children's typical and atypical responses to family conflicts, about family members' needs and feelings, about family dynamics, about the divorce process (emotionally, structurally, and legally), and about the likely future outcomes for children and parents of a variety of different postdivorce family structures. The mediator should be knowlegable about individual psychodynamics, interactional dynamics, family systems, and behavior change, and have a broad general knowledge of psychological functioning. Child custody mediators who are not specifically trained in these areas may seriously compromise the benefits of child custody mediation.

Above all, Wallerstein and Kelly (1980) emphasize that the mediator must remain the *advocate for the children.* Although this point seems obvious, it is worth considering more carefully. The traditional adversarial approach to child custody determination has failed to provide meaningful advocacy for the children of divorcing parents. Attempts have been made to provide legal counsel for children in custody proceedings (Derdeyn, 1976), but the legal system so far has not been able to find an appropriate place for the needs and wishes of the child in the adversarial scheme. Moreover, the lawyers who typically are assigned the task of legal advocacy for the child usually have no special training for this task, and therefore are not necessarily more knowledgeable about, or sensitive to, the needs and feelings of children than are the judges or the parents' own attorneys. Hence, the attorney for the child most often functions only to slow down the legal process, and to confuse rather than clarify the issues.

If the mediator is to be a helpful advocate for the children, it is incumbent on him or her to be fully knowledgeable about how children think, feel, and act, during and after a divorce, as well as in different stages of development. Using only intuitively gleaned assumptions about what the child is experiencing is not enough; indeed, very often it is just such assumptions made by parents that lead to court battles (see Chapter Six). Acting on incorrect assumptions can have devastating consequences. Hence, both insight *and* information about children are essential. While this book can provide perspectives, information, and strategies, supervised training is necessary before one can competently carry out the tremendous responsibilities involved in doing mediation.

A final important attitude in mediation is the degree of positive conviction held by judges and attorneys about the potential effectiveness of child custody mediation. Even after several years of successful voluntary mediation (arranged by attorneys) and a year of successful involuntary mediation (legislatively mandated), numerous judges and lawyers in the state of California remained skeptical about mediation's potential for resolving custody and visitation disputes. This attitude was grounded in a persistent belief that spouses who are divorced or divorcing with a contestation about custody cannot even talk constructively with each other, let alone agree on issues as important as custody. At bottom, this myth assumes that if the spouses could talk constructively and civilly with each other, they would not have gotten divorced in the first place. One attorney who, along with the opposing counsel, sat in on his first mediation session involving a client (the mother), commented afterwards, "I was astounded to see them actually talking nicely and constructively with each other after what I've heard about that SOB from the mother." It is the adversarial approach to such disputes that, in the past, has perpetuated these myths. Since there was no opportunity for nonadversarial approaches, no cooperative solutions were forthcoming. Therefore, it was concluded that, given the hostility surrounding custody battles, cooperative solutions were not possible. However, once the opportunity arises, new solutions are possible.

Without the support of judges and attorneys, the mediation process is extremely difficult. When the mediator is working against an upcoming court date and attorneys who are discouraging their clients and expressing resistance to mediation, either spouse, at the slightest frustration in a session, may run back to his or her attorney and say "Let's go to court, I don't like what she (he) said." Or, knowing that the court date is coming up next week, the spouse might simply sit through the mediation sessions, passively resisting all requests for a compromise. With the support of the legal representatives, the process becomes significantly easier. When a judge is willing to continue, indefinitely, the court date for custody determination, and when both attorneys in the case are firmly and strongly supportive of the mediation efforts, then the mediator's task is markedly easier, and mediation proceeds much more effectively.*

Part of the challenge of mediation is its attempt to stand

*It should be noted that the Honorable Donald B. King, a Superior Court judge in San Francisco, California, has exemplified the ideal degree of legal support offered for mediation, beginning several years before California's mandatory mediation. In his court, he required all couples with custody or visitation disputes to settle their disputes with their attorneys and/or a Family Court mediator before the judge would hear the rest of their dissolution proceedings. He reports over a 99 percent success rate for such mediation efforts, with success defined as settling the present dispute and not returning to court with similar future disputes (King, 1979).

between adversarial law practices and psychotherapy. Mediation work requires the precision and strategic thinking of legal work, coupled with the insightfulness, emotional sensitivity, and supportiveness of psychotherapy. In other ways, however, mediation differs from law and psychotherapy, and the dissimilarities are worth elaborating here, since failures in mediation often are due to unintended slippage by the mediator into one of the other roles.

The task of lawyers functioning in an adversarial role is to protect their client's legal rights and to maximize the client's leverage within a dispute, through various legal maneuvers. In his excellent article, Brown (1982) cites severe criticisms of the adversarial system by a wide variety of professionals who work in the domestic relations field. Among these are the perspectives of Felder (1971, pp. 1–2), a prominent divorce lawyer: "I am in business to win. . . . Once I have been hired, my sole aim is to gain victory; and in doing so, I will do anything and everything I think necessary to serve the interests of my client, to achieve his purpose, to gain him a divorce in which he will come out financially, psychologically, in every way on top. That is what I have been hired to do and if in doing it, I appear cold and calculating, then that's the way it has to be. I am tough because I assume the lawyer who opposes me will also be tough [and] when I take a case, I am not concerned with whether my client is always right. As far as I am concerned, a client is always right." This attitude is firmly trained into lawyers and gets reinforced ethically, through peer esteem, and financially, through winning clients. Moreover, if a lawyer does not advocate to the fullest extent possible for his client alone (typically one parent), he is failing to live up to the American Bar Association's canon of ethics, which specifically requires him to represent only one party in a dispute, with the understanding that the other party is entitled to full representation by separate counsel. Hence, within the adversarial system, a lawyer who eases up on advocacy for his client in a custody dispute, because he understands the systemic nature of such disputes and feels the pain and injustice experienced by the other spouse and the child, may be accused of questionable ethical practices. This clearly places the adversarial lawyer in a difficult dilemma. While, personally, he may fully appreciate the destructiveness of adversarial efforts to resolve such domestic issues, professionally, he is ethically bound to perpetuate such destructiveness.

The lawyer's dilemma is resolved when he assumes a mediator's role. In this role, he can step out of his advocacy position and can work with both spouses simultaneously, legally representing neither of them, but letting them know that each has the right to seek separate attorneys if they feel the need for a legal advocate. However, when lawyers are functioning as mediators, they must work against their professional reflexes to advocate, defend, argue, and win. Lawyers must view success in reaching an agreement not as their client winning, but as the children winning. The errors made by lawyers doing mediation are typically in the direction of either subtly advocating for one of the parents and leaving the other parent feeling unsupported, or of excessively exploring the feelings of one or both of the clients to such a degree that more distress than constructive emotional venting is experienced. Often, the lawyer attempts to deal with the emotions without, perhaps, having the proper training and skills to work through these emotions enough so that negotiation efforts can get on their way. The error in the first case is in behaving too much like a lawyer, and the error in the second is in behaving too much like a therapist. In both cases, the approach is inappropriate and may result in failure of the mediation effort.

A psychotherapist, on the other hand, has the task of helping clients to understand and deal more effectively with emotional distress and behavioral problems. Usually a great deal of support is offered the client (who, typically, is defined as the person who makes the appointment and pays for the therapy), and this unilateral support may well continue even when another significant person in the client's life is brought into therapy (for example, a spouse). Or, if a couple seek therapy together and then, out of discontent, one of the spouses drops out of therapy, the remaining spouse may claim the full support of the therapist in his or her continued individual therapy.

In many therapies, the therapeutic process is open ended,

time unlimited, and exploratory in nature, and it may proceed until an unstated end point is reached (often, when the client drops out of therapy). Moreover, unlike the mediator, the therapist typically has much more information about the couple or family with which to work, is not under any time pressure for resolving the problems, and does not need any support from judges or attorneys to carry on the therapeutic work effectively. Furthermore, because of this, the therapist has a reasonable degree of predictability, within a given session and between sessions, as to what is likely to take place in the family. Hence, a great deal of the confusion and stress experienced in mediation is typically not present in therapy.

The mediator is in a unique position in relation to both the lawyer and the therapist. She is an advocate for the children, but not for either parent. She has an explicit goal to achieve within a clearly designated structure, and in a relatively brief time period. She may give support to either spouse, as long as equal support is always offered to the other spouse. And, she must always remain impartial and objective in all interventions, from the first phone call to the final signing of the written agreement. Emotions are dealt with only to the degree that such intervention contributes to the creation of the final written agreement, but not for any purpose of facilitating personal growth. Emotional venting is considered a potentially disruptive event to the mediation process and is channeled into constructive negotiations. This approach is unlike that of therapy, in which such venting might be viewed as a goal in itself.

These differences between mediation and therapy are important to note because of their practical and theoretical implications. When one is mediating custody and visitation disputes, according to the structure offered in this book, it is very important not to slip into the role of therapist, and to maintain the mediator role throughout the process. Because of the emotionally volatile nature of custody disputes and because the mediator must remain a neutral advocate for the children, it is extremely difficult for the mediator to be concerned with the needs of one or both spouses to the degree necessary for psychotherapeutic benefit for them. If it appears that either or both spouses need therapy before they will be able to negotiate effectively in mediation, the mediator can make an appropriate referral to a marital or family therapist, preferably one who is knowledgeable about the mediation process and is able to sustain the family systems view while working on the emotional issues.

If the mediator is mediating the entire divorce settlement, then the possibility may exist for the mediator to call a time-out, to switch roles to that of a therapist, and to explore, therapeutically, the specific issues that might be blocking the couple from effective negotiations (as suggested by Haynes, 1981). Certainly, dealing with a wider variety of issues (some more and some less emotionally charged), over a greater number of sessions and greater expanse of time, may offer the divorce mediator wider latitude for functioning temporarily as a therapist. However, whether or not a mediator in a case can also function as a therapist for the same clients is in controversy. Indeed, the ability of the particular mediator to remain neutral and balanced may be a more crucial point than whether the two modalities are in fact mutually exclusive. If a divorce mediator feels that switching roles is too difficult for him, then he should, if necessary, refer the spouse or couple to an appropriate marital or family therapist, before proceeding further with mediation.

3

Beginning Mediation: Setting the Context for Negotiations

The single most important tool of mediation is structure. Because couples going through the crisis of divorce tend to be volatile, a mediation process without a solid, well-defined structure is bound to end in failure. One mediator, for example, who had much experience doing long-term psychotherapy but little doing mediation, began to do custody mediation with a couple who were still very emotionally involved with each other three years after their divorce. They could easily be characterized as an enmeshed couple (a term suggested by Kressel and others, 1980). As the mediator began to ask the couple about their early marriage, emotions poured forth. Taking this as evidence of their need to express feelings that probably have been repressed for years, the mediator allowed the spouses to vent. After three sessions of such venting, the mediator began to feel as if he were accomplishing a great deal. However, as he then began attempting to focus the couple on the task of developing a time-sharing plan for their child, they just continued to vent their feelings—all the way through session number *nine*. Needless to say, the mediator felt more and more out of control and unable to focus the couple on any concrete task. Each time he attempted to suggest a resolution, one or the other spouse would divert the topic to an emotional one, which would trigger off the other spouse, and both would become extremely volatile. However, they were no closer to resolving any of the custody issues than when they began mediation. The exasperated mediator finally realized that these spouses thrived on elaborate expressions of their emotions. These were not people who had repressed feelings, but a couple whose style of interaction was best characterized as emotionally volatile. Moreover, although their depth of emotional expressiveness was bottomless, they were unable to provide any structure to their interactions that might lead to effective problem solving. Hence, because the mediator began with an assumption of repressed feelings, as is characteristic in traditional psychotherapy, he failed to provide the tight and clear structure necessary in mediation work, and hence was unable to lead the couple effectively through the problem-solving process that is mediation. While working with this particular enmeshed couple would be difficult even in a tightly structured situation (Kressel and others, 1980), the absence of such a structure leads to almost certain failure in mediation.

General Structural Issues

The particular structure that guides the mediation process will be the basis for a variety of decisions the mediator has to make. Let us consider general structural issues before proceeding to specific issues.

Number of Sessions Needed. Mediators tend to split into groups that claim mediation can be accomplished in ten to twenty sessions, six to ten sessions, four to six sessions, or one to three sessions. These differences are a function of a number of contributing factors that can vary the actual number of sessions needed for a particular case. For example, the number and complexity of issues considered in mediation will partly determine how many sessions will be needed. If the mediator is dealing with every aspect of the divorce settlement, including property division, financial distribution, support issues, and tax considerations, in addition to custody issues, then he or she no doubt will require more sessions. Moreover, if the custody issues are intertwined with property division and/or child support issues, more sessions may be required to assist the couple in separating the custody issues from the financial issues. Fewer sessions are needed, however, if the mediator is dealing only with the custody and visitation issues (generally from one to three sessions). This may be the case when the financial issues are already settled or are being dealt with separately by a co-mediating or consulting attorney, or by the spouses' respective attorneys. It is also the case when financial issues are specifically excluded from the custody mediation work (for example, as provided for under California's mandatory mediation law).

The nature of the referral also partially determines the number of sessions needed. A private mediator who works with couples that voluntarily seek mediation on an hourly fee basis generally has the opportunity—both temporally and economically—to offer more sessions than does a court-connected mediator who may be very backlogged with cases and therefore limited in the number of sessions he or she can offer.

Another factor is the amount of experience that the mediator has had in this area of work and his or her intervention style. In this author's opinion, it appears that more experienced mediators, and those who stylistically are more active and structured in their approach, generally tend to need fewer sessions to reach settlement than do those who are less experienced or less active and structured.

The mediator's view of which issues must be discussed before a satisfactory resolution is possible will also affect the number of sessions needed. At one extreme are mediators who believe that extensive knowledge of the history and dynamics of the couple and their children is essential before the mediator can lead them to agreement. At the other extreme are those who believe that minimal knowledge of the participants yields resolutions most effectively. These mediators feel that prolonged mediation opens a Pandora's box of issues that may forever be unsettled, and may in fact aggravate the situation further, making resolution difficult or impossible.

The expectations of the mediator and the motivation and expectations of the spouses will partly determine the number of sessions. If a mediator views the task of mediation as helping the couple to explore their marital relationship and individual psychodynamics so as to resolve their feelings about each other, then the process will go on for a longer time. Occasionally, a couple who voluntarily seek out a private mediator may specifically request such an approach. However, such couples not uncommonly are seeking reconciliation and are using the mediation context as a forum for marital therapy. A mediator who attempts to mediate a divorce and/or custody settlement with a couple who have not really decided to divorce may find her efforts counterproductive. Many sessions may pass by before she realizes that each attempt at clarifying the divorce and/or custody issues has been frustrated by the strong emotional pull within each spouse for reunification. In such cases it might be best for the mediator to refer the couple to a marital counselor (or, if appropriate, assume such a role herself) until such time as they have definitely decided to divorce or reunite.

For some couples, mediation presents an opportunity for divorce counseling and an opportunity for their children to talk to someone who is objective and rational in the midst of parental subjectivity and irrationality. Often, the mediation sessions are the only opportunity since the separation or divorce for family members to meet together to wrap up the loose ends of the breakup. While an extended number of sessions can occasionally be very helpful to such families who voluntarily seek mediation, there are some circumstances in which extending the number of sessions is counterproductive. For example, extending the number of sessions is very risky when only one spouse wants to explore the divorce issues more extensively, while the other spouse wants the mediation short and sweet. This is often the case when the motives of one spouse are expressive of a reuniting strategy (see Chapter Seven) and that spouse's request for more mediation sessions is an attempt to gain more conjoint time to persuade the other spouse back into the marriage. Often in this situation there will be one session too many, and the other spouse will refuse to continue mediation, resist efforts toward compromise, or demand an immediate and inflexible resolution to the mediation issues. Because this tends to polarize the other spouse, the possibilities for a stalemate are great. This is also frequently the situation in certain court-ordered mediation cases in which neither spouse wants to be there; extending the number of sessions can polarize such a couple even further, forestalling or obstructing a resolution to the custody or visitation dispute.

It is wise for the mediator to heed the warning: mediation is not therapy or counseling. It is a highly structured process for negotiating a temporary or initial agreement from which later decisions can more rationally be made. Very often, the more open-ended the opportunities available for couples in mediation to talk, the greater their chances for justifying their mistrust of each other. Such opportunities can increase the number of negative transactions and thereby increase the difficulty in reaching a settlement. As one therapist put it: "Communication doesn't just mean talking; . . . oftentimes, couples develop 'communication problems' because they talk to each other too much. For them, communication is increased by not talking to each other so much!" (Haley, 1979).

If a mediator views his task as achieving successful resolution to a custody or visitation dispute in as brief and painless a time as possible, then a tight and well-thought-out structure can help to accomplish this task in relatively few sessions. The mediator must, indeed, always aim at being in control, and having fewer sessions necessitates greater control.

Length of Sessions. Mediators should generally allow one and a half to two hours per mediation session. Occasionally, a simple case may take as little as forty-five minutes of a single session, but usually it is difficult to accomplish much of significance in a session of less than one and a half hours.

Once again, there is a wide variety of mediator styles, schedules, and circumstances that will necessitate different lengths of sessions. Some mediators fit their mediation cases into an hourly schedule in the middle of their regular workload. This can work fine if individual sessions are held with each spouse, but it typically is too short a time period to work with the couple together. Other mediators prefer to schedule an entire morning or afternoon for a mediation case. This leaves open the possibility of a marathon session, and gives the mediator more flexibility for expanding on the process while he or she still controls its direction.

Time Between Sessions. A key variable for the mediator is the length of time that passes between sessions. Whereas in psychotherapy the tradition has been to schedule weekly sessions for the course of the therapy, in mediation the time between sessions can often determine whether or not a resolution will be reached.

There clearly is an optimal time period between sessions that maximizes the likelihood of reaching a resolution. This period, especially the one between the first and second sessions, needs to be carefully planned by the mediator. If the time period is too short (a week or less), the feelings generated in the first session often prevent the spouses from working on their problems in a rational manner. They remain stuck in protective, adversarial stances. If, however, too much time passes (several months or more), momentum is lost, legal or personal changes will have been numerous, and the complexion of the case is often significantly different by the time of the second session. If, however, the second session is scheduled an optimal length of time after the first session (usually several weeks), there is time for negative feelings to die down following the first session and for each of the spouses to complete some focused thinking about some possible solutions to their situation.

An interesting phenomenon often occurs after the spouses leave the first session. Even if the entire first session is devoted merely to understanding the specific circumstances of the couple's situation, several other things will also have taken place. For one thing, this is often the first time that the spouses have been together in the same room since their court hearing. For another, it is often the first time since their separation that the spouses have talked together for any length of time without generating more negative feelings toward each other. It is often the first time that the couple have worked on a constructive resolution to conflicts that may have been going on for many years. And, it is often the first time that both have experienced equal participation in discussions about their children and their future and the first time that they have experienced equal respect for their particular points of view. All these factors help a couple to generate new perspectives about their situation, and thoughts of more cooperative solutions begin to develop within each spouse. It is often after this first session that the characteristic unpredictability previously described is first manifested. It is as if the first session has a disorienting effect that temporarily disarms the spouses and is conducive to compromise. Allowing two or three weeks (on the average) to pass until the second session helps the spouses to reorient and prepare themselves to engage in more rational problem solving by the next session(s).

Relationship with Attorneys. The relationship between the mediator and any attorneys of the spouses that may be involved in the custody or visitation dispute is very important. The mediator's task is greatly facilitated if the attorneys are knowledgeable about and supportive of mediation. Indeed, attorneys who are experienced with the successes of mediation almost always become quite supportive of the mediator and are a delight to work with. There is great comfort in knowing that a client's threat to talk to his or her attorney about going to court is an empty one.

When one or both of the attorneys in a particular case are unknowledgeable about and/or unsupportive of mediation—as may be the case in court-ordered mediation—then the mediator's efforts are very vulnerable to being blocked. There are a variety of reasons that a particular attorney might not be supportive of mediation efforts. An attorney who has never experienced, or perhaps even considered, mediation might simply not believe that it could work. An attorney who is himself in the middle of a bitter divorce might tend to project his unwillingness to compromise onto his clients. Or an attorney might have experienced failure in the only two cases that she sent for mediation, and so would remain unimpressed. Finally, an attorney might be so strongly oriented to an adversarial stance that cooperative efforts would seem personally awkward or even professionally unethical. Whatever the reasons, the mediator needs to be aware of potential blockage by an attorney, preferably before starting the mediation process.

If the mediator knows that the attorneys in a particular case are supportive of mediation, then the mediator may simply want to make courtesy contact with them before beginning. If, however, an attorney is not known to the mediator or is known to be unsupportive of mediation, then a more extensive phone call or personal meeting with that attorney is very important. This contact should be intended to assess the attorney's current beliefs and feelings about mediation in general and for this client in particular. It is also an opportunity to make gestures toward cooperation, either by direct appeals or by offers of information about the mediation process and its potential benefits to the attorney and his or her client. For attorneys, the benefits of this approach include freedom from the angry phone calls from clients that are common in custody cases; having clients who are more satisfied because they worked out the custody and/or visitation issues themselves; and being free to counsel their client about legal matters, rather than having to deal with the raw emotions of marital conflict. Contrary to the implication of Coogler (1978) that lawyers may sabotage mediation efforts because of reduced financial rewards for them, it has been my general experience that lawyers welcome the opportunity to reduce the level of emotional tension and acrimony in their cases. They appreciate having someone specifically skilled in resolving emotionally laden issues who can take their clients to the point of being rational enough to work effectively within the legal context.

If the confidentiality agreement (discussed later) between the couple and mediator is to be signed, contact with the attorneys should be made before the first session. This allows the mediator to receive from the attorneys any pertinent information about their clients that they choose to reveal, without the mediator's being tempted to reveal any information about the couple to the attorneys. The mediator can open communication by saying, "Is there anything about your client or your client's situation that might be helpful for me to know?" To this question, the attorney might respond with a negative, or she might indeed share information. For example, the attorney might cite documented allegations or convictions of child abuse, sexual molestation, or dangerous substance abuse or addictions on the part of the other spouse. Or the attorney might point out that her client is a religious fanatic who will not compromise, or is dead set against mediation, or is extremely young and unable to make mature decisions about children without a lot of help. Given such information, the mediator can be alert to safety issues regarding the children when discussing negotiable parameters in the mediation sessions.

In response to this bid for information, the attorney may attempt to influence the mediator to side with her client and to look askance at the opposing client. A mediator can easily detect this intent by listening to the significance of the content chosen by the attorney. If, for example, the attorney says, "I think the father should not have much contact with the kids because he lets the kids stay up until 10 P.M., and he feeds them hot dogs, and he never takes them anywhere fun," then the mediator can understand this more as the attorney's fulfillment of her role as an advocate for her client than as significant concern for the safety or well-being of the children. Such an attorney should be respected for the dedication shown to her client and, in time, educated about the really important needs of children and the benefits of cooperative approaches to custody and visitation disputes. If, however, the attorney says that the other spouse has just been released from prison for the third time on felonious child abuse and drunk driving convictions, then the mediator must be very cautious when leading the negotiations about child care arrangements.

Before beginning the mediation, the mediator should also request the attorneys to refer their clients directly back to the mediator if either should consult them during the mediation process. Knowing that both attorneys are supportive of the mediation efforts and the condition of confidentiality (discussed later), the spouses become more willing to commit themselves to participate fully in the mediation process.

Fees. The fees mediators charge vary according to a number of factors. Mediators who are based within a court (such as conciliation court counselors) receive a flat salary from the county to handle all the contested custody and visitation cases and receive no direct fees from their clients. Private custody mediators may also receive direct referrals from the court and may be paid by the county on a contract basis per year, per case, or per hour. Private mediators who are not court-connected generally charge on a per-hour basis. When the private mediator is dealing only with custody and/or visitation issues, fees typically are paid at the end of each session. It is best if half the fee is paid by each spouse, but other arrangements can be made. In some cases—for example, when a modification of custody is requested years after a divorce—there may be a significant discrepancy between the spouses' abilities to pay half the hourly fee each. One spouse may be willing to pay the entire fee or some greater proportion of it, and the other may be willing to contribute his or her equivalent share in bartered services or a deferred reimbursement to the other spouse. It is best to have each spouse contribute at least a token amount to the total fee, in order to stress that *both* parents are responsible for contributing to the resolution of any dispute regarding their children.

When handling all aspects of a divorce settlement, some mediators receive a lump sum deposit from the couple at the first session, against which all charges are made for mediation fees, advisory attorney fees, and fees for other consultants needed by the mediator. Any unused money is returned to the clients (Coogler, 1978). Other divorce mediators prefer not to collect a deposit but to receive their hourly fees at the end of each session.

Fees for mediation generally are set in accordance with the usual hourly rates for other work done by the particular professional conducting the mediation. Typically, attorneys who do mediation charge more than mental health professionals and, geographically, mediators on the coasts and in large metropolitan areas seem to charge more than those in other locations. Some mediators in both the legal and mental health professions charge a greater fee for mediation than their usual hourly fee for their other professional services. They do this for several reasons: because they have received special training or have acquired special expertise to do mediation; because both spouses are contributing to the fee and therefore can afford a larger fee, or because mediation is generally more demanding than their other work. As a matter of fact, some mediators have felt that the legal risks of doing mediation work call for special malpractice insurance. Malpractice insurance specifically designed for divorce and family mediators first became available in 1982, from Lloyds of London (cited in Brown, 1982).

Private mediators also vary in their policies of charging for telephone conference calls. Some mediators charge both parties for *all* time spent on a case; this is especially true for attorneys, who typically have much greater overhead expenses than do mental health professionals. Other mediators charge only for face-to-face contact time and absorb phone costs as a courtesy extension of their mediation work. Hence, some clients may be charged by both their mediator and their respective attorneys for conferences between them, some may be charged by one and not the other, and some may be so fortunate as to not be charged for any services except the mediation sessions per se.

Scheduling the First Session. Based on information gathered on the phone as well as that received from the court, from the attorneys, and from the spouses themselves, the mediator must decide about several structural issues relating to the first session. The first issue—when to schedule the first appointment—should be decided on the basis of several factors. If the spouses were in court for their divorce only yesterday, are still very acrimonious, and are attending mediation reluctantly (that is, by court order or attorney stipulation), then the mediator would do well to schedule the first appointment for several weeks hence. This would give the spouses a cooling-off period and would allow them to be more rational when mediation begins. If, however, the spouses have been separated for several years, have been friendly and cooperative with each other over that period of time, and are now filing for divorce and want assistance in making the best co-parenting arrangements for their children, then the mediator can feel comfortable in setting an appointment for the very day or week they call. Although there is no guarantee that the latter couple will resolve their issues more quickly than the former couple, the probability for success in the first case would be increased if they had some time to diminish their anger before attempting to cooperate on a plan for their children.

A second issue that needs deciding is who shall attend the first mediation session. On this issue mediators split into those who schedule individual appointments with each spouse before seeing them together and those who schedule the couple together from the start. An advantage of the first approach is that it gives an opportunity for each spouse to vent his or her feelings and concerns before beginning the mediation process. However, there are several disadvantages to this approach. First, there is the potential for stirring up more problems than is necessary in order to facilitate a workable resolution. Second, it may set up the expectation within the clients that mediation is counseling or psychotherapy, which may leave them feeling disappointed when the mediator does not follow through with the individualized personal concern characteristic of therapy. And third, it seems inefficient, necessitating at least three initial sessions instead of one.

The advantages of seeing the couple together for the first and each subsequent session include the implicit message that this is mediation and not individual therapy, that the problem is to be resolved between the spouses right from the start, that the mediator will not sympathize with either spouse to the exclusion of the other, and that the dispute is to be viewed from a systems, rather than individual, point of view. Also, the potential for stirring up unnecessary issues and feelings is minimized by the tight structure of the mediation context. And lastly, this approach is temporally efficient.

Although seeing the spouses together in every session might appear to have the disadvantage of lacking an opportunity for each spouse to vent feelings, that is not in fact the case. Opportunities to vent feelings arise at various points throughout the mediation process. However, such venting is structured in a constructive manner that leads more easily to resolution than to increased anger and frustration. Moreover, there are to date no clinical or research data suggesting that extensive expression of feelings aids in the resolution of custody and visitation disputes. If the spouses, together or individually, express the desire to have counseling or therapy, then a referral is made for them either during or after mediation.

Although factors other than the above may significantly influence the mediator's decisions, careful and strategic planning in scheduling the first appointment can greatly maximize the effectiveness of mediation.

Setting the Context

It has become increasingly clear that the context of mediation is crucial to its outcome. The context is set partly by the nature and source of the referral, partly by the degree of connection with the court system and state and local law, partly by the attitudes of the judges and attorneys involved, and partly by the skills and style of the particular mediator.

The mediator must explicitly elaborate the nature of the mediation context for the couple. This elaboration serves several functions. First, it makes very clear that the mediator is in charge of the entire mediation process and has already worked out how to proceed. This tends to reduce the anxiety level of the spouses, who typically are entering unknown territory. Second, it sets explicit boundaries for the expected conduct of the spouses and the mediator; for example, it specifies that mediation is not psychotherapy, it specifies that there will be no name-calling, accusations, or dredging up the past, and it specifies whether the mediator will make recommendations to the court if mediation is not successful. This allows the spouses to adjust their own expectations accordingly and minimizes the buildup of false expectations or even fear about the proceedings. Third, it gives the couple an opportunity to listen to a significant amount of information about what their children really do and do not need at present and in the years ahead. The conjoint and neutral format for receiving this information decreases the chances that one spouse might later distort what the mediator said. In effect, it serves to "pre-empt" much of the resistance to cooperation (Watzlawick, 1978; Saposnek, 1980). In preempting, the mediator anticipates thoughts, feelings, attitudes, or positions of the client and states them in a neutralizing context before the client has a chance to state them. By pre-empting these utterances, the mediator eliminates or at least minimizes the opportunity for the client to develop and manifest resistance to change or compromise. While there are a wide variety of ways for setting the context, the following presents a format that has worked very successfully for this author.

The Confidentiality Agreement. If the mediator is not expected to arbitrate or make recommendations to the court in the event that mediation is unsuccessful, then a confidentiality agreement should be the first order of business. It is very helpful to begin the first session by explaining the purpose and function of such an agreement (see Appendix D), and then to have the spouses and the mediator sign it. The mediator can explain somewhat as follows: "In order for us all to talk together in an open and honest manner, without feeling excessively defensive, we need to make an agreement that our conversations in this room will be kept confidential. By signing this form, we agree that anything you say here will not be used against either of you by the other or by me in any future court proceedings, if there are any. Furthermore, I will not reveal any of the contents of our talks to either of your attorneys, to the judge, or to anyone else, unless all three of us agree to it. Moreover, I will not testify for or against either of you, my records will not be subpoenaed, and I will not even give a recommendation to your attorneys, to the judge, to a probation officer, or to anyone else."

Although there is some controversy as to whether or not such a signed agreement is legally binding—since it has not yet, as of this writing, been tested in court—it does seem to have a powerful psychological effect on many spouses. It offers a sense of support, security, and freedom of speech that enables the spouses to achieve at least a minimal degree of trust in each other and in the mediation process. Only rarely has a spouse even questioned the value of signing such an agreement, and no spouse with whom this author has mediated has refused to sign it.

In some locales, the regulations require the mediator either to function as an arbitrator, who listens to all the input and then renders a binding decision, or to offer recommendations to the judge as to the preferred custodial parent and visitation plan, in the event that mediation efforts fail. Within such legal structures, the confidentiality agreement is clearly inappropriate. Advocates of the mediator as arbitrator or recommender point out that after spending many hours in discussion with the spouses (and perhaps with the children as well), the mediator has information about them that would be useful to a judge in making the determination of custody and visitation. However, advocates of the mediator exclusively as mediator point out the critical importance of the spouses feeling able to be open and honest in their negotiations, even though the information gleaned by the mediator is sacrificed to confidentiality. Such advocates feel that the sacrifice is worthwhile in that it helps to maintain the couple's belief in the value of a self-determined approach to solving custody disputes. They feel that when the spouses know beforehand that the mediator will function as an arbitrator, the spouses may limit their disclosures of important information and may be less willing to negotiate. Comparative research is needed to determine which approach is of greater overall effectiveness.

Explaining the Mediator's Role. Not uncommonly, couples begin mediation with the belief that the mediator is to make a decision for them about custody or visitation. Their belief follows directly from the usual legal context, which has made them familiar with a judge's role as an arbitrator and with a probation officer's role as a recommender, but not with a mediator's role as a facilitator. It is therefore necessary to clarify the mediator's role early in the process so the spouses will know that they must take full responsibility for arriving at the decisions cooperatively, and that the mediator will simply facilitate their doing so. If, on reaching an impasse, the mediator is required to change roles to that of an arbitrator, recommender, or counselor, then the couple must be informed before the mediation proceeds any further. Failure to clarify the mediator's role can cause the spouses to lose trust in professional help.

Benefits of Mediation. Oftentimes one or both spouses need to hear specifically how mediation can benefit them and their children. It is useful in such cases to explain the benefits by describing California's experience with joint custody and mandatory mediation legislation. The new laws, which are supported by the findings of two major studies on children of divorce (Wallerstein and Kelly, 1980; Hetherington, Cox, and Cox, 1978), reflect major changes in consciousness in the California legal system regarding custody and visitation issues (see Appendixes A, B, and C). I explain as follows:

"Prior to January 1, 1980, the first option for a California judge in a custody dispute was to award sole legal custody to one of the parents. Such decisions were made in favor of mothers 90 percent of the time and in favor of fathers only 10 percent of the time–mostly in response to a long tradition that mothers were the only valid caregivers for children. Wallerstein's and Kelly's longitudinal research on children of divorce dispelled many of these myths by documenting that the children who best survived their parents' divorce were the ones who had regular and continuing contact with both parents after the divorce. Children who had one parent practically removed from their lives–by the absent parent's choice, by a court decision to seriously restrict a parent's contact, or by the actions of one parent who believed it to be in the best interests of their child to restrict contact with the other parent–had a very difficult time adjusting to the divorce. They frequently developed a variety of symptomatic behaviors, including depression, regressive behavior, noncompliance with the custodial parent, and aggressive or withdrawn behavior. Many of these behavior patterns are typical of almost all children of divorce for about one to one and a half years following a divorce, but the children who lost regular contact with a parent suffered for many years longer. So the California Legislature enacted a presumption of joint legal custody. This set up the expectation that after the divorce the parents would continue making major decisions about their children together, as they presumably did before the divorce. So, by law, the judge now first has to consider joint legal custody, and it is only if the lawyers of the spouses (or the spouses themselves) can convince the judge that joint legal custody is not in the best interests of the children that a judge will then consider sole legal custody to one parent. And this is becoming increasingly rare as judges gain experience with the long-term benefits of joint custody.

"Research studies also concluded that children of divorce did best when their parents continued to cooperate with each other over issues regarding the children even if they did not cooperate over the issues of their own relationship. When parents retain control of the decisions affecting their children, the children undoubtedly benefit because the parents are the ones who best know the needs of their children and the circumstances of their children's lives.

"Then the California Legislature enacted a mandatory mediation law stating that before a judge will hear a case involving contested custody or visitation issues he or she must send the case to mediation. Such an action reflects the court's increasing conviction that decisions about custody and visitation that are made by the parents rather than by a judge are more relevant to the specifics of the case, are more meaningful to the couple and their children, are more carefully thought out, and last longer. Also, several years of experience have shown that couples who resolve these issues in mediation typically do not return to court year after year, trying to get back at each other. Finally, there are clear monetary savings to be gained from using mediation instead of emotionally draining court hearings and negotiations by lawyers.

"In order to ensure that the two of you will continue to resolve future child-related issues outside the legal system, the last clause that I regularly include in the final mediation agreement states that if you are unable to resolve any future disputes about the children between yourselves, you will seek mediation before legal action."

California is currently the only state that has a mandatory mediation law, but other states are preparing to follow suit. California in particular is reputed for initiating humanizing laws that, over time, are similarly enacted by other states.

Agreement on Talking with Attorneys. Occasionally in

the course of the custody mediation process, one of the spouses will talk with his or her attorney who may then say something that has the effect of hampering the mediation process. Since the attorneys do not know what is going on in the mediation of a particular case, comments that they might make from an adversarial stance could be damaging to efforts at mediated resolution. Hence, it is advisable to request the spouses at the beginning of the mediation process to refrain from consulting their respective attorneys about the custody or visitation issues. It is fine to discuss financial matters with their attorneys, but the custody and visitation issues must remain the exclusive domain of mediation while it is in process. Although custody and visitation issues are often linked up with support issues, to varying degrees (see section on financial links in Chapter Five), the experience of mediators under California's mandatory mediation has shown that such issues can be effectively resolved separately. These efforts are successful to the degree that the judges and attorneys involved support the mediator's attempts to keep the primary focus on the time-sharing needs of the children. When the links are too difficult to separate, consultation with an attorney can be quite facilitative.

Of course, there are situations in which the issue of custody is linked up with property settlement. For example, a recent California case (In re Marriage of Duke, 1980 101 CA3d 152, 161 CR 444) established a precedent–known as a Duke order–such that in certain circumstances at the time of a divorce a judge can defer the sale of the family house until the last minor child reaches eighteen years of age. The appellate court's opinion states: "Where adverse economic, emotional, and social impact on minor children and custodial parent which would result from immediate loss of long-established family home are not outweighed by economic detriment to noncustodial party, court shall, upon request, reserve jurisdiction and defer sale on appropriate conditions" (In re Marriage of Duke, 1980 101 CA3d 152, at p. 156). Hence, with a Duke order, the parent with primary physical custody of the children would be entitled to remain in the family home with the children until they reached their majority. So, on certain occasions, a parent may need to discuss the legal, property, and tax implications of particular time-sharing arrangements with his or her attorney while mediation is in progress.

Assumptions in Beginning Mediation

Each spouse comes to mediation with a list of adversarial grievances against the other spouse, usually headed by accusations of that spouse's negative influence on the children. The evidence with which the spouses back up these accusations is often based on their interpretation of the child's behavior on returning home from being with the other spouse or on reports of the child's behavior while at the other spouse's house. Moreover, each spouse comes to mediation believing many myths about what children do and do not need in order to thrive. If the spouses are given the opportunity to state all these accusations and mistaken beliefs, then the mediator is put in the defensive position of trying to persuade the spouses to change their stated views. However, if the mediator begins the mediation by telling both spouses in an informed and authoritative manner what is currently understood of children's needs following divorce and noting the irrelevance of the couple's own interpretations, then their resistance can be pre-empted to a significant degree. If, for example, the mediator presents the finding that children need regular and continuing contact with both parents, it then becomes very difficult for one parent to state that the children do not need the other. The assumptions that I state and explain at this point include all or some of the following, depending on the particulars of the case.

"I'm going to assume that the two of you absolutely despise and hate each other and furthermore that each of you wishes the other off the face of the earth." At this point, one (or both) of the spouses invariably laughs and says, "Well, it's not *that* bad; I don't 'hate' him/her." My assumption is stated in an exaggerated fashion (although sometimes it is actually not much of an exaggeration) in order to compel them to moderate the statement toward the mean, thereby making an implicit move toward cooperation. In order to further compel cooperation, I reaffirm the original assumption by saying, "Well, I'm going to assume that anyhow."

I then go on to say, "But we have found, through much experience, that people can hate each other as spouses and still cooperate together as parents in making important decisions about their children. To the degree that you separate the parenting relationship that you share from your spousal relationship, you will be able to make good decisions for your children. It is possible to be a caring and effective parent even if your marital relationship has not been satisfactory. To the degree that you make decisions based on your children's need for parenting rather than on your own need to get even, to gain power, or to satisfy your own needs first, your children will benefit. Remember that children are always easy pawns in marital battles, and they are especially prime targets for leftover marital battles. Keep them out of those battles and you will help to protect their psychological health."

These statements give spouses the hope of being able to separate their negative feelings for each other from potential agreements on co-parenting. This also begins to disarm them from using the children to get revenge on each other.

"I'm going to assume that both of you love your children equally well, in your own styles, and that both of you want the best for your children. Is that accurate?" I find it important for each spouse to verbally acknowledge this assumption at this point in the presence of the other spouse. This focuses their concern on the children and establishes a neutral territory that is framed in a positive way. It also blocks either spouse from accusing the other spouse of not loving the children. And their explicit assertions of love for the children are an anchor to which I can later return if negotiations take a turn toward self-interest or noncooperation.

"I'm also going to assume that your children love and need both of you. As I explained, research has consistently demonstrated that children need regular and continuous contact with both parents even if the parents disagree with each other on many issues. Your children can handle the reality of each of you quite well, but when denied a chance to check out the reality of a parent's being, they will fill in the missing parts with fantasy. And we do know that children's fantasies are very frequently distorted, since children have such minimal experience to draw from in accurately assessing people. Their fantasies tend to be polarized; the absent parent is viewed either as a wicked person who is clearly unfit to take care of a child or, more likely, as a saint who can do no wrong. Often, against the protests of the custodial parent, the child's view will be sustained and will only get stronger over time. It will often be tucked away in a secret fantasy storage place but will be quickly retrieved whenever the custodial parent challenges the worth of the absent parent."

This assumption and discussion helps to decrease the fear that either parent might have of losing the child forever if a compromise is reached. The negative effects of either parent's being refused access to the child are explicitly substantiated, which often elicits a smile of relief from one or both parents. They experience momentary relaxation on hearing that the final resolution will assure each of them a significant degree of involvement with the children.

"My main concern is for your children. In custody hearings, judges typically deal with children in stereotypical ways and often do not take their individual needs into account. In mediation, though, we have the opportunity to develop a plan that can fit your children's individual needs, as well as your own needs. I am going to keep our primary focus on your children and their specific needs before focusing on each of your needs. I am going to act as an advocate for your children."

This statement serves to reassure both parents of my intent to protect the best interests of their children, in spite of their own motives and confusion. It also serves to reduce the attempts of the spouses to get me to side with each of them, by explicitly stating that their interests are a lower priority.

"Children seem to have an intuitive sense of justice regarding their parents. In my experience, if one parent badmouths the other, more often than not it backfires on the badmouthing parent. The child will most often come to the defense of the parent who is put down and will refuse to accept anything negative about that parent. Sometimes this will happen right after a divorce, and sometimes it will happen a few years down the line in the child's development. Trying to convince the child of the faults of the absent parent just leads the child to confirm the absent-parent-as-a-saint fantasy. So even though you may have put down the other parent to your children in the past, it is advisable to refrain from doing it in the future, because it may well backfire on you." This assumption is intended to prod the parents into supporting each other's parenting role.

"While children do not like their parents to bad-mouth each other, the children themselves will carry out a variety of behavioral strategies against their parents for some time following their parents' separation. In well-functioning, intact families, children almost always play one parent against the other at some time. It is a natural way of learning the limits of their own power and that of their parents. In effect, they are asking several questions about their parents: Will they be in agreement in their decisions? Will they be consistent? Will they act calmly? Will they lose control and hurt or kill me or each other? Will they stay around to love me? Will they still love me and stay with me even if I cause this much trouble? The children will often present their parents with aggressive, demanding or resistant behavior as a test to see whether their parents will remain united. They hope for the feeling of security that they experience when their parents cooperate with each other for their children's sake.

"Following divorce, children use these same strategies but frequently exaggerate them, even to the point of destructiveness. They will tell mom the awful things that dad does and then turn around and tell dad the terrible places that mom goes. They will feed your disagreements with each other and will distort and sometimes even lie about events that happened at the other parent's house. All of this is done not because your children are evil, but in their attempts at emotional survival. Partly they are expressing their anger and frustration about your divorce, but mostly they are asking for clarity about your relationship with each other and your feelings about and commitment to them. These are simply normal behaviors exaggerated to crisis proportions as the children try to take care of themselves through the emotional crisis of divorce.

"So it is important to take what your children say about the other parent with a grain of salt and not to jump to conclusions about the unfitness of the other parent. Many a court battle has been initiated by a parent who overreacted to the innocent but distorted words of their child and failed to check out the reality of those words with the other parent.

"In spite of the terrible things your child may tell you about the other parent, and in spite of what you may remember about the ineffectiveness of your spouse's parenting skills when you were all together as a family, consider the fact that a parent often is more effective with his or her children when alone with them, and less effective when the other parent is also present. This is because children will regularly play one parent against the other when both are physically together, but they cannot so easily do it, nor are they as motivated, when alone with one parent. So it is quite possible that each of you is actually more effective with your children rather than less effective, when the other parent is not there.

"Also, consider the fact that it is rare for one parent to be really effective with children of all ages. Usually each parent is more effective in parenting children of certain ages, and less effective with children of other ages. For example, one parent may be wonderful with infants and have a harder time dealing with the challenging and demanding behavior of a three-year-old. Another parent may not know what to do with a child under two but be marvelous with an older child who can talk and reason. Some parents are great with teenagers, and others give their best nurturance to younger children. Parents who are aware of these strengths and weaknesses can best help their children grow up by each helping the other to get through his or her rough periods in the children's development."

These statements serve to forestall each parent from using the children's verbal and behavioral strategies as evidence for reducing their access to the other parent. The children's behaviors are put into a normalized perspective, reducing their value as ammunition against the other parent.

"Children almost always have a secret wish that their mom and dad will get back together some day. A well-known family therapist, Carl Whitaker, once said, 'Kids whose parents get divorced stop wishing them back together when the kids are about eighty-one years old.' And your children will often use their behavioral strategies to try to reunite the two of you. Although children do not like their parents to fight, at the same time they often believe that as long as mom and dad are dealing with each other intensely, even if that means fighting, there is a chance that they will get back together. But if you play into their game and fight with each other, you actually make it even worse for them by creating more tension and insecurity, which in turn encourages them to provoke you more. This leads to a vicious circle in which everyone loses."

This assumption serves to elicit in the parents an acute awareness of the consequences of their divorce on the children and is intended to influence them to soften the emotional trauma for the children by minimizing further conflict. It also serves as a paradoxical challenge to stay apart, by not fighting with each other. By showing that the children take their conflicts as evidence both that the parents have succumbed to the children's manipulations and that they will get back together, this maneuver subtly encourages the parents to reduce their fighting and cooperate with each other.

"Individual differences among your children are important. Each child is a distinct person with unique feelings, attitudes, tolerances, behavior patterns, habits, and preferences and, as such, deserves to be considered in terms of his or her special needs. Your children's ages, sex, and temperament characteristics such as activity level, attention span, approach to new situations, and adaptability need to be taken into account, as do their behavioral styles, interests, tolerances, established friendships and relationships with relatives, feelings about their neighborhood, attachment to the house, adjustment to school, quality of the school they attend, involvement in sports activities, and so forth. Considering all these factors before your own needs will result in the best decisions for your children."

In discussing individual differences of children with their parents, it is particularly helpful for the mediator to be informed about temperament characteristics. In addition to the four characteristics listed above, Thomas and Chess (1977) detailed five more characteristics—intensity of responses, distractibility, rhythmicity of bodily functions, sensitivity threshold, and general quality of mood, in their twenty-five-year longitudinal research study. They found that these nine temperament characteristics are measurably present a few months after birth and remain relatively stable through development, interacting predictably with other people's reactions to these characteristics. Knowledge of these dimensions can be quite useful for helping parents to maximize compatibility ("goodness of fit") for day-to-day living. Ironically, a divorcing couple are in the unique position to maximize these research findings to the benefit of themselves and their children, of course notwithstanding the many other variables that are also necessary to consider.

This assumption about individual differences among children encourages parents to focus on the specific needs of their children. It reduces the tendency to view the children as a generalized package for which to fight, and it gets them to view each child respectfully, as a real and unique person.

"A key factor to consider in your decisions is flexibility. As time goes by, children grow and their needs change. They enter different developmental stages and they change friends, schools, and interests. Your needs and your life situations will also change over time. It is best to view your decisions about your children as part of an ongoing process, rather than as a once-and-for-all event. Both children and adult development are ever-changing processes and if we constrain the process by forcing static, one-time decisions on it, it will not work effectively."

"Presently both of you are in a crisis and no doubt feel vulnerable, as if you potentially have a lot to lose. Your flexibility is probably not as evident now as it could be but is very important to keep in mind as we progress. Some couples choose to make year-by-year or biyearly agreements to meet again, either between themselves or in mediation, in order to reassess the changing needs of each family member. If need be, we can arrange to reevaluate your plan in six or even in three months."

This assumption serves to prevent the parents from viewing the mediation as a crucial, one-time event and their decisions as ones that must endure forever. Such an attitude encourages intense competition to win, which is contrary to the necessary spirit of mediation.

"Neither of you *owns* your children. So the concept of custody is archaic, yet it has tended to guide our perspectives and has encouraged us to view children as possessions. To the degree that you possess your children, you lose them. Both of you are, and will always be, parents to your children, and when you divorce, you simply restructure your family, not abandon or destroy it. It is important to think about the words we use in our negotiations. Phrases like 'getting custody,' 'keeping my kids,' 'giving them up,' 'having visitations,' and so forth all imply that the children are owned and loaned. We will begin to use phrases like 'sharing time with the children,' 'being with the children,' 'having the children be with you.' This will help us look at the situation differently—in a more cooperative, sharing way."

These statements lead into the difficult task of getting the parents to reconceptualize their family relationships, using cooperative rather than competitive concepts. This assumption must be repeated periodically throughout the mediation process, and the mediator herself must consistently follow through in using the new language and new concepts in all discussions that follow. She must serve as a convincing and consistent model for the parents of how to think and talk about cooperative co-parenting.

"Young children going through a divorce have two great fears. One is of being rejected or abandoned by one or both of their parents; often, they will secretly think, 'If my daddy left,' then maybe my mommy will also.' The other fear is of not being taken care of—that is, fed, clothed, sheltered—and loved on a day-to-day basis. Very often, children will not tell you what is upsetting or scaring them but they cannot help but show it somehow through their behavior, questions, comments, and general attitude. Sometimes they may show their fears by acting excessively clingy, and at other times by acting withdrawn and uncooperative. They may also act demanding, challenging, or irritable or show symptomatic behavior such as bed-wetting, insomnia, stealing, lying, fighting, or poor schoolwork. Sometimes they may not even show their fears and insecurities until years later when they wind up in psychotherapy to try to undo all the damage that has been done. So it is important that you both help them to feel as secure as possible by cooperating together to work out a plan for your children to have regular and continuing contact with both of you."

These comments are intended to arouse one of the greatest concerns of most parents: that of psychologically harming their child. It is often very effective to offer the parents such dire predictions of psychological damage as a means of encouraging them to cooperate with each other; and few therapists would question the validity of such predictions.

The Ground Rules. In presenting these assumptions, it is helpful to end by setting the ground rules for proceeding with negotiations. The following are the two I consider essential:

1. "There is little value in talking about the past, since it only leads to fighting and arguing, as I'm sure you both know." (I obtain explicit acknowledgment of this fact from each of the parents before continuing.) "Our focus will be on your children's needs for the future and on how you two can satisfy those needs. I will need some background information for my own benefit, which I will ask for, but unless I specifically request it, we will talk about plans for the future."

2. "In talking with each other, we will use I-messages, that is, statements that begin with the word *I,* such as 'I want . . . ,' 'I need such and such . . . ,' 'I get angry when such and such . . . ,' rather than statements that begin with *You,* such as 'You are ignorant,' 'You are incompetent,' 'You are irresponsible,' and so forth. Such statements are accusatory in nature and only lead people to become defensive and angry. Clearly, this will lead us nowhere in our negotiations. So speak for yourself and about yourself and we will proceed much more easily."

After the ground rules are presented, the mediator is ready to begin the first phase of the actual mediation process.

4

Phases of Mediation: From Gathering Information to Reaching Agreements

Beginning Phase

Gathering Information on the Phone. As every clinician knows, gathering information and generating hypotheses begin well before the first office visit. Moreover, the more short-term and structured intervention approaches require a more rapid assessment of the clients and their particular situation. Mediation, which is among the most structured and short-term of all interventions, necessitates the most efficient and rapid assessment of important variables.

The richest source of initial information about the clients' situation can be the first phone call with each spouse. The arrangements for these initial calls are determined by the particular source of the referral to the mediator. In private mediation, referrals may come directly from the spouses or through their attorneys. In the former case, one of the spouses phones the mediator and requests mediation for the couple, who previously have agreed between themselves to seek mediation. In the latter case, an attorney representing one of the spouses phones the mediator and requests mediation for the couple, in accordance with an agreement developed between the attorneys. In both cases, it is wise for the mediator to telephone each spouse and each attorney involved in the case to inform them of his or her procedures and expectations and to gather essential information. In mandatory mediation, the mediator may receive a written court order or minutes from a court hearing with the names of the spouses who were ordered to mediation. Typically, the spouses or their attorneys call and provide phone numbers by which to reach the parties. The mediator then phones each spouse to explain procedures, answer questions, inform them of the time of the first appointment, and gather information.

From these calls the mediator can get basic information, such as the names, ages, addresses, and phone numbers of the parents and children, the names of the attorneys involved, recent and pending court dates, and current custody and visitation arrangements. The mediator can also assess the important issues between the couple; the degree of motivation to negotiate; the degree of resistance to participate; the presence of any special allegations by one parent against the other (such as child abuse, incest, battery, alcoholism, drug abuse, or homosexuality); the interactional dynamics of the couple; the degree and duration of their custody battle; the degree of adversarial attitudes; whether the children have an express preference for where to live; whether joint legal custody is a feasible option; the degree of enmeshment of the custody and/or visitation issue with financial, marital, and other issues; the current status of the divorce proceedings; the degree to which the spouses each have accepted the fact of divorce; the degree of their respective levels of personal maturity (ability to recognize and deal with the needs of others before, or along with, their own); and which issues have already been settled before mediation.

A word of caution needs to be offered regarding information gathered in the initial phone call with each spouse. Frequently, during these initial calls, each spouse gives slanderous information about the other spouse that goes well beyond what is helpful to the mediator. Such information may bias the mediator or even generate hostility within him toward the reporting spouse (much as the child might feel when hearing one parent put down the other parent), and it may create more difficulty for the mediator in the early sessions. Moreover, in listening to such accusations, the mediator implicitly condones the spouse's tactic. However, *not* listening to such information (including, perhaps, allegations of child abuse, molestation, neglect, and so on) may cause the mediator to overlook or unintentionally screen out important information about the children's safety or well-being. Hence, not listening errs in the direction of missing significant data, while listening encourages distortion, hostility, and noncooperation. The mediator can best handle this dilemma by striving for a balance of input.

Gathering Information in the First Session. The next important information to gather is the nature of the couple's marital and premarital relationship. In asking the spouses to describe the way they met, courted, married, and divorced, the mediator quickly achieves a number of very important steps in gaining essential information. First of all, the immediate emotional climate often changes from hostility to warmth and friendliness as the spouses reminisce about good times past. This frequently stimulates the couple to a more cooperative attitude. Second, the spouses reveal (both verbally and nonverbally) the nature of their best ways of relating and solving problems together. This is useful as a predictor of their potential for cooperation and as an anchor to which to return if they later become too hostile. Thirdly, the mediator gets a quick historical and developmental picture of the stages of their marital relationship, of the long-term marital issues and interactional patterns, of the interactional strengths and weaknesses of the couple, and of their manner of regulating the emotional distance between them (Kantor and Lehr, 1975).

I generally begin the exploration of the premarital relationship by asking, "How and where did the two of you meet?" The couple's demeanor when asked this question is similar to those mildly altered states of consciousness that we drift into and out of all day long, described by Erickson and others as trancelike (Erickson and Rossi, 1979; Zeig, 1980). This discussion almost always elicits good feelings between the spouses, as they describe what are frequently the best times of their lives. After they describe the beginning of their romance, this next question is rapidly offered: "What first attracted each of you to the other?" This gives further opportunity for the spouses to warm to each other, as each relates the other's most positive aspects. I draw out these descriptions until I sense resistance, at which point I casually summarize and repeat the positive characteristics of each one.

Then I inquire about their predivorce relationship by asking: "How would you each describe the course of your marriage (or relationship, if never married)? Divide it into thirds—a beginning third, a middle third, and a last third. For example, some couples say that it was great at first, then in the middle gradually got worse, and at the end was a disaster. Others say that it was terrific until the day the partner left, or that it was horrible from the very first day they met, or that it was like a roller coaster ride, good times alternating with bad times. How was it for you?" I add that "it's not uncommon for each of you to have a very different perspective on it."

They thus are each encouraged to present their personal perspective briefly and in a highly structured manner. From this the mediator gains access to their marital dynamics, which often parallel their stances in the custody battle.

The mediator can then ask, "How did the decision to divorce (or separate) get made?" Stating the question in this neutral form allows either spouse to respond and implies no judgments or criticisms by the mediator. Often this discussion opens up and clarifies the feelings that each spouse has had, and currently has, about the other. But since the feelings typically are already very familiar to the couple, they need only be expressed briefly, as reacknowledgement. Paying too much attention to these feelings and their expression may result in an escalation of the negative feelings. The mediator must then take charge, neutralize these feelings, and redirect the discussion.

At this point, it is important for the mediator to explore the degree of finality of the divorce plans and the degree of acceptance of those plans by each spouse. If one spouse is unwilling to accede to the divorce, further negotiations over the custody issues are pointless, since the divorce issue will block any talk about the children. Among the typical reasons that one spouse will resist the divorce are hurt, anger at being abandoned by the other spouse, religious beliefs, love for the other spouse, panic over being alone, excessive dependency on the other spouse, confusion over why the other spouse left, and hope that the estranged partner will return to the marriage.

The mediator should be aware that it is rare for couples going through custody mediation to reconcile their marriage. Generally, by the time they come for custody mediation, one or both spouses have experienced too much pain for reconciliation to be possible. In addition, various postseparation changes typically occur that exclude the other spouse permanently; these may include changed values, a new mate, and numerous other irreversible decisions.

However, because the decision to divorce must be settled squarely before meaningful negotiations about the children can take place, a brief inquiry into this issue is helpful. The mediator asks such questions as "What percent probability would each of you give as to your getting back together within the coming year? within the next five years?" "What would it take for you to get back together?" "How likely is it that those changes will happen?" These questions allow the spouses to assess the likelihood of reunification by focusing on the concrete changes required (which they both usually know all too well). Frequently one spouse states a zero percent likelihood of reuniting. This then functions both as a clarification and as a challenge to the other spouse either to accept this position or to try to persuade the spouse to reconsider. If persuasion is seriously attempted, the couple is requested to go home and think about the divorce decision for several weeks. Usually, allowing time to pass dissipates resistance to the reality of the divorce (if it is a reality) and provides an opportunity for the resistant spouse to reevaluate the situation so as to be able to return to mediation at a later date.

If the decision to divorce is relatively well accepted by both spouses, the mediator proceeds to the next line of questioning, which concerns the children. Either at this time or during the inquiry about the course of the marriage, the question is asked, "How did the decision to have children get made?" This elicits any unusual circumstances surrounding the conception and birth of each child, and it serves as an indicator of the original motivations behind and feelings about the birth of each child. If, for example, one spouse describes never having wanted the children and also fails to express any current positive feelings for them, the mediator can hypothesize (and listen for) other motives for wanting custody, such as revenge, assertion of power, or desire to keep a hold on the other spouse.

Then the parents are asked, "What are your children like? Give me a capsule description of each of them." Addressing this question to both parents gives the mediator information about how much each parent knows and cares about the children. The mediator notices which parent initiates the descriptions, the degree to which each parent feels attached to and positive about the children, and how realistically each parent describes the positive as well as negative characteristics of the children. When parents are asked this question, they almost always have an emotional response that is similar to the one they show when asked about their early courting. Since each parent typically is vying to have the children live with him or her, or at least to maximize their time together, each tends to portray the children in positive and competent terms. Moreover, both parents usually perceive the children in similar ways, except for differences in emphasis on certain characteristics. The similarities of the parents' descriptions provide important leverage for the mediator later in the negotiations. Coming back to the agreed-upon positive characteristics of their children at times when the negotiations are stuck can help the parents get on with cooperative efforts. Moreover, the particular way in which each parent describes each child reveals useful information about the degree to which they are matched or mismatched. This is useful in the middle phase of mediation, when decisions are made about sharing time with the children.

It is important to remember that in intact families the degrees of positive or negative compatibility between each parent and each child are constantly being expressed. As Thomas and

Chess (1977) noted, being aware of the various areas of poorer compatibility allows parents to develop ways of working around them. For example, consider a boy who has a high activity level and whose mother is also very active but whose father likes to sit quietly and read. If the parents chose to work smoothly with these temperament characteristics, then the mother and son would probably spend a good deal of time being active together—perhaps playing sports—and would not expect the father to participate. The son and father might well enjoy quiet time together in the evening. However, if the parents expected to fit more traditional sex roles, with the father being more active and the mother more passive, then the child's activity might well be viewed by the father as a constant annoyance and by the mother as a frustrating reminder of her own desire to be more active. Furthermore, the mother might subtly or overtly encourage the child to be more active, which would further irritate the father and could well cause marital discord.

Hence, even when there are difficult temperament matches between a parent and child, if the parents are aware of the potential problems and work together to minimize them, they can share equitably in parenting their children.

When the mediator is helping a couple design a parenting arrangement that will approximately equalize each parent's time with the children, it is often useful to discuss temperament differences among the children so that the time-sharing arrangements can be planned with due consideration both to the children's needs and to their own tolerance levels. For example, if one of the children has always had particular difficulty in adapting to changes and has been extremely slow to warm up to new situations, then the time-sharing arrangements should be designed to minimize transfers between the parents' houses. For that child, alternating houses on a biweekly, triweekly, or even monthly basis might work out best, while for the child's more adaptable sibling a weekly alternation might work out quite well.

There are occasions when behavior and temperament are of relatively little importance to the mediation work. For example, when the spouses are very hostile to each other and cannot even consider such issues as temperament matches (as is frequently the case for couples who are in court-ordered mediation), discussion of these issues may backfire and be used tactically by one spouse against the other—for example, "Jennifer cannot handle changes, so I'm going for full custody." In such cases, the mediator must limit the amount of information offered to what the couple can handle constructively. However, if the mediator is obliged to make recommendations in the event that mediation efforts are unsuccessful, then information about temperament compatibilities can be useful in formulating meaningful recommendations.

Middle Phase

Describing the Options. After the necessary background information has been gathered, the mediation process enters the middle phase. In this phase, the actual negotiations will begin. In order to make sure that the negotiations proceed with correct information and in order to avoid getting caught in conflict based on misunderstanding of the options available for resolving the custody dispute, the mediator should describe those options. While the range of available legal options varies from state to state, I will present those that are available under California law, since this state currently offers the greatest number of options.

The choices presented for parental consideration are based on the information that has previously been gathered about the needs, preferences, and tolerances of each parent and child. If the parents have agreed that one of them will retain sole legal custody, and they are merely in disagreement about visitation schedules, I may lightly explore the possibility of joint legal custody, or I may not even mention it unless it is brought up by one of the spouses. While not mentioning it can bring up moral issues for the mediator if he or she feels that it is not fair for one parent to have sole legal custody when there is a judicial presumption of joint legal custody, it is more important at times to consider what is *feasible* rather than what is *fair*. Oftentimes, emphasizing what is fair only functions to imbalance the mediator's position, because it injects his or her own values into the couple's struggle. For example, cases come up in which one parent wants sole legal custody of the children and the other parent wants joint legal custody. In one such case, I spoke of the benefits of joint legal custody as if it were in fact a neutral position. However, this was construed by the mother as evidence of my partiality to the father's position and, therefore, of my lack of neutrality. As she continued to express her preference for sole legal custody, I spoke further about the benefits of joint legal custody. The father sat back, smirked, and watched me argue with his wife. From that point on, it was very difficult for the mother to trust me to be fair (from her point of view), and she subsequently refused to cooperate further with the negotiations. The importance of looking at the available options from the couple's point of view rather than from the mediator's becomes apparent. This occasionally becomes a full-blown paradox: the mediator who attempts to be fair is perceived as being unfair, while one who refrains from asserting what would seem to be fair is perceived as being fair.

If, as is more often the case, the couple has implicitly agreed to joint legal custody, I describe the range of ways for sharing the children's time, from the most ideal to the most workable solutions. I say: "Joint legal custody means that each of you will have equal privilege and responsibility for making major decisions about your children. Of course, the minor day-to-day decisions need to be made by the parent whom the children are with at any particular time. We will develop a comprehensive agreement that describes how each of you will share time with each of your children. The design of this agreement is completely up to your creative imaginations. You can literally create any sort of plan that works for you and your children, and as long as it is not totally inappropriate, the judge will almost always approve it. So allow yourselves to be flexible, creative, and compromising. Consider the needs of the children first, then design the plan to suit both of your schedules and life-styles. The best plans actually are those that also accommodate the needs of each of you.

"Experience has shown that at first you may both need to

agree to a time-sharing schedule that is highly structured and firmly maintained. It is important at first to keep the dates and times of the schedule absolutely sacred, until each of you proves to the other a degree of trust and cooperation that would then allow you to build in more flexibility. Over time, you may well be able to help each other more in sharing child care responsibilities. When one of you is not available to be with the children, the other parent may be able to spend that time with them, which benefits all of you.

"The most ideal arrangement is for the parents to live at opposite ends of the same block, have bedrooms for the children in each of the homes, and allow total freedom for the children to choose where they will sleep on any particular night. This allows the children to remain in the same school, stay in the same neighborhood, play with the same friends, see both parents on a regular and frequent basis, and feel the support of both parents maintaining access to each other. The closer your approximation to this ideal, the better the plan. If you live at opposite ends of town, this will mean more driving and coordination of schedules, but it can work as well. Some couples choose to share the children on a daily basis, so that one parent is with them during the daytime and the other with them in the evenings and nighttime. Some couples have the children with one parent three days a week and with the other four days, alternating every other week or month. Some have them with one parent for a week and then with the other parent for a week. Some alternate every two weeks, three weeks, month, two months, year, or two years. Whatever will work for you can be arranged."

If young children are involved, the parents are given the following advice: "Because young children have a very limited sense of time, it is very desirable for them to be able to see each of you on a fairly frequent basis. If one of you moves far away, it becomes very difficult, although not impossible, for your children to have such frequent contact. So if it is possible for the two of you to remain within the same geographical area until the children are somewhat older, that would be a nice sacrifice for you to make for your children. If this is not possible, then I know that your children will still survive. In any case, please give this some serious consideration in making your plans."

Cautions Regarding Co-Parenting. In general, while co-parenting to the maximal degree feasible is the ideal goal toward which the mediator should strive, there are circumstances in which the mediator may choose to soften her advocacy of this goal and perhaps even omit describing it as an option. In addition to circumstances in which co-parenting is obviously not possible, such as when one parent is incarcerated or hospitalized for extended periods of time, the mediator should be alert to circumstances in which the best interests of the children would not be served by a high degree of co-parenting. These may include situations in which one parent is unavailable to the child for extended periods of the time that the child might be in that parent's care—for example, when extensive travel is necessary to the parent's work, or when the parent's work hours necessitate leaving the children with sitters for extended periods of time. In addition, when a child tells the mediator of being afraid of one parent's unpredictability or abusiveness (input from the children will be discussed shortly), or when a child consistently refuses to spend time with one parent, the mediator must heed the warning and very cautiously assess the degree to which co-parenting may or may not be in the children's best interests.

Obviously, these situations can pose a dilemma for the mediator, especially if her role is exclusive of arbitrating or making recommendations. She must guide and shape the available choices to best serve the children. As an advocate for the children, she must maneuver the parents to accommodate to the needs of their children while being sensitive to the parents' own needs. If appealing to reason does not suffice, then more confrontive suggestions can be offered. For example, consider a parent who works as a traveling salesperson and is on the road five days out of seven. If that parent insists on having the children alternate weeks for an even fifty-fifty split, even though it will involve the children staying with sitters most days and nights, the mediator must convey to this parent the negative effects such a plan will have on the children. The mediator should elaborate on the more workable possibilities for maximizing that parent's time with the children when the parent is available (for example, the two days at home per week, holidays, school vacations, summers), and should inform the parent of the value of children being with the other parent rather than with sitters whenever possible. The mediator may have to help the parents recognize the destructiveness of asserting their parental rights over their children's needs. It may also help for the mediator to venture an experienced guess about how the local court might view such a plan.

In describing the options available, the language that the mediator uses is critical. As Ricci (1980) points out, the language that the spouses use largely determines the conceptual way they will deal with each other. By the same token, the way the mediator uses language will determine the way the negotiations proceed. If the mediator continues to use concepts like custody, visitation, the children's home, the custodial parent, and so on throughout the negotiations, the spouses will remain in adversarial stances and the mediation process will be bumpy. If, however, very early in the process the mediator begins to shape his or her language to reflect the change in consciousness from ownership of children to sharing in parenting, the couple will soon follow suit. Although they may, in times of anger and resentment, revert to the older language, the mediator's regular use of the new language will continually reinforce the new conceptual way in which the couple are implicitly and explicitly being encouraged to think and act. Asking the couple how they would like to share time with their children and what specific plans they can arrange in order for the children to be with their mother or spend an extended amount of time with their father can go far in helping them view their relationships with the children and with each other in a more cooperative manner.

One problematic issue is the frequent parental interpretation of joint custody as meaning the children will spend exactly 50 percent of their time with each parent. The mediator must quickly get the parents to abandon this interpretation because it often leads to an impasse in the negotiations. The psychological implications of exactly equal time are powerful to a resistant parent and will hamper the making of more flexible and workable plans. Avoiding the concept of percentage of time spent with the children and focusing instead on specific, scheduled time can greatly facilitate the process of mediation.

The Children's Input. There are a number of situations in which it is very helpful to get input from the children. If one of the parents indicates that the children have consistently expressed a preference for residing primarily at his or her house and the other parent disputes this, the children can be interviewed either separately or together with the parents, or both. If one or more of the children have specifically requested to speak with the mediator, that request should be honored. If the parents have been unable to comprehend the destructive consequences to the children of their continued hostility and, instead, adopt self-righteous attitudes, then having the children present in a session with the parents can give the parents the necessary firsthand feedback (see section in Chapter Nine on leveraging the children).

Adolescents generally have clear preferences about where they primarily would like to reside and how they would like to share their time with their parents. They should be given the opportunity to express their wishes to the mediator if they have not already explicitly expressed them to one or both parents. Moreover, because of the relative independence of their lives, and because of the importance of their peer relationships and social, school, and athletic activities, the preferences of adolescents should be seriously considered in developing the final parenting agreement.

In contrast, children under the age of five or six will generally abide by the joint decisions of their parents and seldom need to be included in the mediation process. Although the express preferences of children of these ages often are transitory and situationally specific (depending on whom they are with and how they are feeling at the time the preference is expressed), if a child has expressed a consistent preference over a significant period of time, then the mediator should take heed. He or she should assess the intent and importance of the child's preference and should make certain that it gets conveyed effectively to the parents.

Children between six and twelve are much more varied both in their desires for input and in their tactical usefulness to the mediation process. Wallerstein and Kelly (1980) concluded that children below the age of adolescence are not reliable judges of their own best interests and that their preferences should not, therefore, be relied on in making decisions about postdivorce parenting arrangements. To support their conclusion, these researchers cite evidence of erratic emotional reactions, decisions, and judgments regarding parents, especially in children between the ages of nine and twelve.

While there is clearly validity to the Wallerstein and Kelly findings, the decision whether or not to include the children in the mediation process must be made individually for each specific case. There is no doubt that there are ten-year-olds, and even children as young as seven, who have well-thought-out, valid reasons for preferring one parent's home over the other. These reasons need to be considered in the final decisions.

When a mediator decides that it is important to interview the children, a number of factors become important in planning the approach. If there has been a specific request by a child to be interviewed alone, or when the mediator suspects it will be more helpful for the child to be interviewed without the parents present, the mediator should get both parents to agree to the interview. This can reduce the probability that one of the parents will invalidate the child's preferences by claiming that the other parent primed the child beforehand. Although it happens only rarely, if one parent refuses to give permission for the child to be interviewed, the mediator should discuss with that parent his or her concerns. The parent may be worried that interviewing the child will be too stressful, or that the child might express something that parent does not want to hear. If the mediator feels that it is important for the child to be interviewed, he must address these concerns. Although he cannot guarantee that the child will not be under stress, he can reassure the parent by relating his own experience in dealing sensitively with children in such situations. Moreover, the mediator can inform the parent of the approach that he will take in the interview. The mediator can also assure the parent that he will place any expressed preference of the child within its appropriate context but that if the child has some particularly strong feelings about how he or she wants to share time with the parents, it should be acknowledged, or else whatever arrangements the parents make may not work out. If the parent remains unpersuaded, the mediator can suggest that the child be interviewed with the parents present. If this is still unsatisfactory, then the mediator may have to proceed without interviewing the child.

When proceeding with an interview, and when there is more than one child at issue, I generally find it more useful to interview all the siblings together. This structure offers several positive benefits: It provides sibling support to each of the children in talking about very uncomfortable topics; it gives the mediator data on the interactions, emotional bonds, and general relationships among the siblings; it usually gives the mediator a more accurate assessment of each of their needs and desires, since siblings will tend to keep each other honest and accurate as to incidents, attitudes, and feelings; and it is a more efficient use of the mediator's time. However, it is best to interview the children individually when there is a wide age gap between them; when they have previously expressed clearly different preferences; or when one child is extremely talkative and/or overpowers the others, effectively preventing them from comfortably sharing their feelings when together.

When it is deemed more helpful for the children to be interviewed together with the parents, the parents are instructed to request the attendance of the children by saying "We'd like you to help us understand your feelings about the arrangements for spending time with each of us, so that we can make better decisions for you." It is most important that neither parent directly ask the children to decide which parent they want to live with. Such a request is almost always interpreted by children as being asked to choose which parent they love more. Furthermore, it does not accurately represent the need for the child's input in the mediation process, since it is the parents, not the children, who must make the decision.

Having the parents present when the children are interviewed gives the mediator a very powerful leverage, for the mediator can orchestrate the children's verbalization of preferences in such a way that the parents will pay attention to them. If the mediator does not know whether the children have strong preferences, he or she should plan to interview them apart from their parents first, and then on the basis of the information obtained, decide whether to interview them also in the presence of their parents.

Telling their parents directly of their feelings about various time-sharing arrangements is, no doubt, one of the most difficult, frightening and risky tasks for children, but it is also often one of the most important, since it can open up communication between them.

In all communications with children, building rapport is crucial in order to establish the level of trust required before a child will share feelings that are difficult to express. Talking about the child's interests, skills, friends, and pets is an easy and reliable way to build rapport. Guiding the child to talk about comforting and familiar things is relaxing for the child and also shows respect and support for his or her world. When the child appears reasonably comfortable, the mediator can begin to talk about issues of importance.

The particular language and words used must be addressed to the age of the child. In general I say the following: "As you know, your mom and dad are having trouble talking with each other and making decisions together about how to share time with you. It seems to me that they need to know how you feel about these arrangements. Your feelings are important to know so that your parents can make the best arrangements for you. The final decision about how your parents share time with you will be made by your parents, but it would be helpful if your parents knew first how you feel about it. Even if you don't have any strong feelings one way or another, that would be helpful for your parents to know, too."

As the child begins to elaborate upon his feelings, I gently probe and listen for whether the child has a particularly strong bond with one parent; how comfortable the child feels with each parent for short and extended periods; the nature and duration of neighborhood friendships; the nature and duration of bonds with any relatives who live close to the home; the child's degree of ease in handling changes of homes, neighbors, schools, and so on; the best and worst consequences of extended stays at each parent's home; and rapport with siblings, stepparents, and stepbrothers and sisters.

If the child is not very verbal or is hesitant to express his or her feelings about the situation, I attempt to address the child's fear, discomfort, anger, embarrassment, mistrust, and other difficult feelings by telling the child what I know about how other children feel in this situation. I will empathize with the child's feelings, present anecdotes about other similar-aged children, talk about the benefits to the child of helping the parents with their decisions, and generally encourage the child to share at least some feelings, even if it is only how rotten it feels to be interviewed about these feelings. For example, to a six-year-old girl, I might say: "You know, about three weeks ago I saw a girl in my office who was sitting right in that chair that you're sitting in. She was a little bit older than you are—she was, I believe seven years old—or was she only six and a half? I don't remember. Well, her mom and dad got divorced too, and, you know, she was very upset. She told me that when her mommy left, she thought she'd never see her again. But she soon learned that she was going to see her again. Then, you know what she said to me? She said that secretly she was real mad at her mommy for leaving her daddy. She felt confused, and later she felt sad, and she cried in her bedroom a lot. And you know what? She thought that she was the only girl in the whole world who felt that way when her mommy and daddy got divorced. But, you know, when I told her about the many other girls that I had seen who also felt those ways when their parents got divorced, she was surprised, 'cause she thought she was the only one. And then she didn't feel so all alone anymore. Now, I don't know if you've felt any of those ways or not . . . (pause) . . . *Have* you felt mad, or confused, or sad about your mommy and daddy not living together?"

At this point, the child usually will tell of similar feelings. A discussion of these feelings can then take place, which can lead to a discussion of her feelings about sharing time between her parents. This topic is very delicate, and must be pursued with sensitivity. The timing and pacing of questions about time-sharing preferences must be carefully monitored, and the exact words used must be carefully selected so as to avoid any suggestion that the mediator is pressuring the child to choose between her parents. Oblique questions are much less intimidating to children than are direct questions, especially about sensitive topics. For example, the mediator can ask, "What does it feel like when you are with mommy, at her house?" or "What does it feel like with daddy, at his house?" Such indirect questions are preferable to such direct questions as "Who do you want to live with, your mommy or your daddy?"

Throughout the interview, I will offer generous amounts of emotional support, give reassurance of the parents' love for the child, and try to explain what it does and does not mean for the child that her parents got divorced. I will also reassure the child that her negative feelings do not mean that she cannot or should not continue to love both parents.

If, after interviewing the children alone, the mediator feels that it would not be productive to have the children express their feelings directly to the parents, the mediator can meet alone with the parents and report the children's feelings, serving as an advocate for them. The wording of such a report is crucial, since the parents are going to feel vulnerable to criticism or rejection by their children. For example, if a particular child says he loves his mother more than his father, the mediator should deemphasize this statement and instead relate things the child said that were favorable to the father. Or if the child's stated preference seems to be based on coaching by one parent, or on momentary anger at one parent, then the mediator should be very careful in reporting the child's expressed feelings to the parents. Doing so could imbalance the negotiations to a stalemate, with the child gaining nothing but more parental conflict. Hence, the mediator must assess very carefully the sincerity, intent, and meaning of a child's stated preference for a particular time-sharing arrangement. Of course, if a child reports being scared to death of a parent or reports that the parent beats him or is always drunk or unconscious when with the child or has been regularly molesting him, the mediator would surely need to confront the parents with this information.

If, after interviewing a child alone, the mediator feels it would be productive to have the child relate his or her feelings to the parents, the mediator should explain this to the child and get the child's explicit permission to invite the parents in. The mediator should also rehearse with the child several ways that the child might express his or her feelings. The mediator must always offer support to the child in this task, by saying, for example: "I know this is going to be difficult, but I will help you say what you want to say." The mediator can then invite the parents in and help the child to express his or her feelings to the parents and, if possible, encourage a limited dialogue between the parents and child about those feelings. The parents are prompted to be supportive of the child's expressions, even if one or both do not like what the child is saying.

It is important for the mediator to be aware that a child may be criticized or punished later by one or both parents for what the child says during this interview. To decrease the probability of this, the mediator should discuss with the parents the negative consequences to the child of their doing so. Obtaining in the child's presence their acknowledgment of this problem and their commitment to refrain from such criticism or punishment can help the child to speak more freely. Experience has shown that when the mediator deals with this issue explicitly, most parents respect this need of their children. If criticism is forthcoming, it is usually directed at the other parent, rather than at the child.

The mediator must then decide whether to have the child remain or leave the room while the parents negotiate. This should depend largely on the parents' responses to the feelings expressed by the child. If the parents appear very defensive, hurt, and quiet, it is best to ask the child to wait out of the room while the parents have time to digest what they heard. If, on the other hand, the parents are very understanding of the child's utterances and there seems to be an affectionate communication between the child and the parents, then the child could be encouraged to remain in the room while they all negotiate. In general, however, younger children (under five or six) should not be encouraged to remain during these negotiations, since they are too likely to misinterpret things said during the parents' discussions.

Requesting Proposals. The mediator is now in a position to request from each of the parents proposals for workable co-parenting arrangements. The timing of this request is critical, since it is the first point in the process where the parents are asked to offer explicit statements of their respective positions. If this request is made too early, when one or the other parent is still resistant or perhaps upset about something said earlier in the session, the proposal made by one or both parents may be unreasonable. If the request is made too late, there may have been too much opportunity for accusations or expressions of hostility, with the result that the mediation process is further delayed. With experience, a mediator learns to time the request for proposals so that it comes at an opportune moment.

Often, by the time this stage is reached, the mediator has some idea of the proposals that will be made. If this is so, then the mediator can leave many aspects of the proposals implicit. Doing so can allow the couple some degree of face-saving. As Haley (1973, 1976) has written, asking clients the obvious about their feelings or beliefs is often just being rude and disrespectful under the guise of being clever and insightful. If, for example, the children currently are living primarily with the father and have expressed a consistent desire to remain there, the mediator might entertain proposals by asking the father, in a manner that is indirectly but strongly supportive of the mother, "How do you propose to arrange it so that the children are with their mother on a regular and frequent basis?" Implicit in this question are the fact that the children need regular access to both parents, the understanding that the children are likely to remain residing primarily with their father, and support for the mother's rights in the veiled form of a pre-emptive challenge to the father to develop a constructive solution.

If, however, the mediator has no idea about what proposals might be offered at this time, the request can be stated: "Now, I'd like to hear some proposals about how you two are going to share time with your children." Phrasing the request in this manner implies that both parents will work together on this task and that the children will be shared, rather than competed for or taken from one parent by the other. While such phrasing clearly helps to reduce the struggle in which the parents will engage, there is still likely to be a struggle, and one that will persist until both parents feel reasonably secure that their respective needs have been satisfied.

Some mediators prefer to have the parents submit their proposals in writing. Although this does give the spouses more time to think out their proposals, it has the disadvantage of consolidating their defenses early. Social psychology research has demonstrated that people feel obliged to defend a position once it is formulated (Festinger, 1957). Hence, if the formulation of the parents' positions can be guided by the mediator within the mediational context, they will feel somewhat more compelled to offer cooperative rather than adversarial proposals from the start. So I prefer that the parents present their proposals orally, under the mediator's guidance.

Ending Phase

Shaping the Proposal. Once the children have given their input (if any) and the parents have offered their proposals, the mediator is ready to shape the proposal into a workable agreement. The sense of the mediator *as mediator* is most apparent at this point in the process. It is here that the delicate balance between the spouses can be thrown off by one wrong move on the part of the mediator. During this phase, the mediator must utilize all the information gathered in the beginning phase of the process and maintain awareness of the current dynamics and past issues of the couple. The tension is heightened as the couple approaches either resolution or a costly trip to court.

The mediator needs to offer the couple suggestions of alternative ways to arrange their plan. These suggestions must be fully enlightened by details of the parents' life-styles, tolerances, feelings about each other, resistant areas, and so forth. The mediator's suggestions should be geared to be maximally acceptable to both parents. The mediator should support each suggestion offered with an indication of the benefits to the children and to both parents.

The mediator must anticipate the specific issues and details that should be included in a given proposal. Some couples, for example, need to have a fairly lengthy list of very specific agreements, since they are likely to quibble about every detail that is not spelled out in black and white. Other couples need very few areas specifically delineated, since they tend not to argue about details but only about main points. The mediator should offer many suggestions to the first kind of couple, and few to the second kind. Offering too few suggestions to the first couple can result in no agreement being reached or in a recurrence of conflict in the weeks following the sessions because of lack of specificity in the agreement. Offering too many suggestions to the second couple can stir up old conflicts and create new conflict between the couple, resulting in no agreement being reached.

The suggestions offered by the mediator often are quite simple and logical solutions to a particular conflict. It can seem baffling to the beginning mediator why a couple did not think of a particular suggestion before the mediator brought it up. However, with experience, the mediator comes to see how very blind a recently divorced parent can be. There often appears to be a cognitive freezing whereby rational ideas do not come forth easily. The emotional resistance that is present can prevent the parents from solving even the most elementary problems. Judith Wallerstein aptly characterizes the recently separated spouse as manifesting a "diminished capacity to parent" (Wallerstein and Kelly, 1980). So in offering suggestions, the mediator should try more to be informed and sensitive to the particular dynamics of the couple than to be particularly creative in the solutions presented.

In attempting to maintain balance when offering suggestions to the couple, the mediator should consider two kinds of balances on which to focus: natural marital balances and mediator-initiated balances. Natural marital balances are those that exist between the spouses; usually, they have existed throughout the marriage. These are largely based on power differences, tolerance differences, and differences in the significance of particular issues to each of them. Any stable pattern of balances between the couple will manifest itself during the negotiations, and the mediator simply needs to note the decisions that result naturally from it. For example, if a father proposes having the children stay at his house six days a week and the mother and children do not seem to object, then the mediator should think twice before suggesting, for example, that the couple split the week in half between the mother and the father.

Mediator-initiated balances, by contrast, develop when the mediator makes a suggestion that tips the balance from an extreme spousal position to a more moderate or equalized position. Using the same example, if a father proposes having the children with him six days a week and both the children and mother strongly object, then the task of the mediator is to present to the father the benefits of a more equal sharing of time with the children. The mediator can use research information, clinical experience, and the express feelings of the children and the mother as backup, all the while supporting the father for his obvious devotion to the children. The mediator can reemphasize the importance to the children of more frequent access to both parents and also stress the importance to the father of having time to himself. In essence, if there is an uncomfortable imbalance between father and mother, then the mediator must initiate a more reasonable balance in order for a satisfactory resolution to take place.

Getting Agreements. The mediator should choose the path of least resistance and seek agreement on the easier issues first. Typically, these are issues like arrangements for transporting the children between the parents' homes, arrangements for the children to have phone access to both parents, the particular clothes and children's belongings to be regularly transferred between the parents' homes, and sharing of special days. Usually the parents will inform the mediator, either explicitly or implicitly, which are the easier issues. In spite of the many disagreements that a given couple may have, there are usually at least several issues upon which they agree. Initially, their agreements may be based on a desire to relieve some of the tension by settling something. Still, an agreement of any kind is helpful in that it seems to reduce the general resistance of the couple to engage in discussion.

Although as the spouses come to agreements about these issues of lesser importance they often realize how much easier it is to agree than to disagree, they still maintain some resistance as a form of self-protection. The mediator should proceed to the next issue as if there were no resistance at all. It is always better to move into another area of potential agreement than to get stuck arguing with a parent who is resistant in one area.

In the event that one parent offers resistance to a comprehensive or long-term plan, the mediator should suggest a temporary agreement. This can be either the same comprehensive agreement plan already proposed or a scaled-down version, but enacted in either case for a time-limited period. The period can be anything from one year to as little as two weeks. If need be, this can be framed as an experimental or probationary period, depending on what concepts are needed to help the parents feel safe and justified in acquiescing to the temporary agreement. Offering such a temporary agreement almost always functions to reduce the resistance of the parent. A temporary agreement serves several purposes: it gives the resistant parent an escape clause, by offering a sense of security and control, and helps the parent save face in submitting to the compromise; it yields an agreement, which serves to defuse the present power struggle; and it allows a real-life test of a cooperatively made plan for sharing the children. Moreover, experience has shown that on reevaluation at the end of the designated time period, the temporary agreement is rarely thrown out entirely; typically, it is only modified so as to be more effective. In fact, it is most often the case that once the parents come to a temporary agreement, they do not even need to renegotiate. The reasons for this are not clear, but it is likely that over time, life events change perspectives so profoundly that the original power struggle no longer seems important or worth the effort.

The "Last" Issue. Occasionally, after all the minor issues and most of the larger issues are settled, there loom one or two holdout issues. These are the issues that one parent hangs onto until the very end—the last stronghold of resistance. Not infrequently, this issue is the designation of legal custody. In California, the joint custody law has reduced this particular last-minute struggle for sole control by making joint legal custody a presumption. Hence, most couples in California do not quibble over this particular issue any longer. However, in states that do not have a presumption of or preference for joint legal custody, couples may argue intensely about the designation of legal custody.

Saving this issue until the very end serves several purposes. It allows the couple to experience cooperative efforts in finding areas of agreement before tackling the tougher issues; it gives the mediator time to reinforce the couple's cooperativeness; and it gives the mediator the leverage of the couple's earlier successes to use in encouraging the final agreements.

By far the most effective approach for settling this last issue is for the mediator to remain subtle and indirect. It often happens that if the mediator draws too much attention to this last point one of the parents is challenged to take a rigid stance, bringing the mediation process to a standstill. The psychological and symbolic connotations of the concepts of sole legal custody and joint legal custody are often greatly disproportionate to their real significance. Sole legal custody connotes that there is a winner and a loser, a competent parent and an incompetent one, a loved parent and an unloved one, while joint legal custody connotes cooperation, compromise, and balanced power. One parent may dread joint legal custody while the other may fear sole legal custody, and each may feel that the wrong designation will result in irreparable harm to the children. However, the direct ramifications of legal custody seldom determine the psychological well-being of a child. The parent with legal custody has a say in the major life decisions of a child, but the day-to-day decisions—which are, in fact, much more psychologically meaningful to a child—are made by the parent with whom the child happens to be staying on any given day. The mediator can usually minimize the importance of the exact designation used by providing an appropriate perspective on the issue. It is often helpful to remind the parents that the degree of postdivorce parental cooperation is a much more important determinant of the psychological health of the children.

If all the earlier agreements look cooperative, then the mediator can assume that the parents are implicitly agreeing to joint legal custody. At this point, the mediator can say something like: "So we will call this joint legal custody, all right?" Usually, if asked in this fashion, both parents will agree. If, however, the mediator were to present this final decision as a major and difficult one, it could be predicted that if either of the parents wanted to have one last issue of contention, he or she would seize the opportunity to stalemate the process.

An inexperienced mediator may feel quite disheartened when a couple works out all the details of a parenting agreement and then gets unexpectedly stuck on this last, symbolic issue. If, after exploring each parent's understanding of and concerns about the legal custody designation (see section on designation of legal custody in Chapter Five), neither parent will budge, the mediator can try using one or more of the impasse-breaking strategies presented in Chapter Nine. If nothing seems to work, then a partial agreement can be written up (see Chapter Five) and the issue of legal custody referred back to the attorneys and/or the court for a decision.

Fortunately, however, it seldom happens that the couple cannot resolve this issue and must go back to court. With the settlement of this last issue, the mediator gets to experience one of life's pleasures, the resolution of human conflict.

5

Drafting the Mediation Agreement

Agreements reached through the mediation process are formalized in a written mediation agreement. This document represents all the hard work of both the couple and the mediator. As such, it must be relevant, clear, and useful. It must stand as a lucid statement of the parenting arrangements to which both spouses have agreed.

Many couples, before entering mediation, have already made parenting agreements with each other that have failed. Some of these are oral agreements, some written. Both types typically break down for some or all of the following reasons: absence of a mutually acceptable context of cooperation; hidden motives that can lead to sabotage of the agreements; differing interpretations of the agreed-on clauses due to lack of precision and clarity of wording; inclusion of inappropriate, insensitive, imbalanced, or unworkable clauses; exclusion of certain appropriate and necessary clauses; absence of an agreed-on format for making modifications.

Oral agreements often break down the first time one parent irritates the other. For example, suppose that for the second or third time in a row a father returns the children home an hour later than the orally agreed-on time. The mother confronts the father, who then retorts, "I didn't know that you really meant five o'clock; it didn't sound like it was that important when we talked about it." The argument often escalates because the fact that nothing was put in writing leaves wide open the possibilities for distortion by both parents to justify their respective interpretations of the agreement.

Written agreements about parenting arrangements, while more definite and clearer than oral agreements, typically have been made either by court order or by attorney stipulation. Such agreements often suffer from excessive rigidity and insensitivity to both marital dynamics and the spousal strategies for sabotage. Because the context in both of these circumstances is adversarial, there is no precedent for flexibility or cooperative modification of the agreement in the future, should circumstances change. As instruments of the legal system, these agreements usually cannot deal very responsively with the children's and parents' needs and circumstances.

In contrast to these agreements, the mediation agreement derives from a supportive, cooperative, nonadversarial context, within which the marital dynamics, hidden motives, needs, and less guarded desires of the children and the parents have been systematically taken into account. Moreover, the agreement itself is born out of a *direct* communication between the parties involved, rather than by court imposition or by the indirect, almost inferential process of adversarial negotiations. This provides the couple with a sense of direct control over every detail of the agreement. It frequently gives a psychological boost of mastery to the parents, in the midst of feelings of helplessness. Hence, if the mediation process is well done, the mediation agreement is the most valid and useful kind of agreement about parenting that is possible to achieve.

As every therapist knows professionally and as all of us know personally, interpersonal conflict is increased by disorganization and the absence of mutually acceptable rules of conduct and is decreased by organization and structure. Before such conflict can be reduced, there has to be a common focus on the elements of structure that are necessary to create order out of disorder. Focusing is recognized as an important element of self-healing as well as a tool for behavior and attitude change across a multitude of therapy approaches (Butcher and Koss, 1978; Budman, 1981; Saposnek, in press). Whether it be the acupuncturist's needle, the behaviorist's assigned behavioral task, or the hypnotist's repeated words and images, the point of focus serves to create ease out of dis-ease, order out of disorder, and harmony out of conflict. The mediation agreement serves as the common focus for the conflicting spouses. Through sensitive and responsive design, it directs the attention of each spouse to the specific issues that have in the past created conflict, and through careful wording, it offers concrete and workable resolutions to this conflict.

Structure of the Agreement

Different mediation agreements generally are written up for the different types of referral. For the self-referred couple who draw up their own divorce settlement and consult a mediator solely to assist them in making co-parenting arrangements that will best meet the needs of their children, the written agreement can be in the form of a simple typed list of clauses to which they agree. They each receive a copy, and the mediator keeps a copy for his or her records. Since spouses who choose these self-divorce procedures typically are quite amicable, it often is not even necessary for them to sign the written agreement. The document serves as a simple clarification of what they already agree to in principle and in spirit, and they usually follow through on these agreements quite successfully. If there are any issues that might require legal perspectives or advice (for example, financial issues), the mediator should refer the couple to one or, if need be, two consulting attorneys to review the agreement. This will also safeguard the mediator against any allegation that he or she may be engaging in the unauthorized practice of law—an issue currently in great debate among mediators.

A second type of mediation referral is the divorcing couple who have each retained an attorney to work out their dissolution and are in conflict over custody and/or visitation issues. As part of their negotiations, the attorneys stipulate private mediation for the custody and visitation issues, and the spouses come to mediation with varying degress of willingness. The written agreement from this mediation can be in the form of a letter drafted to the attorneys that includes the agreements reached and a brief discussion of the issues over which no agreement was reached. The spouses may sign such a document, but that is not really necessary, since the agreements will usually be rewritten and included as one part of the comprehensive marital settlement reached by the lawyers.

Then there are the couple who have been ordered by a judge to attend private mediation after having had a court hearing on an Order to Show Cause regarding custody and/or visitation. In these cases, the judge usually requests either a written mediation agreement or an evaluation and set of recommendations for the court as to the custody and visitation arrangements that the mediator thinks would best serve the interests of the children. If agreements are reached, it may be helpful but not necessary for the couple to sign the document before sending it to the judge.

Mandatory mediation laws result in several types of referral. In some cases, there is an automatic referral by the court at the time of an OSC hearing regarding modifications of custody and/or visitation. Under California's mandatory mediation law, some counties instead allow attorneys to stipulate mediation before a court hearing, thus saving court costs. Some counties even allow divorcing or divorced spouses to stipulate mediation simply by filing with the court a signed one-page petition and paying a nominal filing fee, saving both attorney and court costs. In each of these cases, the mediation agreement is signed both by the spouses and by the mediator, with copies going to the judge, to each attorney, to each spouse, and to the mediator. In the event that no agreements are reached, some counties require the mediator to send recommendations to the court and to the attorneys, and other counties allow the mediator to retain the privilege of confidentiality and simply send a statement back to the court and attorneys that says: "No agreement reached–referred back to court," with no further details of the content of the mediation sessions.

Occasionally cases are referred under mandatory mediation in which the couple are able to reach agreement on many or most issues, but not on all. The mediator can then write up a partial agreement. The clauses are written up in the same order and fashion as in a full agreement, but at the end a separate section is included that describes the issues on which no agreements were reached. In order to retain a positive, cooperative stance, this last section can begin: "Because the parents are unable to reach agreement on the issue of ________, they agree to request that the court make the decision for them on this last issue."

If the mediator is able to help the parents formulate a number of possible options to resolve a particular issue, even if they cannot agree on which option to choose, these can be included. For example, the agreement can state: "The following possible plans for sharing the children were developed by the parents: [*plan a, plan b,* and *plan c*]. Because the parents were unable to decide among these options (*a, b,* and *c*), they are requesting the court to decide this matter for them."

Although a partial agreement still may necessitate a court hearing (albeit brief), the benefits of a partial agreement over none are several. First, there appears to be a psychological advantage to the couple in signing a statement that includes even a few agreements, even if not all the matters were resolved. This gives them at least some hope that further cooperative efforts may be possible. Second, it saves time, money, and stress for the couple by reducing the number of issues needing to be argued by their respective attorneys. Third, it facilitates the work of the attorneys and judge by separating the issues of contention from other issues.

The importance of words in shaping our thoughts, beliefs, attitudes, emotions, behaviors, and relationships cannot be overstated. The history of humankind has been significantly influenced by the strategic use of language (see Watzlawick, 1976). More recently, words have been discovered to have therapeutic potential for dealing with problems both physical and psychological in origin. The crafts of the diplomat, the politician, the lawyer, the poet, the therapist, and the mediator are basically grounded in the precision of words chosen. The greater the precision of words used, the more influential the craftsperson can be.

An agreement as significant as the one developed in mediation must be written very carefully. The exact wording chosen for the various clauses of this document is a delicate matter and can make the difference between a workable plan and one that quickly elicits an escalation of old marital conflicts. Four aspects of the wording are particularly important: the clarity of the clauses, the degree of detail in the clauses, the balance of spousal concessions, and the attitude and perspective connoted.

In order for the mediation agreement to be more workable than previous oral or written agreements, the conditions of each clause need to be spelled out clearly. For example, a clause written "Father will get the children every other weekend" allows many possible misinterpretations. The father may interpret this as meaning Friday after school until Sunday bedtime or even Monday morning, while the mother may interpret it as meaning Saturday morning until early Sunday afternoon. If, instead, the clause is written to reflect days and times that are convenient for both spouses, there is little or no possibility for differing interpretations. For example: "The children will be with father on alternate weekends beginning the weekend of January 1, 1983. On his weekends, he will pick up the children from mother's house between 4:30 and 4:45 P.M. on Friday and will return them to mother's house on Sunday between 6:30 and 7 P.M. If he ever anticipates being late for either of these transfer times, he agrees to call mother at least one-half hour before the pick-up or drop-off time." Because conflict so often arises over the pick-up and drop-off times, it is generally a good idea to negotiate and write down a time period within which the transfer of children will take place. This gives some room for lateness and helps keep the issue from inciting conflict. The time period must be negotiated between the spouses until it is acceptable to and truly workable for both spouses before entering it on the written agreement.

A second important aspect of the agreement's wording is

the degree of details written down. As a general rule, the more detail that is included, the less the spouses will have to fight about later. However, there are several reasons that too much detail can be counterproductive. For one thing, excess detail may unintentionally convey the message to the spouses that there will be debilitating conflict without a written exposition of every last transaction to be made between them. Such a message can effectively destroy the potential for a cooperative joint custody arrangement. The spouses may be left feeling that unless they carry their mediator around with them at all times, there is no hope for a cooperative co-parenting relationship to develop.

Another reason for avoiding excessive detail is that some spouses are offended by highly structured arrangements, viewing them as rigid. Following mediation, such a spouse will often systematically and subtly sabotage each clause of the agreement, not because the clauses are unworkable, but because their high degree of structure triggers off rebellious feelings in the spouse, who may be yearning to be free after the divorce. To such a spouse, an overly detailed agreement may also feel demeaning and condescending. He or she may feel that the intent of the mediation process—to give control back to the parents—has actually backfired, in that the mediation agreement has become even more restrictive than a judge's decree. Moreover, the potential for spousal conflict may rise even higher if the other spouse uses the written agreement as a weapon of revenge against the rebelling spouse and sticks rigidly to each detail.

Some couples require very little detail in their written agreement. These generally are couples who have a fairly smooth and organized child-sharing routine worked out, either by chance compatibility on this matter or by previous private negotiations between themselves. They typically come to mediation over a single major issue, or just a few minor issues, such as a need for clarification of the specific days that the children will be with each parent, a need for a plan to share holidays equitably, or a need for written acknowledgment that both parents agree to consult each other before moving out of the area. Typically, such couples have a basic trust in each other's parenting abilities, and they respect each other's right and need to stay significantly involved in the children's lives. Although they may have strong negative feelings toward each other, they seldom have many doubts about the welfare of the children while in each other's care. Moreover, they have usually maintained a level of postdivorce communication such that they can negotiate directly with each other to work out the necessary details for sharing their children. For instance, once the number of regular days that the children will spend at each of their homes has been settled, they frequently have no need to include a written plan for sharing holidays and special days with the children. By mutual consent they maintain that they will have no difficulty in developing their own workable plan outside of mediation. Since the mediator can trust their declarations, he or she need not include such details in the written agreement.

There are, however, some couples who have such basic disagreements, mistrust, or doubts about each other's intentions, abilities, and resources for taking care of the children that it becomes necessary to include numerous details in the agreement. Each spouse may insist that his or her long list of conditions be included before he or she will agree to those of the other spouse. While such details often appear quite petty to the mediator, they may have great significance to the spouses, both personally and strategically. For example, in one case, the spouses needed to include a plan for dividing the baby clothes and baby pictures of their teenage children before they could agree on a joint custody plan. After forty-five minutes of negotiations, they finally were able to resolve the issue by developing a plan for joint custody of the baby clothes such that they would alternate possession of one half of the clothes every six months. Moreover, copies of the baby pictures were to be made from the original prints, for which each spouse was to pay half. However, because the copies would not be as clear as the originals, the couple agreed to have a neutral third party randomly assign half the originals and half the copies of all the pictures to each spouse. Then, because one spouse had negatives for about one third of the pictures, it was decided that whichever spouse had the copy of a particular picture after their random division to the spouses would be entitled to claim the negative for his or her own. This spouse would then have the option to have a print made directly from the negative, at his or her own cost. Even though these issues were closer to property division than to child-sharing concerns, their symbolic significance, which related to the resolution of their feelings about sharing their children, was so strong that the mediator felt it was important to include these details in the agreement. (Examples of agreements with differing amounts of detail are presented in Appendix E.)

The third important aspect of the written agreement's wording is the balance of spousal concessions. Just as it is crucial for the mediator to maintain a balance between the husband and wife throughout the negotiations, so is it critical to preserve this balance in the final written agreement. Because the mediation process requires both spouses to compromise to some extent if it is to be successful, the agreements that are included in the written document represent a list of concessions made by each spouse. If, however, the concessions made by one spouse significantly outweigh the concessions made by the other spouse, renewed conflict may erupt.

Sometimes a single concession by one spouse can be equivalent to several concessions by the other. For example, a wife yielding sole legal and physical custody of a child and reluctantly agreeing to joint legal and physical custody with a spouse for whom she feels a great deal of mistrust may feel recompensed by an extensive, detailed list of provisions for the care, welfare, and education of the child when in the husband's care. Hence, the importance of achieving a balance of spousal concessions does not necessarily mean including one concession by the wife for every concession by the husband; rather, it means including an equivalent value of concessions for each spouse.

Occasionally, one spouse refuses to be singled out on disproportionately many conditions even when his or her concessions are balanced by a single major concession on the part of the other spouse. This is especially true if the spouse allegedly has been involved in alcohol or drug abuse, child neglect or abuse, violence, and so forth. In these cases, the mediator must carefully monitor the number of concessions that the accused spouse can tolerate on the written agreement. Occasionally, one too many concessions asked of this spouse will trigger off heavy resistance and possibly refusal to complete mediation. If this happens, the mediator must back off and negotiate a way for this spouse to concede these points in a face-saving way. One technique is for the mediator to word the one spouse's concessions in a way that is tactfully inclusive of both spouses and focuses on the children's welfare. For example, instead of writing, "Father agrees to refrain from using cocaine or alcohol while driving the children or while in the presence of the children," the mediator could write, "Both parents agree to protect their children by not exposing them to any use of drugs or liquor while the children are in the care of each, and they agree not to drive the children while under the influence of alcohol or any illegal drug." Sometimes the other spouse will resent being included in such a clause if he or she does not partake in substance abuse. In such cases, the mediator can usually negotiate an acceptable phrasing between one that singles out one spouse and one which includes both spouses.

The final point to remember in wording the written agreement is the importance of emphasizing the cooperative attitude and child-centered perspective of the mediation approach to custody and visitation decisions. Whereas the legal wording of such written documents almost always takes the point of view of the parents' rights and privileges, the mediation agreement can and should be written largely from the perspective of the child. For example, the traditional wording of a custody and visitation agreement is something like this: "(1) The parties shall have joint legal custody of the minor child. (2) Physical custody is awarded to the mother. (3) The father shall have visitation with the minor child alternate weekends, on Wednesday of each week, and alternate holidays." The mediator, however, can shift the perspective by writing it up like this: "(1) Both parents agree to share joint legal custody of their child, Alicia. (2) Alicia will share her time with her parents according to the following schedule: (a) She will be with her father from Friday after school at 3 P.M. until Sunday evening between

7 and 7:15 P.M. on alternate weekends. She will also be with her father from 4:30 P.M. on Wednesday until her father takes her to school on Thursday morning, each week. (b) She will be with her mother from Sunday evening until Wednesday afternoon, and then from Thursday to the following Wednesday, except on the alternate weekends that she will spend with her father. (c) Alicia will share her holidays with her parents by spending the first week of Christmas with her father, and . . . ."

In this example, the focus is on how the child will share her time with each parent. This represents a conceptual shift from parents owning their children to children sharing their parents. Such a shift is in the true spirit of mediation. Such wording may also help to influence the perspectives of the attorneys and judges involved in the case. While some attorneys and judges still prefer, or even insist, that any legal document be worded in legalese, perhaps enough examples of child-centered co-parenting agreements can eventually modify the spirit of the law, at least on these particular domestic issues.

Content of the Agreement

The primary goal of child custody mediation is to develop a plan that will reduce spousal acrimony and increase cooperative decision making, and the secondary goal is to maximize the children's access to both parents. In order to achieve these goals, the final document needs to include five areas of content: a designation of legal custody; a plan for regular time-sharing of the children; a plan for sharing time on holidays and special days; adjunct clauses to facilitate cooperative time-sharing; and a clause that specifies the procedure for future modification of the mediation agreement.

The first clause included in the mediation agreement (but the *last* clause negotiated) is the statement of how the spouses have decided to designate legal custody. Except for the traditional designation of sole custody (which implies both legal and physical custody) to one parent and reasonable visitation to the other parent, other designations of custody have had few clear legal definitions. Generally, it is assumed that legal custody entitles the legal custodian to make decisions about the child's educational and religious upbringing and to give consent to medical, dental, and psychological treatment for the child. Moreover, physical custody is assumed to entitle the custodian to the companionship of the child (MacGowan, 1981). However, controversy continues over the actual demarcation between legal custody and physical custody, in terms of the real nature of parental influences on the child. The controversy is especially great over the designation of joint custody, which, as a general term, implies shared legal *and* physical custody. However, as Clingempeel and Reppucci (1982, p. 103) note, "Practically speaking . . . this may translate into a multitude of variations and does not mean that physical custody is necessarily divided evenly between parents or that there is an equal sharing of child-care responsibilities. The pattern of alternating between parental homes (including the duration of stays with each parent and the frequency of environmental changes) varies widely [so that] one parent may have physical custody a greater percentage of the time (and thus have greater responsibilities with regard to daily care and activities . . .)."

Unless the actual daily care and daily responsibilities for the children are relatively equally shared, the designation of joint legal custody may be limited in its practical significance for the child's upbringing. However, some fathers' groups have asserted that unless there is joint physical custody in the ideal sense (equal time with each parent), then joint legal custody is not really meaningful to them. In fact, the California state legislature recently went so far as to pass a bill (AB 2202) that yoked joint physical custody with joint legal custody; however, it was not signed into law by the governor. It was defeated as too inflexible a law to be workable. Nevertheless, as mentioned earlier, the psychological benefit to a parent achieving a joint legal custody, with its connotation of equal legal power, may be extremely important for certain parents and should be seriously considered by the mediator.

Other designations of legal custody that may be approved by a court are *alternating* (or *divided*) custody and *split* custody. Alternating custody permits each parent to have one or several children for a part of a year, or for alternating portions of a year, or for alternating years. Each parent alternately assumes the responsibility given to a sole custodian during the time period when the child is with the respective parent. Reciprocal visitation rights are given to the noncustodial parent. It should be noted that alternating custody is *not* joint custody, since the parents do not ever at the same time have legal custody of any particular child. Split custody, which applies only to families having two or more children, allows each parent to be the sole legal custodian of at least one child all the time. For example, the mother might assume custody of one child and the father of the other two, and each parent would have visitation rights for the child or children not in his or her custody.

Of the legal custody designations available, certainly joint custody remains the most controversial in terms of its definitional ambiguity, its legal, theoretical, and practical significance, and its sociological implications. In spite of its problematic nature, however, it appears to best reflect the ideal spirit of shared parenting that, in varying forms, is implemented by mediation. As such, joint legal custody generally seems to be a more desirable legal designation than sole, alternating, or split custody, unless specifically contraindicated by circumstances, as previously noted.

The next clause included in the mediation agreement is the plan for how each of the children will share time with each of the parents. This written plan will stand as the descriptive substitute for the legal designations of *physical custody* and *visitation.* While such designations may be required in the formal court order of particular jurisdictions, the connotations of ownership of children and of the insignificance of the visiting parent are contrary to the spirit of shared parenting. They also seem contrary to the intent of the joint custody presumption currently held in a number of states. When such legal designations are necessary, the mediator can begin the wording of the clause as follows: "Both parents agree to share physical custody (and visitations) of their children according to the following schedule: Jessica will be with her mother on . . . and with her father on . . . ." With such wording, the focus shifts back to the child after the required legal opening.

The variety of ways for divorced parents and their children

to share time with one another is limited only by the tolerances of their individual schedules. If the couple have difficulty coming up with possible ways to share time, the mediator can suggest a variety of ways that reflect the greatest degree of sharing that the couple seems able to tolerate. These can range from the children's having total open access to two homes within walking distance of each other, to the children's staying in one home and the parents' alternately moving in and out of the house according to a set schedule, to the children's spending equal or disproportionate amounts of time at each parent's home. Or, if the couple needs something more traditional, the children can spend the school year at one home and part or all of vacations at the other.

When the children are going to spend the great majority of their time at one parent's house (for example, during the school year), then the weekend times should be carefully considered. The mediator should alert the parents that, next to holidays and vacation times, weekends are typically the most flexible periods for children to spend time with either parent since most parents do not work (and the children do not attend school) on weekends. If at all possible, it is generally advisable for parents to share the weekends in some sort of alternating fashion, with the children spending at least one full weekend per month with each parent.

Included next in the agreement is the plan for sharing special times during the year with the children. These include regular school vacation times, national holidays and their occasional extended weekends (New Year's, Presidents' Day, Easter, Memorial Day, Independence Day, Labor Day, Veterans' Day, Thanksgiving, Christmas), special festive days (Valentine's, St. Patrick's, Mother's Day, Father's Day, Halloween), special personal days (family members' birthdays and unanticipated special occasions), and special religious and cultural days (Martin Luther King Jr.'s Birthday, Good Friday, Cinco de Mayo, Rosh Hashonnah, Yom Kippur, Chanukah, and so on).

Most couples do not celebrate or find personal significance in all such special days. Moreover, most court-ordered decrees primarily specify schedules for regular school vacation times and, occasionally, the national holidays, since these occasions usually include days off from work and school which parents and children can share together.

In developing a plan for holidays and special days, the mediator first needs to ask each parent which holidays or special days are of particular personal significance to him or her. For example, one spouse may traditionally spend a particular holiday with the extended family, while for the other spouse that holiday does not have any special significance. Often, many of the major holidays can be divided up equitably according to the parents' personal preferences. Then the special days that are not particularly special to either parent can be subsumed under the regular time-sharing plan.

For the holidays and special days on which both parents want to share time with the children, the mediator can suggest several workable solutions. The most traditional solution is to alternate the holidays within a year, reversing the alternation every year.

Another plan is to divide the longer holiday periods into two phases so that the children spend part of each holiday with each parent. For example, Easter week can be divided in half (or into two separate week-long periods, if there is also a spring school break), and Christmas vacation, which is typically two weeks long, can be divided so that the children can spend the first week (through Christmas Eve) with their father and Christmas night through New Year's with their mother. The schedule can remain the same or switch every year.

A third, less desirable plan is to have one child with one parent and the sibling(s) with the other parent for a particular holiday, and then switch every other holiday and/or year. This can work if the siblings do not enjoy each other's company or if each parent insists on having at least one child with him or her throughout every holiday. However, this plan deprives the siblings of contact with each other during times that are usually fun and special.

Summers can be shared in a more flexible way, since the time available for the child to spend with each parent is almost completely a function of the parents' availability. Summer is the ideal time for a child to share more extended periods of time with each parent, particularly one whom the child may be with less frequently, or not at all, during the school year.

Depending on the time-sharing arrangements made for the school year, the child can spend large portions of the summer with each parent, on a rotating basis—for example, six weeks (or four weeks) with one followed by six (four) weeks with the other. Occasionally, summers can be divided by the child's scheduled summer activities. For example, the father may want to take the child on a camping trip for the first three weeks of summer vacation, and then the mother may want to take the child to her parents' home for four weeks, then to return home to enroll the child in swimming lessons for two weeks at the neighborhood pool. This kind of arrangement best accommodates both the child's opportunities and the parents' schedules.

Because of the flexibility usually possible during holidays and vacation times, the mediator should try to optimize creative solutions in the written plan for these times. This gives an extra sense of control to the parents as it expands the available options for everyone involved.

In two kinds of cases, the mediation agreement needs to contain additional clauses to be workable. In one kind of case, the spouses have been in significant conflict in a wide variety of areas regarding time-sharing with their children and need the additional structure provided by adjunct clauses that will regulate their conduct with each other and with the children. In the second kind of case, one spouse has made a very large concession to the other spouse and needs the security of knowing that the other spouse will be expected to fulfill a number of extra conditions before the concession will go into effect.

In both of these cases, the adjunct clauses do not relate directly to scheduling, but to issues that are of concern to both spouses or to one spouse about the other. These typically include the children's phone access to their parents ("Both parents agree to allow access by phone for both children to call either parent at any time"), communication about a child's health ("Both parents agree to call each other at any time if there is any special health concern regarding Patrick that needs sharing with the other parent"), communication about a child's whereabouts ("Father agrees to keep Mother informed about any extended trips with Aubrey out of the county"), child care responsibilities ("Both parents agree that the parent with whom Jonathan stays at any particular time is fully responsible for arranging and paying for child care in the event that that parent is unable to be with Jonathan directly"), safety ("Both parents agree to keep Sara restrained in a seat belt during any transportation in a motor vehicle"), health ("Mother agrees to take Richie to a doctor immediately if he is injured or sick"), cleanliness and neatness ("Both parents agree to return the children to the other parent's house bathed and dressed in clean clothes"), shared resources ("Mother agrees to send certain listed items of the children's clothing to Father's house, to remain there for the children to use on subsequent stays at Father's house"), restraint from harassment ("Both parents agree to remain in their respective cars during pick-up and delivery of the children to each other's houses and not to enter each other's house uninvited by the other parent"), restraint from drug or alcohol use ("Both parents agree to use no illegal drugs or alcohol in the presence of the children, especially while driving"), and restraint from verbal degradation ("Both parents agree to refrain from bad-mouthing each other to the children or to anyone else while in the presence of the children").

When discussing these clauses, the mediator should attempt to elicit a balance of concerns from both parents while being careful not to push too deeply into sensitive terrain. As stated earlier, too many clauses can trigger off resistance in one parent; too few clauses could leave the other spouse feeling excessively vulnerable.

As discussed earlier, the mediation agreement should not be viewed as a final decree. Hence, provisions must be made for future modifications of the agreement should any of its clauses not prove tenable for any reason. If necessary, the mediator should include a clause that states: "Both parents agree to reevaluate the above plan in one year's time [or any other reasonable interval] in order to reassess the changing needs of the children and the living situation of each parent. This will take place in a discussion between the parents, or if necessary, with the assistance of a mediator." Interestingly, not many couples return for this follow-up session. The expectation that in a year's time they will return to mediation rather than to court may well set a context for the parents to take responsibility for resolving future problems on their own. This hypothesis is supported by the findings of Frank (1974, 1978), who confirmed that expectancies have a powerful positive effect on potential psychotherapy clients and can elicit improvement in them without treatment. The expectation of help alone often induces change.

To encourage the couple to continue solving their problems in a cooperative rather than an adversarial mode, the last clause in the agreement should read: "In the event of any future dispute regarding the children which the parents are unable to resolve between themselves, both parents agree to seek mediation before legal action." Couples rarely return for such mediation. Occasionally, a parent will phone the mediator with a minor question or problem. Most often, the mediator can resolve the issue satisfactorily on the phone. If a mediation session is deemed necessary, the mediator can usually begin at the ending phase of mediation (see Chapter Four) and proceed directly to negotiations. Needless to say, resolution typically is reached much more quickly the second time around.

It is important that the mediator inform the parents that if they modify their agreement on their own, it is advisable to put the modifications in writing in the form of an addendum to the mediation agreement. This document should be dated and signed by each parent, and copies should be sent to the mediator, to the court (for inclusion in their file), and to each of their attorneys (for their records). This will ensure that such modifications are formally acknowledged and that each parent has a clear agreement in hand in the event that the other parent has a change of heart later and violates the agreement or tries to deny that the agreement was made. Moreover, by filing it with the court, the doctrine of *parens patriae* (which requires the court, as the legitimate representative of the state, to approve any custody arrangement) is legally satisfied.

Financial Linkages

When negotiating and designing the mediation agreement, the mediator should be aware of the broader context within which custody mediation takes place, which may involve certain financial matters. In addition to cases in which property settlement and custody may be linked (see discussion in Chapter Three on talking with attorneys), the mediator will most likely encounter cases in which the financial issue of child support is intertwined with custody and visitation issues. This link is usually present for one of two reasons, according to Mnookin and Kornhauser (1979). First, each parent may be willing to exchange some amount of time with the child for an increase or a reduction in income. Second, one parent may keep the child from spending designated time with the other parent in order to enforce the collection of support payments. And, conversely, the other parent may withhold support payments in order to assure a maintenance of the time designated to be spent with the child. While such bargaining over children may seem offensive to some, Mnookin and Kornhauser suggest that it may well be preferable to going to court as a way for couples to enforce support and visitation. These authors further suggest that withholding support payments to ensure that the other parent will not interfere with court-ordered visitations is not as potentially damaging to the child as the legally sanctioned alternatives of having the sheriff take the child from the custodial parent or of filing a contempt order that would put the custodial parent in jail until the designated visitation time is fulfilled. In most states, parents are not legally permitted either to cut off visitation if child support payments have not been made or to withhold support payments on the grounds that the custodial parent withheld visitations. Hence, the parents often are left to their own informal tactics to maintain an equality of bargaining leverage between themselves. When one parent shifts the balance by initiating a court action for enforcement of a promise to comply, an escalation of many peripheral issues often ensues, presenting the mediator with a challenging bundle of issues to unravel.

Links between financial and custody or visitation issues

also arise when there is an agreement between parents for equal time-sharing, yet one parent, who has a larger income, is still expected to contribute child support payments to the other parent. Often, these parents (typically fathers) resent having to pay child support when the time shared with the children is exactly equal. Moreover, they feel that they are being exploited by the other parent. Their preference for *everything* being equal (including financial support of the children) is based on not wanting to put out more than the other spouse, rather than on wanting to share proportionately in the financial support of their children. This resentment may present itself to the mediator in disguised form, as strategic resistance (see Chapter Seven).

Yet another financial link exists when one parent, because of low income, is receiving money under the Aid to Dependent Children program, as part of welfare benefits. Since this program was developed before joint custody arrangements were legally sanctioned, welfare regulations have not been specifically developed to accommodate the newer custody arrangements. In facilitating a time-sharing arrangement that gives the child equal time with each parent, the mediator may unwittingly be terminating welfare support money for the children because such benefits can be issued only to a parent who has primary custody of the children. If the parents share equally in physical custody, *neither* parent may be eligible for such aid. For example, the regulations may require that one parent have the children at least 51 percent of the time in order to retain eligibility. This imbalance may be unacceptable to the other parent, who may not only insist on sharing time equally, but also want to be the recipient of the welfare benefits.

In light of the possibilities for such financial links, the mediator should be informed about local regulations and practices regarding such matters and should help the spouses to separate out time-sharing issues from financial matters. Moreover, there are advantages to excluding financial questions from the mediation agreement. For one thing, some jurisdictions (for example, those under mandatory mediation) restrict mediation exclusively to time-sharing arrangements and leave financial problems and child support to the attorneys and judge, who typically are more skilled in negotiating such issues. For another, it seems tactically preferable for the mediator to keep negotiations about parenting and child sharing separate from the bargaining inherent in money negotiations. This helps the parents focus more exclusively during mediation on the psychological, emotional, and social needs of their children. Financial arrangements can then be accommodated to the child-sharing plan, rather than vice versa.

6

How Children Contribute to Custody Disputes

Children's limited comprehension of the meaning and implications for them of their parents' breakup creates terrible confusion and emotional upset and generates characteristic attempts to cope with the disruption. However, the limited means they have for expressing their needs makes it difficult for their parents to accurately recognize and address those needs.

For example, in her attempts to control her fear of losing both her parents, four-year-old Kirsten tells her father at his visitation time, "Mommy doesn't have any more food in the 'frigerator–could you come over tonight and bring us peanut butter and jelly sandwiches?" In a characteristically childlike way, Kirsten is trying to convey to her father that she is afraid she will be completely abandoned, no longer fed or cared for (she feels that since daddy left, maybe mommy will also). To assure her continuing survival, she tries to mend her parents' relationship by getting her father to offer nurturance (food) to her and her mother, while reuniting them at the family home. However, the parents are unable to understand the emotional basis or functional intent of Kirsten's utterance, but instead interpret it in accordance with their mistrust of each other. Her father takes Kirsten's comment as evidence of her mother's parental incompetence and neglect. Her mother takes it as evidence that Kirsten's father is continuing to spoil her by letting her think she can get anything she wants from him. As a result of their respective misinterpretations, Kirsten's father may file a court petition for sole custody and Kirsten's mother may file a counterpetition for a reduction of visitation times—each believing he or she is doing what is best for Kirsten.

It is these very fights over differing interpretations of their child's needs and behavior that frequently drive spouses to court. The complications that arise from these disputes are for the most part not due to parents' being callous or uncaring about their children's needs. The vast majority of parents are very concerned about the emotional well-being of their children and are able to set aside their own needs so that they can try to satisfy the needs of their children first. Even when faced with the pain and anger of divorce, these parents still maintain a sense of fairness, understanding, and compassion and may even convert the trauma of divorce into a growing experience for each of the family members. However, some parents who become involved in custody or visitation disputes have difficulty focusing clearly on the needs of their children. Often the stress of divorce narrows their perception of their children's needs, and their anger at the ex-spouse clouds their ability to separate their own needs from those of their children. This is particularly the case with couples who are ordered to mediation by the court, but it may also be true of couples who attend mediation voluntarily. Let us now attempt to clarify what becomes so problematic for these families by exploring the nature of the strategies that children use to express their needs.

Children's Strategies

In intact families, there are some occasions when a child willfully provokes conflict between his or her parents. There are other occasions when a child is merely an innocent victim of parental disputes. However, a third and even more common occasion, in accord with family systems theory, is when a child is an *innocent but functional contributor* to conflict between the parents. From this perspective, it appears that the child, in attempting to get his or her needs met, initiates and participates in a behavioral sequence that results in overt parental conflict. The child's action is neither clearly willful nor clearly an instance of victimization, but partly both—hence the term *innocent but functional contributor.* Such a conceptual formulation does not aim at making children blameworthy, but rather focuses on the perspective that within a family system all the members are contributors to the interactional process. By maintaining such a view, the intervenor (whether therapist or mediator) has the decided advantage of neutrality over fault-finding and side-taking and maximizes her leverage as a result of her more comprehensive view of the functional rules of the family system. So, for example, when a mother accuses the father of turning the child against her and subsequently refuses to let the father see the child, the mediator may be able to defuse this accusation by pointing out the innocent but functional part that the child may have played in telling his mother that he wanted to live at his father's house.

Early theories of the etiology of child and marital problems assumed unidirectional cause-effect relationships. That is, it was always presumed that dysfunctional marital relationships caused dysfunctional behavior patterns in children. However, more current formulations within the field of developmental psychology point to the unmistakably circular nature of causality in family interactions (Bell, 1968; Thomas and Chess, 1977; Lerner and Spanier, 1978; Hetherington and Parke, 1981). And in the past fifteen years, family systems theorists and therapists have developed such interactional theories to quite sophisticated levels (Minuchin, 1974; Watzlawick, Weakland, and Fisch, 1974; Watzlawick and Weakland, 1977; Haley, 1976; Minuchin and Fishman, 1981; Madanes, 1981).

From this systems perspective, it appears that children and parents tend to express distress during times of natural developmental family crisis such as the birth of a sibling, the beginning of adolescence, or leaving home for independent living and that each family member subsequently responds to the responses of the others in a circular rather than linear fashion. If these interactions are based upon clear communications, understanding of each other's needs, empathy, and the absence of overreactions, then the natural developmental stresses are resolved in a constructive fashion. If, however, there exist unclear or distorted communications, lack of understanding or empathy, or blatant overreactions, then the stresses escalate into crises that are greater than those typically experienced during these transitional stages in family life. It is out of these negative, escalating, interactional loops that serious family conflicts and, specifically, child behavior problems most often arise. The child's behavior functions as a strategy to communicate distress and to escalate the family conflict to a climax and resolution. Hence, what may appear as irrational, self-defeating, and antagonistic behaviors on the part of the child when viewed from an intrapersonal perspective appear as functional strategies when viewed from a family systems perspective.

The extraordinary crisis of divorce elicits all the strategies that children normally use, but in exaggerated form, to cope with the unpredictable and uncontrollable aspects of divorce (see Visher and Visher, 1979; Clingempeel and Reppucci, 1982).

In their classic longitudinal research study of children of divorce, Wallerstein and Kelly (1980) detailed the various characteristic ways that children responded to the separation of their parents initially, after eighteen months, and after five years. Such responses were clearly developmentally linked and expressed the emotional issues typical of each age range. After the initial marital separation, children three to five years old primarily manifested behavioral and emotional regression (thumbsucking, bedwetting, whining, clinging to caregiver). Children six to eight years old primarily expressed pervasive grief (crying, sobbing, yearning for the departed parent). Older children (nine to twelve years old) primarily manifested intense anger at the parent whom they perceived as responsible for the divorce, as well as a variety of psychosomatic complaints. Adolescents aged thirteen to eighteen expressed grief and anger in a more sophisticated and dramatic manner, blaming their "selfish" parents for leaving them prematurely and hence removing the opportunity for the reverse and more natural developmental event to occur, the children leaving their parents.

These characteristic initial reactions tended to subside within eighteen months and to diminish significantly within five years as more integrated acceptance of the reality and permanence of the divorce took place. However, it is within the first year following the separation that most custody and visitation plans are made, and hence, it is on the children's initial expression of their needs that parental negotiations are typically built. Moreover, while the Wallerstein and Kelly findings have shown us that it is normal for children of divorce to manifest the above characteristic responses for up to the first year and a half following the separation, most parents are unaware of this fact. Not uncommonly, each parent will interpret such behaviors as evidence of harm to the child caused by the other parent.

Added to the children's general manifestations of emotional distress are more specific and individualized reaction patterns, to which we refer here as coping strategies. These strategies are the manifestations of a combination of factors, which include the emotional needs of the child, the social and intellectual skills of the child, the temperament of the child, and the child's awareness of the emotional triggers of each parent.

To reiterate, such strategies are functional but not necessarily intentional. Their significance lies in the conflict that results from the parents' interpretations of their meaning. In general, the clarity of meaning of children's strategies is age-linked. The younger the child, the more ambiguous the meaning of the child's behavior and the more open to differing adult interpretations. However, it is not infrequent that older children (even those well into adolescence) will show behaviors that are ambiguous and open to conflicting interpretation. This can be the case when, for example, the child changes his mind several times about his preferences for living arrangements, or when an older child does not easily express herself verbally and consistently says, "I don't know." Such instances of ambiguous meaning will often polarize parents.

Because of the importance to the mediator of understanding children's strategies, I will discuss some of the more typical ones. Although the examples presented below are not comprehensive in scope, they are representative of the common strategies dealt with by mediators.

Reuniting

As stated earlier, it is common for children of all ages to wish to get their parents back together. Even in intact families where there is marital discord, children will attempt a variety of strategies for keeping their parents together even if it necessitates developing symptomatic behavior so that the parents have to remain together to solve the child's problem. Children of all ages (but especially younger ones) would often rather have their parents fight than have them separate. The child reasons: "As long as my parents are dealing with each other, they are more likely to remain together." This is a family variant of the more widely acknowledged emotional wisdom of childhood, "Negative attention is better than no attention." The desire for parental reunion is most intense for the children of divorce, and the strategies for attaining it are quite diverse.

For very young children who do not have the verbal sophistication to express their needs, their behavior is their means of expression.

Example A

Behavior: A three-year-old boy, on returning to his mother from an overnight stay with his father, wets the bed, sucks his thumb, clings to his mother, and is excessively whiny and prone to tears.

Underlying emotion: Fear of abandonment; anxiety about his own survival without his mother and father together.

Function: The emotional distress should appeal to both mother and father and urge them to reunite to make child feel better.

Mother's interpretation: Contact with father is disruptive

and destructive to the child; child feels insecure when with father; contact with father should be terminated.

Father's interpretation: Child misses his father very much and deeply loves him (perhaps more than does his mother); mother is not caring well enough for the child; contact with father should be increased.

For school-age children, reuniting strategies are more active yet often still disguised.

Example B

Behavior: An eight-year-old girl tells her mother how her father has changed: "He's so nice now, he has lots of money now, he doesn't yell anymore, and he takes us to nice places."

Underlying emotion: Sadness and grief at loss with hope of parental reunion.

Function: Child's description of perceived changes in father should attract mother to father once again and result in reuniting them.

Mother's interpretation: Father is trying to buy the child's love; he is pretending to show real interest in the child but is not sincere; he is conveying a false image of himself to the child; he should have limited contact with the child until his life gets settled and the child can see him for what he really is.

Father's interpretation: Child really wants to live with him; child will continue to be poisoned against her father if she continues to live at her mother's house; custody should be given to father.

With adolescents, reuniting strategies are even more active and intense although, again, often disguised.

Example C

Behavior: A thirteen-year-old girl reports to her father that her mother is very unhappy and that she is afraid her mother will not be able to take care of herself or her household responsibilities.

Underlying emotion: Fear of losing nurturance and fear that she will not be provided for.

Function: Father should feel worried about mother and should return home to take care of her.

Mother's interpretation: Child is just manipulating the parents to get out of doing her chores; she needs firmer discipline, unlike what her father provides.

Father's interpretation: Mother is unfit and incompetent to parent. She obviously is suicidal once again and it will be harmful for the child to be around her; child should live with the father and have minimal or no contact with the mother until she seeks treatment and is certified by a competent psychiatrist as not suicidal.

Reducing Separation Distress

For some time after the marital separation, young children often experience separation distress each time they make the transition between their parents. Each time such a child leaves one parent to go to the other, he experiences the emotional loss of the parent he is leaving, even if he is going for just a day. Often such a reaction reflects a particularly close bond with both parents, but it can also be reflective of the child's own adaptability. Children who are less adaptable tend to have a more difficult time dealing with the transition from one parent's house to the other's. Because of the increased emotional stress following divorce, any lack of adaptability is likely to be exaggerated.

Example

Behavior: A four-year-old girl cries each time she is transferred from her mother's to her father's care (or vice versa); child appears to be happy while in the care of each parent, after the transition time.

Underlying emotion: Child reexperiences intense separation anxiety each time she has to make this change from one caretaker to another.

Function: To signal distress about these changes so that

parents will somehow reduce the number of changes or help her to decrease her discomfort in dealing with such changes.

Mother's interpretation: Child is crying when leaving her because she doesn't like having to leave her mother so often; she cries upon returning to her mother because she is upset at having to stay at her father's so much, and she no doubt has a terrible and stressful time with her father; contact with father should be reduced until child feels more comfortable around him.

Father's interpretation: Child cries when leaving him because she does not want to go back to her mother's house so soon. She cries upon coming to her father because her mother probably has told her bad or frightening things about him; contact with father should be increased in frequency and duration so that child can enjoy even more time with him.

Detonating Tension

Very often, the tension between hostile separated parents feels to the children like a volcano waiting to erupt. In intact families, such marital tensions are often resolved or at least temporarily reduced by the child providing an excuse—such as disturbing behavior—for both parents to yell and even hit out, thereby diffusing the tension between them. In effect, the child unconsciously (and sometimes quite consciously) offers himself temporarily as a scapegoat to absorb the hostility between his parents.

Children of divorced parents utilize this strategy as well, but in different ways.

Example

Behavior: A seven-year-old boy tells his father that his mother has been sleeping with two different men at the house within the same weekend.

Underlying emotion: Fear that father's chronic jealousy and anger at mother may result in mother and child getting hurt or killed.

Function: To get Father to blow up once and for all; the

reality would be easier to handle than the fantasies that the child has generated in response to the chronic tension over his father's jealousy.

Mother's interpretation: Child is just angry at mother for the divorce and is jealous that his mother shares her attention with other people in her life. Child needs to refrain from telling father about her personal life, and father needs to keep out of her life. Now there is even more reason to be guarded in dealing with father, since he is so intrusive.

Father's interpretation: Mother is an immoral person and incompetent parent; child's contact with her should be limited or restricted until she gets her life straightened out. She should not be allowed to set such an example for her son.

Testing Love

Wallerstein and Kelly (1980) have pointed out how both parents are frequently emotionally unavailable to their children for about a year following the separation. During this phase, children often feel emotionally neglected and will occasionally test their parents' love for them.

Example

Behavior: A five-year-old boy who lives with his father calls his mother on the phone frequently and, in a driven manner, tells her he loves her. Throughout his stays with her, he repeats this utterance.

Underlying emotion: Fear of rejection by his mother for wanting to stay with, and feel love for, his father.

Function: To find out, in a child's characteristically backwards fashion, whether his mother still loves him. The statement is intended as the question "Do *you* still love *me,* Mommy?"

Mother's interpretation: Child desperately wants to live with mother; he is probably afraid of, or is not being nurtured enough by, his father; custody should be changed to mother, since father obviously cannot satisfy the emotional needs of a young child.

Father's interpretation: Child is just trying to make mother feel better because mother has been complaining to the child how unhappy she is. Mother must stop encouraging and using the child to satisfy her own needs. Contact between child and mother should be restricted until she stops burdening the child with her own problems.

Proving Loyalty

Not infrequently, the emotional unavailability of both parents frightens a child enough to willingly sacrifice a relationship with one parent, at least temporarily. The child feels tremendously torn between her parents and feels that she cannot love both of them if they do not love each other. She feels that she has to choose between her parents, withdrawing love from one and investing it all in the other. She allies with that parent and proves her loyalty by actively participating in the ongoing marital conflict. This results in the development of a dysfunctionally close bond with one parent and a dysfunctionally distant one with the other.

Example

Behavior: A nine-year-old girl refuses to have any contact with her father and spends a lot of time and energy disparaging him to her mother and agreeing with and supporting the mother in her own disparagement of the father.

Underlying emotion: Fear of being totally neglected by both parents.

Function: To prove to her mother that she will fully support her in her feud with the father, in exchange for being taken care of and loved by her. Child also assumes that her father will somehow understand and be patient until she feels reassured of her mother's love, at which time she can then reestablish an affectionate relationship with him.

Mother's interpretation: Child knows the truth about how rotten her father is; contact between father and child would be seriously destructive to the child and should therefore be terminated.

Father's interpretation: Mother has poisoned the child's mind against him and should be forced to stop this; custody should be given to the father so that he can undo the damage and normalize his relationship with the child.

Seeking Fairness

Children of almost any age will often attempt, to the point of self-sacrifice, to make everything come out exactly even between their parents. They will take it upon themselves to monitor fairness for both their parents no matter how embroiled the parents may be with each other. They feel burdened with the task of keeping parental peace and pressured to balance concessions to each parent. They fear confrontation between their parents and repress their own needs and sense of individuality in order to keep their parents from overt conflict.

Example

Behavior: A fourteen-year-old boy insists on staying exactly one week at his mother's house and one week at his father's, even though his parents live a sizable distance apart; this creates considerable inconvenience and distress for the boy, and his school work and friendships suffer markedly, but he maintains the preference.

Underlying emotion: The boy wants both his parents to keep loving him equally well; is afraid of losing one of them.

Function: To make the time-sharing arrangements so perfectly equal that mother and father will stop fighting over the boy and resume showing their love for him.

Mother's interpretation: Son is unquestionably afraid of confronting his father because father may have a temper tantrum and intimidate him; boy's own life is suffering from this bouncing back and forth between houses, and the arrangement must be changed; boy should live at his mother's house and visit his father every other weekend only if he wants to.

Father's interpretation: Son understands what is fair and

loves both parents equally; his problems at school and with friends are natural for children following divorce and have nothing to do with the time-sharing arrangements; the arrangements should remain as they are.

Protecting Self-Esteem

Unfortunately, some parents are quite insensitive to the feelings of their children. Because children often hide their own feelings, some parents mistakenly assume that children either do not have significant feelings or are so resilient that they can easily recover from any hurt feelings. In the case of divorce, when parents are just looking for places to vent their anger, children are easy, available targets. And if such anger is exacerbated by a parental style that is already insensitive to children's feelings, the emotional ambience for a child can be quite threatening. This problem is complicated further by the fact that children often have difficulty in identifying, let alone verbally expressing, the source of their discomfort when around a parent who threatens their self-esteem. Hence, they will commonly resort to strategies that protect their self-esteem.

Example

Behavior: A ten-year-old girl resists going to her father's house and develops psychosomatic illnesses whenever time with him is anticipated; when asked why she resists, she says, "I just don't feel like it today."

Underlying emotion: Child fears being criticized by her father; she loves him but always feels uncomfortable and guarded around him.

Function: To protect child's self-esteem and hopefully persuade father to change his style of dealing with the child.

Mother's interpretation: Father is putting down child just the way he used to put down mother; child should not have to tolerate such abuse from someone whom she does not even care about; until father changes, contact between father and child should be restricted.

Father's interpretation: Mother is once again poisoning the child's mind against father; child and father used to have a very good relationship, which mother is clearly trying to sabotage; child needs more contact with father to get her away from her mother's influence.

Protecting Parents' Self-Esteem

Children often are acutely aware of the fragility of their parents' self-esteem, especially following a marital separation. Partly out of genuine empathy and love for each parent, but mostly for their own emotional survival, they will make efforts to protect the self-worth of each parent. Such efforts are particularly characteristic of children who tend to be more sensitive to their parents' feelings. Children using these strategies generally are not aware of the resulting inconsistencies of their actions toward their parents.

Example

Behavior: An eight-year-old girl, when with her father, tells him that she really wants to live at his house and see her mother once in a while. When with her mother, the girl tells her that she really wants to live at her house and see her father once in a while.

Underlying emotion: Child feels badly for each parent and is scared that something bad will happen to each of them unless the child emotionally supports them; also, child fears being emotionally abandoned by either or both parents.

Function: To boost self-esteem of both parents so that they will remain emotionally strong enough to care for and love the child.

Mother's interpretation: Child wants to live at mother's house and is afraid to tell father; father should give child to the mother.

Father's interpretation: Child wants to live at father's house and is afraid to tell mother; mother should give child to the father.

Permissive Living

A mediator may occasionally come upon older children and adolescents who appear to deal with the divorce by manipulating the marital dissolution to their own immediate advantage. They appear to be in little or no emotional distress and state preferences for their living arrangements that tip the marital balance into conflict. Although these youngsters may actually have repressed their emotional distress over the divorce, it is very difficult for the mediator to ascertain this. The motivation for their strategies may be a lack of any particular bond with either parent, an exceptional degree of manipulative skill or self-centeredness, or a simple withdrawal in response to feeling trapped between conflicting parents. In any case, these youngsters appear to push a decision that will work to their own advantage.

Example

Behavior: A sixteen-year-old boy consistently states a preference to live at his father's house and see his mother every other weekend. When asked why, he gives a variety of inconsistent reasons.

Underlying emotion: Boy has withdrawn his emotional investment in his parents and now wants the most comfortable life-style that he can get.

Function: To structure his postdivorce living situation so as to maximize his financial resources and minimize daily responsibilities and demands for conforming behavior.

Mother's interpretation: Father clearly has made unrealistic promises that life will be easy for his son if he lives with him. This is just another of the father's tactics to get revenge on the mother; father sets no example of discipline for his son; youngster should live at his mother's house, where he will learn responsibility and self-discipline.

Father's interpretation: Boy loves his father more than he does his mother and does not want to live with her; he is old enough to make his own choices and should live with father if he so wishes.

Conclusions

Certainly, each of the children's behaviors in these examples is open to differing interpretations. Still, they exemplify the near-incredible degrees of misinterpretation that conflicting parents are capable of. The unfortunate consequence for the children is the pain and anguish they must suffer as a result of not having their real feelings recognized or their emotional needs met. Moreover, the children may unwittingly contribute actively to the leftover marital feud by fanning their parents' flames of wrath and mistrust with behaviors that are confusing and unintentionally provocative to the parents.

The mediator is in a position to utilize this information to reduce acrimony between parents. By offering a thorough, detailed explanation of the general nature of children's strategies and by discussing the particular ones used by their child, the mediator can help parents unravel the sequence of events that led up to the present custody or visitation dispute. Sometimes it is most effective to carry on this discussion after interviewing the children, to confirm the data and muster further confidence in the mediator's perspective. It is not uncommon for a couple to be drawn together somewhat by a shared recognition of their child's innate cleverness in initiating these strategies. It should be repeatedly emphasized by the mediator that children's strategies are not malevolent or blameworthy, but merely their way of taking care of their own needs. This emphasis is intended to reduce any tendency in a parent to displace his or her anger at the ex-spouse onto the child for contributing (however innocently) to the dispute.

It is of great significance that the parents' various misinterpretations of their children's behaviors are *exactly* the arguments that would be utilized by the parents' respective attorneys in arguing their case in court. The lawyers build evidence to support each misinterpretation and then construe this as reality. They then offer this construction, based on distorted assumptions, as "in the best interests of the child."

From this perspective, it can easily be seen that such legal recourse frequently has little to do with what is in the best interests of the child and much to do with what is in the best interests of the adult client. Ultimately, however, even this approach is likely to backfire on the parents, since if the legal argument presented by the parent's attorney is based on false assumptions of the child's needs, then pursuing that position in court may yield an unhappy child. Certainly no parent, no matter how motivated by anger, could feel satisfied in winning such a bitter victory.

Once in a while, the mediator has occasion to observe children who are in such severe emotional distress that they seem in need of psychological treatment. However, before making a referral for such treatment, the mediator should consider several factors. While it is possible that the child's emotional difficulties predate the divorce, it is highly probable that they are a reaction to, or at least exacerbated by, the ongoing parental conflict. Treatment for the child alone may therefore be of only minimal help if the spousal feud continues. Moreover, the child's therapist may unknowingly add to the problem by siding with one of the parents (typically the one who brings the child for therapy), thereby escalating the conflict.

Because the child's problems are embedded in the family's dynamics, it is important that those problems be viewed within the context of the family system. Hence, if therapy seems appropriate, it is helpful for the mediator to refer the child to a therapist who will deal with the child within the family perspective. Ideally, the therapist should be sensitive to and experienced with the systemic nature of custody and visitation disputes. This will help to ensure that he or she will remain neutral with respect to the parents while treating the child's distress. A sensitive, knowledgable therapist can help the child get through the crisis of the divorce and custody dispute. In addition, if the parental feud continues, the therapist may be able to help the child develop coping strategies that take a less severe psychological toll than the ones he or she may already be using.

7

Parents' Motives and Methods in Custody Disputes

The emotions experienced by divorcing spouses have been thoroughly detailed by other authors (Bohannan, 1970; Kessler, 1975; Weiss, 1975; Federico, 1979; Haynes, 1981). Among the many difficult feelings experienced are hurt, rejection, anger, loneliness, depression, anxiety, lowered self-esteem, and guilt. Although many of these emotions are transitory, there is a great deal of individual variation from one person to another in terms of the intensity and duration of each of these feelings. In one person, the rejection, hurt, and anger may be experienced for only a few weeks or months following the separation and then be processed in a relatively healthy way, freeing the person to begin the task of building a new life. In another person, the rejection and hurt may turn into a lifelong vendetta against the ex-spouse, and the anger to chronic bitterness, affecting new relationships and other aspects of his or her life.

There are two factors that tend to keep the spouses' negative feelings alive and are central in spurring them to take up adversarial postures following the decision to divorce. One is the almost universal presence of varying degrees of mistrust between the spouses; the other is the traditional legal process for reaching divorce settlements, which actively encourages this mistrust by restraining the spouses from communicating directly.

Mistrust, which builds rapidly after the divorce decision, arises as a result of the traumatic breach of interpersonal security in suddenly losing a mate. During the last phase of the marriage, there typically is a breakdown in communication between the spouses and, therefore, in their trust that they could resolve their conflicts together. Even when conflict resolution skills break down, they might at least be able to trust each other's commitment to being a "married couple," with the inherent security that comes with maintaining the semblance of their social and financial life-style. At the point of the divorce decision, however, even this commitment is breached, and the spouses often can no longer trust each other to negotiate for their common interest. They may suddenly become adversaries, at a time when they are feeling most vulnerable. Moreover, they may project their own vulnerability onto their children and fight intensely to protect the image of their children thus created, even if such actions are not in the children's best interests.

Some spouses (largely those voluntarily seeking mediation), in spite of their negative feelings toward the ex-spouse, are able to contain their hostility and mistrust enough to consider the legitimate needs of their children as well as the needs of each other. During mediation, they may want to discuss such reasonable and important concerns about their children as safety and health, social, emotional, and cognitive development, behavioral styles, interests, tolerances, and so forth. However, many spouses entering mediation (largely those court-ordered to mediation) have not drawn such clear boundaries between the valid needs of their children and their own hostility to and mistrust of each other. Furthermore, they may have a great deal of difficulty in coping with these negative feelings within themselves. Confused and overwhelmed by the negative feelings that erupt following the separation, they grapple with their ex-spouse to gain some sense of security, personal power, and dignity. Often, they feel a sense of disillusionment at the actions and reactions of their ex-spouse following the separation, and they may even be surprised and disheartened by their own reactions. This may be accompanied by a sense of personal failure and guilt over their own actions leading up to the divorce, and they may displace these feelings onto the ex-spouse. Such feelings interact with their individual emotional styles to yield a wide array of responses. While some spouses can utilize their insight into these feelings to check their expression, others appear to have little control over the expression of negative reactions. For these spouses, the mediation process becomes an arena for protecting their own vulnerable feelings under the guise of seeking what is in the best interests of the children. These interactional maneuvers with hidden personal agenda are similar to the functional strategies of children discussed previously. Because adults have more sophisticated cognitive abilities, their strategies generally appear to be more consciously motivated, albeit unspoken. However, if such a strategy is pointed out to the spouse by the mediator, the spouse typically denies any hidden motive and even more firmly proclaims the maneuver to be solely in the best interests of the child. Some typical strategies manifested by spouses before, during, and, unfortunately, even after mediation are given in the following sections.

Reuniting Strategies

In most divorces, one spouse wants a divorce and the other spouse does not. This often leaves the remaining spouse with little or no leverage over the departing spouse. However, custody mediation does provide a forum for attempting to persuade the other spouse to return to the marriage. In assessing the degree to which each spouse wanted the divorce (see sections of Chapter Four on gathering information), the mediator should listen for any extreme position taken by a spouse—for example, "I'll do anything to get her back." Such an assertion should alert the mediator to the possibility of reuniting strategies initiated by that spouse. Although it is rare for couples reaching the stage of custody mediation to reunite (McIsaac, 1981), spouses will attempt a variety of strategies in hopes of bringing about a reconciliation.

Requesting Extended Mediation. Under the guise of having many issues concerning the children to work out, a spouse may request mediation. In the first phone contact with the mediator, this spouse indicates that his wife left him and the children are unhappy. He says that they need to see their mother more often and that he wants to work out a schedule with her, but she has been unwilling to talk with him since she left. When told by the mediator that she will meet with the two of them for one or two sessions to work out these issues, the man expresses distress, saying, "I had hoped we could meet for more sessions—she needs you, or someone, to explain to her that she's making a terrible mistake in going through with the divorce."

In the mediation sessions, the husband persistently tries to talk about the marriage, bringing up issues that elicit talk of the past. Even in the face of repeated clarifications of the wife's determination to end the marriage, and of repeated requests by the mediator to refrain from talking about the past, the husband persists in eliciting talk of feelings rather than proceeding with the task of negotiating co-parenting arrangements. He may try to convince the wife that she really still loves him, or he may try to induce guilt feelings by telling her that the children are suffering greatly and need their father and mother together. If all else fails, he may threaten that she will never be able to make it on her own.

Because of the wife's determination to divorce, his strategies are met with resistance, determination to hasten the divorce, and increased reluctance to participate in further mediation sessions. If the mediator allows the husband to continue expressing his feelings about the marital relationship, the wife may well get up and walk out or at least be extremely reluctant to cooperate in any co-parenting agreement.

Pursuing Sole Custody. If a husband feels that appealing to his wife's feelings is futile, he might initiate a reuniting strategy by declaring that he wants sole custody of the children. Once in mediation, he presents a host of reasons that the children should live with him and remain under his legal control. Although the reasons may appear valid, they are offered in a context of bitterness and refusal to compromise. Further inquiry may elicit a statement such as "Just because *you* want your freedom doesn't mean that the family must split up. We will stay together, and when you are finished doing your thing, we would like you to return to the family."

With this strategy, the husband attempts to maintain unilateral control over the children and the family, with an eye toward coercing the wife to reunite with him or lose her controlling interest in the children and be excluded from the family.

Pursuing Joint Custody. Sometimes a husband tries to reunite with his wife by insisting on joint legal and joint physical custody and presenting the plan as in the best interests of the children. Previous to the divorce decision, this father had little or nothing to do with the children, but suddenly he is extremely interested in sharing time with them. It should be noted that in their longitudinal study, Wallerstein and Kelly (1980) found that the interest of fathers in their children, postdivorce, was unrelated to their relationship with them during the marriage. Fathers who had been distant with their children during the marriage often began visiting them after the divorce with surprising regularity. The clue for the mediator to whether a particular husband's pursuit of joint custody is motivated more by a genuine interest in the children than by a reuniting strategy is the nature of the particular plan proposed by the husband. If, for example, he proposes daily contact with the wife and, against her protests, persists in trying to convince her of the importance of regularly sharing information about the children between themselves, then the latter motive may be safely inferred.

This strategy is aimed at giving the husband another chance to prove his marital worthiness to the wife by setting up frequent contacts between them. The husband hopes that he will be able to use such contact to reopen the marital relationship and eventually persuade the wife to reunite with him.

Yielding to All Demands. If active strategies do not seem likely to work, a husband might take the approach of giving in to all of the wife's demands, which may be quite specific regarding the care of the children when they are with the husband. Even when some of these demands are unreasonable, the husband offers no resistance and agrees with each of them just as they are presented by the wife.

The mediator may be surprised at the husband's passive

response but soon notices that he is not taking any of these demands too seriously because he wants and expects to get back together with his wife. Her demands are irrelevant to him, but he appeases her in as sincere a manner as he can in the hope that she will eventually realize that she and he belong together. His strategy of yielding keeps down the marital conflict while he waits for the reunion.

Refusing to See the Children. This less frequent strategy is typically used by husbands who are less emotionally mature. If the husband wants a reconciliation but direct efforts have failed, he may refuse to see the children unless his wife reunites with him. The effectiveness of this strategy relies on the wife's feeling strongly about the importance of continuing contact between the children and their father. The mediator can recognize the presence of this strategy by observing the wife's response to the husband's threats. If she becomes worried and upset, then the husband's (implicitly coercive) threat of psychological damage to the children may indeed function as an effective tool for attempting reconciliation. This tactic, however, rarely achieves its goal of reconciliation. As the wife comes to realize her own leverage in not succumbing to her husband's threat, she neutralizes his strategy.

With all such reuniting strategies, the mediator must repeatedly clarify the degree of certainty that the divorce decision is final. Often it takes numerous repetitions of this fact throughout the mediation process before the unwilling spouse can accept it. Sometimes the spouse cannot acknowledge it in the presence of the other spouse and simply needs more time apart to process the painful reality. Scheduling sessions many weeks or even months apart can help resolve this emotional block, which otherwise often prevents agreements from being reached. Occasionally, it is helpful to refer the spouse who desires reunion to a counselor for help in accepting the divorce before further mediation efforts are attempted.

Emotionally Disengaging Strategies

For many spouses, although it is easy to get a legal divorce, it is extremely difficult to get an emotional one. It is probably a truism that one is never completely emotionally divorced from a spouse. Carl Whitaker (1982) stated it even more emphatically, saying "Divorce does not exist." By this he meant that spouses (or even young lovers) who have had a deep emotional attachment will never completely lose that feeling, even if the primary feeling that lingers is the intensification of all the anger and pain experienced in the relationship. Nevertheless, having such deep feelings, whether positive or negative, is very different from having no feelings either way.

It is striking to see couples who have been divorced for ten or fifteen years come to mediation for modification of custody or visitation arrangements and reengage the negative aspects of their emotional relationship with (according to the clients) the same intensity that existed at the time of divorce. Clearly, time sets no boundaries for such emotions. To a spouse who wants to divorce and get on with his or her new life, the lingering intensity of negative feelings can feel like a curse—or, as one spouse put it, like being condemned to a life sentence of anger, frustration, bitterness, and general misery. Especially when they have young children at the time of the divorce, spouses can feel overwhelmed at the thought of having to maintain regular contact with the ex-spouse for up to eighteen more years. Each contact with the ex-spouse may reignite their negative feelings, generating repeated reminders of their unhappiness in the marriage. Even when a spouse understands the benefits to the child of regular contact with both parents, his or her emotional response to the idea of such contact can generate defensiveness. Emotionally, the spouse may wish the other spouse would disappear forever. As one spouse put it, "I know that my son needs his father too, but I wish deep in my heart that he would move to the other end of the country, get remarried, have some of his own kids, and leave us alone forever."

Whether fresh from the divorce or many years down the line, spouses use a variety of strategies to emotionally disengage from the other spouse. In some ways, the disengaging strategies of one spouse can be complementary to the reuniting strategies of the other.

Taking or Giving Sole Custody. In an attempt to minimize contact between the spouses, one spouse may enter mediation insisting on sole custody. Initially, she argues that it would be too disruptive to the young child to have to deal with the confusion of two sets of rules and with changing back and forth between houses, as would be the case with joint custody. As the negotiations proceed, she adds that she would have an extremely difficult time dealing with her ex-spouse on any more frequent a basis than visitation times every other weekend. She further insists on being the one to receive sole custody, explaining that she is clearly the superior parent for the child. However, she enters the second mediation session declaring that she has decided to give sole custody to the father and that she will retain visitation rights every other weekend. While maintaining that joint custody would be worse than sole custody to the father, she berates the ex-spouse even as she offers him sole control over the child.

There may be several reasons for such a switch. In one case, the wife rightly interpreted the husband's efforts to work out a reasonable solution involving co-parenting as his attempt to remain emotionally engaged with her. The threat that she felt from this bid for closeness (since her own ambivalence may have been tipped in the direction of reuniting) was noticed by the child during the interim between mediation sessions. The child then displayed a reuniting strategy of her own, telling her mother that she wanted to live with her father, which compounded the mother's feelings of threat. The mother's response was a desperate attempt at disengaging. Her initial motive to protect the child became displaced by her need to be emotionally at peace and truly divorced from her ex-husband. She was willing to sacrifice legal and physical control over her child in order to distance herself permanently from her ex-husband.

Such desperation typically subsides over time, as the freshness of the divorce trauma fades and time mellows chaotic feelings. Hence, scheduling extended time periods between sessions often helps in these cases.

Labeling and Invalidating the Spouse. It is well known that when we apply a negative label to a person—such as thief, drug addict, pervert, schizophrenic, liar—we are able to distance ourselves emotionally from that person (Aronson, 1980). This principle may be taken up by a spouse who wants to discount the ex-spouse. For example, a husband who repeatedly refers to his wife as crazy or a wife who refers to her husband as violent throughout the mediation sessions may each be attempting to invalidate the other as a person worthy of regard. Within the arena of custody negotiations, these labels function as attempts to enlighten the mediator about the unfitness of the other spouse for parenting responsibilities. Typically, the accusations are generalizations from previous difficulties between the spouses that are extended into assumptions about parenting competence. However, while a marital relationship may certainly evoke violent or crazy behavior between spouses, there is no necessary or direct connection between such behavior and each spouse's relationships with and caregiving to the children.

In labeling a spouse, the other spouse builds an emotional case for not trusting the other. Such mistrust then functions as a defensive strategy for maintaining emotional distance from that spouse. If she is crazy, then he wants less to be involved with her. If he is violent, then she has good reason to stay away from him.

Spouses frequently present reasons to mistrust each other and may well expound on this mistrust all the way through the conclusion of mediation. However, the presence of such mistrust does not necessarily preclude development of a workable parenting agreement. Often the expressions of mistrust can be translated into something like "If I trust you at all, then I might be pulled back into a spousal relationship, which I do not want." As long as the mediator views these labels as strategies for emotionally disengaging rather than as charges to be investigated (assuming that the charges are unsupported), then he or she can guide the process to a successful agreement in spite of the labels.

Buffering. When one spouse is unable to maintain emotional distance from the other spouse any other way, he or she will sometimes resort to a strategy of forcing the other spouse to communicate only through other people—the children, a new spouse, a lover, a lawyer—who function as interpersonal buffers.

For example, a husband might propose that all arrangements between his ex-wife and children be made through his new wife. Or, with older children, a wife might insist that her ex-husband make arrangements directly with the children. Although such arrangements occasionally work out, it is usually necessary for the ex-spouses to deal directly with each other, especially during the first year or two following the separation. Moreover, further problems are likely to emerge as a result of the miscommunications and misinterpretations that frequently occur when spouses deal with each other through third parties, since each of these other people has vested interests that may differ from those of the spouse in charge of the children. Hence, buffering strategies for preventing emotional involvement between the ex-spouses make for difficulties in constructing a workable plan for co-parenting. Moreover, because a buffering strategy prevents direct exchange of information between the spouses, there is increased probability that the other spouse will become resistant. The mediator must try to maintain the highest level of direct communication between the spouses that feels satisfactory to both.

Sabotaging Visitations. If all other methods of emotionally disengaging fail, a spouse may attempt to sabotage visitations between the children and the ex-spouse in hopes of driving the ex-spouse away. If a wife, for example, is successful with this strategy, her need for emotional distance from her ex-husband will be satisfied, albeit at the cost of severing their father from the children's lives.

During mediation sessions, a husband may complain that the children always seem to be sick or busy with a planned activity, or to have just left to go somewhere, whenever his visitation time comes around. The wife retorts with "Well, the children *do* get sick, and they *are* very busy." In such cases, the mediator must help the wife understand the importance for the children of regular contact with both parents, and he or she must help the spouses work out a plan that minimizes contact between them while maximizing contact between the children and each of them.

Emotional Survival Strategies

The pain that parents experience in suddenly being apart from their children for extended periods of time is less apparent than the pain that children experience following the separation of their parents. Indeed, the mediation process has as its central goal to reduce the suffering of children following parental separation by maximizing access to both parents. This is a necessary priority because children do not on their own have the power or resources to arrange continuing contact with their parents. But it is also true that just as children need access to their parents, so do parents need access to and continuing contact with their children.

Many parents, especially mothers, who have built their lives around their children throughout their marriage, will, on being informed that their spouse is leaving, cling ever more tightly to the children. Frequently, they have never cultivated adult friends other than their spouse and they have not worked outside the home for many years, if at all. Hence, the only significant relationships remaining for them are those with their children. Moreover, the thought of being completely alone, without either spouse or children, is more than they can bear. When mediation begins, these spouses often panic and develop rigid strategies for their own emotional survival.

Resisting Mediation in Favor of Court. One strategy that these spouses attempt is flat resistance to mediation. In the first phone call from the mediator, these spouses typically say things like "I am not giving up my children; my children want to stay with me. I am keeping custody, so there is nothing to mediate." When the mediator suggests that mediation is almost always a more constructive approach for deciding parenting arrangements for children, such a spouse may say, "Well, *I've* already *decided* on the parenting arrangements—I'm keeping my children. Besides, I'm sure that any judge would let me keep my children—a judge wouldn't let *him* take them from me, so I'd rather go to court."

Usually, with further explanation of the mediation process, this spouse can be persuaded to attend a first mediation session. The mediator must deal sensitively with a mother's emotional panic at the prospect of losing her child, by rephrasing the idea as "keeping your child but also allowing the opportunity for your child to keep his father."

If the mediator cannot persuade the spouse to attend even a first mediation session, a phone call to her attorney will usually resolve the problem. However, on occasion, the spouse will attend the first mediation session but will either not participate sincerely or will resist all reasonable offers by the other spouse during the negotiation phase. In such a case, the mediator must delicately probe the nature of the resistance. If such probing reveals the resistance to be an emotional survival strategy, the mediator needs to sensitively help the spouse by framing the negotiation efforts as an opportunity for opening ways for the children to share time with both parents, and by discussing the consequences of sharing the children. If, on the other hand, such probing reveals that the spouse's attorney advised her to attend mediation but not agree to anything, then the mediator must confer with the attorney to explore the reasons for the attorney's resistance to mediation. Sometimes the attorney may need more information about the process of mediation, and sometimes the attorney may need more of a sense of participation. If the latter seems true, then the mediator can invite both attorneys with their clients to the next mediation session, in order to elicit explicit cooperation from the attorneys (see section in Chapter Nine on leveraging with attorneys).

Demanding Sole Custody. A demand for sole custody may persist in spite of all the mediator's efforts. The reasons offered by the spouse are likely to be weak and inconsistent and may not even be accompanied by any particular accusations about the other spouse as a person or as a parent. With further probing, the mediator usually elicits tears and unveils the spouse's panic at losing the children. At this point, the other spouse typically backs off and responds sympathetically to the panic. A husband may offer affirmation that he has no desire to take the children away but that he does want to maintain involvement in their lives. The wife may then soften her stance and appear more ready to negotiate an agreement.

Manipulating or Invalidating the Children's Preferences. When children have indicated a preference for living with one parent, the other parent, feeling hurt and abandoned, may attempt to manipulate or invalidate the stated preferences of the child. This strategy takes several forms. The father, for example, may refuse to bring the children to the mediation session when requested, saying he does not want them traumatized by having to answer painful questions. Or he may agree to bring them but show up without them, saying something like "I forgot that they had Little League practice today." In this instance, the father knows that the children would express a preference for living at their mother's house, but he does not want to face it. He may even say that the children have told him they want to live with him—and the children may actually have said so, in an attempt to protect either themselves or their father.

Another form of this strategy is for the father to *insist* that he bring the children to the mediation session. He may also claim a particular day as the only time he has available for that session—which just happens to be on the last day of an extended stretch of time during which the children will have been with *him*. Of course he does not state his hidden agenda, but he is exploiting what we may call the recency effect—the tendency of children (particularly young ones) to express, behaviorally or verbally, a preference to live with the parent with whom they most recently spent time.

A last and more desperate form of this strategy is enacted after a child states a preference within the mediation session to live with the other parent. The threatened spouse may refuse to accept the expressed feelings of the child, claiming that the child has been brainwashed by the other parent, or was too uncomfortable to state his or her real feelings, or didn't want to hurt the parent's feelings. The spouse might even blame the mediator for providing such an artificial setting as an office for the child to talk about difficult feelings.

All of these strategies are difficult for the mediator to counter, since the spouse tends to invalidate any perspective offered by the mediator unless it supports that spouse's own perspective. Sometimes the support of a counselor, a sensitive attorney, or even a trusted pastor can help the spouse accept the child's real needs and desires.

Financial Survival Strategies

Along with a divorce come radical changes in life-style due to financial stress. Both spouses experience the economic crunch, but in different ways. Not uncommonly, the wife will need to rely on child support payments, since the spousal support alone may be inadequate for her to live on comfortably and both payments together allow her to manage a meager living. The wife may become acutely aware that she needs the children to live with her if she is to survive financially.

The husband also experiences financial difficulties in having to pay out a significant amount of money in child support and spousal support. Oftentimes, he feels cheated because he is forced to make regular payments to his ex-wife, toward whom he may have very bitter feelings, and for his children, whom he may see only infrequently. Hence, he is often motivated to develop more financially advantageous arrangements for himself.

While financial survival strategies may be used by a spouse for self-serving ends, they are also used when there is a legitimate need to establish or modify spousal support or child support payments. This is especially true for mothers, who usually receive the bare minimum of financial support following a divorce and whose earning power is considerably less than that of their ex-spouses because of underdeveloped job skills. When such financial needs are not dealt with elsewhere, they sometimes enter into the custody negotiations.

Wanting Primary Physical Custody. Although the parent following a financial survival strategy usually seeks sole physical custody, legal custody is not usually an issue. A wife, for example, may be quite willing to have joint legal custody as long as the children primarily reside at her house. Only when challenged by the husband or the mediator does the wife reveal the real reason for her position: that she will not be able to survive financially without the child support payments.

The husband's parallel strategy of requesting physical custody is rooted in his belief that it would be less costly to him to be the primary caregiver than to make the payments to his ex-wife. For him also, the issue of legal custody is irrelevant as long as his child support costs are minimized by retaining physical custody.

Because of the negative impression conveyed by a parent who makes postdivorce parenting arrangements primarily on the basis of financial concerns, neither parent is straightforward about his or her motives. Instead, their discussion centers on which parent can offer better caregiving to the children and on other appropriate issues. Sooner or later, however, a connection between money and time with the children is usually established. Such a connection should cue the mediator to the hidden agenda.

Wanting Shared Physical Custody. This strategy is typically employed only by the husband. Using the excuse that the children need to spend time at both houses, the father attempts to cut in half his child support payments, since the wife would have the children only about half the time. This strategy is again rooted in the belief that being the primary caregiver for even half the time is less costly than making the equivalent child support payments to the ex-spouse. Again, the cue to the mediator is the frequent mention of money issues while discussing optimal living arrangements for the children.

Wanting the Children Most of the Summer. The wife who is financially dependent on child support payments may argue for the children being with her through the summer, except for two weeks, or at the very most one month, with the father. She may claim that the children have all kinds of summer activities planned and really want to be with her for the summer. Her hidden agenda is a fear of reduced child support payments if the children were to spend the summer with their father.

Conversely, the husband may argue for having the children with him for the whole summer because they don't see enough of him during the school year. Father's hidden agenda is the hope that he will not be required to make child support payments during that period.

Both these strategies are weakened by the fact that even if the children do spend the entire summer with their father, he will still be required, by most judges, to pay a significant proportion of the regular support payments. Courts do recognize that the mother's bills keep coming in even during the summer.

Because these strategies can color the negotiations over the parenting agreement, the mediator must remain aware of financial motives behind the spouses' positions. If it appears that the couple are able to reach an agreement that is constructive for the children in spite of the fact that their primary motives are financial, the mediator need not intervene. If, however, financial concerns prevent the couple from even considering the needs of their children, then these issues should be dealt with separately by a consulting attorney, by the spouses' respective attorneys, or by the mediator, if appropriate. After the financial issues are clarified and perhaps negotiated to the point where the parents are able to consider parenting arrangements on the basis of their children's time-sharing needs first, then time-sharing negotiations can resume. As previously noted, financial considerations can and should be arranged to accommodate such parenting decisions, not vice versa.

Power Assertion Strategies

While most spousal strategies have some inherent element of a power struggle, there are a number of strategies in which an assertion of power is the primary goal. These strategies proceed from any of several motives. A spouse who felt dominated by the other spouse throughout the marriage may view the custody mediation as the first opportunity to assert his or her own power in a manner that is equal to or greater than that of the other spouse. This view may be encouraged by the spouse's attorney. With the confidence inspired by the attorney, the spouse may feel strong enough to prove to the other spouse that he or she will no longer be pushed around. Conversely, if one spouse has been the dominant partner throughout the marriage, he or she may try to preserve that status following the divorce by staking out an aggressive claim regarding the custody issues.

Wanting to Win Sole Custody. There are occasions when one or both spouses retain an adversarial stance throughout mediation and consider some or all of the issues in terms of winning and losing. They each arm themselves with aggressive, high-powered attorneys, and the content of what they win is less relevant than the win itself. Not infrequently, a spouse will push for sole custody until he or she wins over the other spouse, and then will turn around and allow the other spouse to retain custody of the children. The trigger to such behavior may be the initial divorce, a remarriage by either spouse, a move by one spouse out of the state, or any number of more minor incidents. In each case, the urge to dominate the other spouse is strong.

Occasionally, these spouses are able to work out every aspect of the parenting agreement except the designation of legal custody. If they each appear too concerned with winning such a symbolic victory, it is advisable for the mediator to refer this one issue back to their attorneys. Sometimes, unfortunately, the craving to win will be satisfied only by a judge's decree, in which case they must go to court for a decision.

The "50–50 Percent Split." In another kind of strategy, one spouse (typically the husband) will insist on joint custody in an absolutely literal interpretation of the term. Although the mediator may explain that joint custody really means 50 percent legal responsibility, not 50 percent ownership, and that the parents can design a time-sharing arrangement so that each of them is with the children for significant amounts of time, this spouse continues to argue for an exact 50–50 percent split in time-sharing even though it will be inconvenient for the children, for the wife, and even for him.

A father using this strategy may argue that the children need him as much as they need their mother. Even after it is revealed that because of his work schedule he will be able to be with the children only infrequently, and that they will be staying with baby-sitters much of the time while at his house, he does not budge from his position. In effect, his intention is to assert to his ex-wife his equality of power in parenting the children, even if he, the children, and the ex-wife all suffer as a result.

If the husband cannot be persuaded to stop thinking in terms of percentages, and if the wife will agree to an even split for the time being, then a short-term agreement can be developed that specifies a reevaluation in three months to a year. The mediator's goal would be simply to get past this particular power struggle and hope that over time the husband will relax his strategy. Moreover, other circumstances that may well change can allow for a more flexible arrangement in future months. Sometimes the initial arrangement eventually works itself into a satisfactory permanent arrangement, and sometimes, unfortunately, the children have to suffer some distress before the father will reconsider.

The "51-49 Percent Split." A couple may be fairly open and flexible in negotiations about all aspects of sharing their children. They may even agree to joint legal custody and to the idea of equitable sharing of time with their children. However, as the details of the number of days that the children will spend at each parent's house are discussed, one spouse begins to resist and deadlocks the negotiations.

In one such case, the couple worked out a compromise to within three fourths of one day's difference in their respective times with the children each week. However, the wife subtly kept resisting working out the final details as to specific days. Because there seemed to be no apparent motive for such resistance, the mediator probed her reasoning. She then revealed her motive, relating a conversation she had had with her attorney. In their discussion of strategies for future custody battles, her attorney had advised her to keep more than 50 percent of the time spent with her children so that if she ever moved out of state, she would stand a greater chance of retaining physical custody, since the children would have become more attached to her.

Clearly this advice was incompatible with mediation efforts. And, in fact, this wife was perfectly willing to share her children equally with her ex-husband, and she had no intention of moving from the area. Yet she was in an intense conflict between her own desires and her attorney's advice to keep the edge of power for future court contests. The resolution of this issue entailed inviting both attorneys to the next mediation session, where the wife's attorney was obliged to give explicit permission and encouragement to compromise.

Use of Cliches for Justification. Cliches give an impression of wisdom and sanctimony and make the person uttering them appear confident and decisive. The only problem is that there are many cliches that contradict each other, and a spouse can simply pick the ones that support his or her desires and ignore the ones that contradict them. Furthermore, cliches are not open to rational discussion, but only to argumentative debate.

Some of the more typical cliches used by spouses in mediation are: Young children need to be with their mother; young children just need any loving parent; girls need their mother; boys need their father; children need one primary parent; children need both their parents; children need one place to call their home; children are adaptable; children need one consistent life-style and cannot handle bouncing back and forth between two homes; children are resilient; quality of time shared is more important than quantity; children need extended periods of time with a parent to develop a really close relationship.

When cliches are being used as justifications, the mediator should point out the overgeneralized nature of their truths and stress the importance of considering each child as a unique person with unique needs. Ideally, such cliches should be preempted by the mediator's opening monologue in the first mediation session (see Chapter Three).

Changing the Child's Last Name. On occasion, a mother who feels particularly bitter toward her ex-husband will assert her power in a subtle but powerfully symbolic fashion by changing the child's last name. Usually the change is from the father's last name to her own maiden name, or it may be to the name of her new husband. With this action she attempts to stake out an exclusive claim on the child and at the same time negate the father's claim on the child; she may also be trying to protect herself against the negative emotions associated with the sound of his name. Typically, this occurs in cases in which the mother, at least temporarily, has sole legal and primary physical custody of the child and is in mediation at the father's initiation to increase his time with the child. During mediation, the mother may compromise on many aspects of the parenting agreement, apparently despite the deep bitterness that she feels. Then, in between mediation sessions, the father learns indirectly from the child's school or some other source, or directly from the child, that the child is being called by the mother's or her new husband's last name. Needless to say, the father comes into the next mediation session incensed and resistant to any agreements. He may then force an impasse by insisting that the child retain his last name. In such a case, the mother's unexpected cooperation is due to the fact that she has already secretly and symbolically asserted her power by depriving the child of the father's name. Had the father not discovered the name change during the course of mediation, a workable parenting agreement might well have been reached. However, when the father eventually discovers this fact, the agreement will no doubt break down and require further mediation.

If the conflict over the name change does not escalate beyond the possibility of negotiation, the mediator may suggest a more contemporary resolution—a hyphenated last name, combining those of both parents. If this is not an acceptable compromise, the issue can be referred back to the attorneys for negotiations, or to the court for a judge's decision.

Secret Phone Calls. A spouse will occasionally attempt to gain some power by phoning the mediator on the sly. If the call is made before the first mediation session, it may be to reveal incriminating information about the other spouse's habits and treatment of the children. If the call is made between sessions, it may be to denigrate what the other spouse said and to reveal what was omitted in the previous session.

The goal of such phone calls is to gain relative esteem in the eyes of the mediator and consequently to gain power by biasing the mediator in the spouse's favor. Such strategies will not be used if the mediator consistently expresses his or her disinterest in hearing accusations about either spouse and declares that there will be no secrets withheld from either of them.

"Holier than Thou" Impression. Another way of attempting to bias the mediator in favor of one of the spouses is by the strategic use of "impression management" (Goffman, 1959). To convey an impression of being self-assured, in good self-control, rational, and reasonable, a spouse dresses neatly or even formally for the sessions and consistently keeps his or her cool during emotionally laden discussions. One goal of this strategy is to provoke the other spouse to lose control and appear incompetent, overly emotional, irrational, or even crazy. Such behavior is then used as evidence of unfitness to care for the children.

Thus provoked, an ex-wife, for example, may decide to break the rule against talking of the past and tell how the ex-husband's previous life included drugs, wife-battering, sexual perversions, or a criminal record, right up until a few weeks or months earlier, when, for example, he underwent a religious conversion. The wife then berates him for his holier-than-thou attitude, asserting that he has not really changed a bit. The mediator should ignore all such accusations, refrain from judging the validity of either spouse's claims, and refocus the couple on the task at hand.

Retaliation Strategies

Whereas strategies of power assertion are aimed at proving oneself as strong as or stronger than the other spouse, retaliation strategies appear to have as the sole intent the desire to hurt the other spouse. They are by far the most unpleasant of the strategies the mediator has to deal with.

Sole Custody as Revenge. In a typical case, a previously uninvolved father vigorously seeks sole custody upon being divorced by his wife. Even though he admits to not being very close to the children and to not having much time to spend with them, he insists on sole custody nonetheless. In probing further, it becomes clear that he is seething with anger at his wife for leaving him, and although he is fully aware that his wife would feel deeply hurt by being separated from the children, he feels that she deserves it. Then he uses some cliche or rationalization to show that the children would be better off with him.

It is helpful for the mediator to facilitate a discussion of the husband's hurt and resentment in such a way as to stimulate a controlled and face-saving venting of feelings. Sometimes this helps stabilize the husband enough so that he can get on with reasonable negotiations. However, if he appears too overwhelmed by his feelings and seems unable to negotiate in a reasonable manner, then a referral for counseling can be helpful. It may also be helpful for the mediator to alert him tactfully to the likely outcome of a court decision if he wants to push the issue that far. Since such a decision is unlikely to favor him, the father may be persuaded to reconsider his position by the next mediation session.

Point-Counterpoint. A classic strategy is a retaliation move provoked, for example, by a wife's taking her ex-husband to court to request an increase in child support payments. Feeling threatened, insulted and angry, the husband files a counterpetition for sole custody of the children. As the story unfolds in mediation, he explains that his wife just pushed him one step too far. He proceeds to elaborate on his plans for having the children live with him.

Once the mediator probes the husband's motives, his anger usually reveals his retaliation motive. Some sensitive clarification of the situation by the mediator can often persuade the wife to offer a more compromising way to satisfy her need for more money, and the husband to back off from his rigid position. Often he then acknowledges that he is not set up to have the children live full-time with him anyway. A compromise is soon reached and the strategy ended.

Joint Custody as Revenge. Occasionally, an embittered spouse (usually a husband) will push for joint legal and joint physical custody while at the same time manifesting no real intention of being actively involved with the children. As he discusses his plans for regular and frequent contact *with his ex-wife,* she appears horrified—continuing contact with her ex-husband is the last thing she wants. It may be that she left him for another man, and consequently his primary intent is to punish her—perhaps for years to come. Usually, at some point, the wife expresses real distress and refuses to go on with mediation if she will have to deal with her ex-husband so regularly. If the mediator then deals sensitively with the revenge motive and suggests a method of sharing the children with minimal spousal contact, the husband will probably back off. Even though he wants to taunt his ex-wife, he does not really want much contact with her either, for it only regenerates his own feelings of hurt and anger.

"Bait and Switch." Sometimes, at the outset of mediation, a husband will offer a cooperative sharing of custody and time with the children. The wife is pleasantly surprised, since the husband had previously been quite uncooperative. However, in the second session, as her hopes are up to finalize the cooperative plan, he suddenly switches gears and decides that he

wants sole custody and will go to court if necessary. His ex-wife is puzzled and upset by this sudden move, especially as he refuses to give her further information about his sudden change of heart.

On probing, the mediator usually is able to reveal that in the interim between sessions the husband started to feel resentful of the idea that he should even consider sharing anything with the woman who left him. Moreover, he is not going to give her the satisfaction of having it easy! With help from the mediator in discriminating between spousal issues and child-related issues, the husband will usually reverse his position once again and work out a reasonable compromise.

Frustrating Visitations. The strategy of frustrating the spouse's visitations is used mostly by wives who already have sole custody of the children. It often arises in situations in which a husband who had not been involved with the children for some time since the divorce files a petition to clarify his visitation rights. The wife resists such visitations in every way that she can and resists efforts in mediation to work out a plan to accommodate the children's schedules to the visitation plan proposed by the husband. Using excuses from "ballet practice," to "gymnastics," to "playing with friends," to "birthday parties," to "camp," to "doctor appointments," she frustrates all efforts.

In such situations, the mediator often finds that the wife desires to punish the husband for leaving her to raise the children all by herself. As one woman put it: "I don't want to share the kids with him—he left me and I always just wanted to be a mother. I'm working full-time now only because I *have* to—I'd rather be a full-time mother. He doesn't deserve to see the kids." While these feelings may be intense, the mediator usually is able to help resolve them by pointing out that the children are the ones being punished, and that she needs to consider the possibility that the husband may now be ready to help her by participating in the children's lives.

Another common motive for frustrating visitations is to punish the other spouse for not keeping current with child support payments (see Chapter Five). The wife may feel that if the ex-husband is unwilling to fulfill his responsibilities for financial support of the children, then he does not deserve to see them. If such a motive is revealed, the mediator should alert the wife to the illegal nature of her action and also inform her that it is not in the children's best interests, psychologically. Moreover, visitation is not only a right of the parent; it is also a right of the child. The mediator should then help the wife to deal with time-sharing and support as separate issues. Often such a discussion gives the husband an opportunity to clarify his reasons for being in arrears on support payments, and the spouses can develop a plan for solving the two problems independently of each other.

"Pushing to Lose" Strategies

Following a divorce, spouses sometimes feel pressure from their extended families, their friends, their neighbors, and even society at large, to fight for custody of the children. Not uncommonly though, upon divorce, an individual finally feels free to live as a single person, unencumbered by spouse or children. If he or she succumbs to the social pressure to pursue custody, it is often with much ambivalence. Such ambivalence frequently leads the spouse to use strategies that are almost certain to result in a failure to gain custody of the children.

Typically, these strategies involve an initial declaration to the judge, the ex-spouse, and the mediator of an intent to obtain sole legal and physical custody of the children. However, from the time of the initial separation all the way through the mediation process, this spouse fails to establish suitable housing for himself and the children, fails to find or keep a job with which to provide for the children, and fails to spend any significant time with the children. In spite of having been informed of the importance of these factors, he makes no changes in lifestyle while still declaring his intention of gaining sole custody. When the other spouse refuses to agree with such an obviously unsuitable proposal, he responds with one of two strategies: a martyrdom strategy or a face-saving strategy.

Martyrdom Strategy. The essence of the first strategy is to present oneself as a wronged victim. Upon receiving the expected refusal by his ex-wife, the husband expounds on how difficult his life has been, how his own parents never gave him enough love or support, and how he always gets fired from his jobs for insignificant and unexplained reasons. If he plays out this strategy to the end, he may appeal to his ex-wife not to take away the "only things that matter to me—my children." Upon her refusal even to consider joint custody, he accepts her decision with a show of defeat and passively signs the agreement giving his ex-wife sole legal custody and leaving the general visitation plan open and conditional upon his finding a job and suitable housing.

Face-Saving Strategy. The husband who employs this strategy is much more aggressive in his pursuit of sole custody. Throughout the mediation process he pushes his position to the maximum, attempting to prove to his ex-wife and to the mediator his sincerity in wanting to be the sole custodial parent. However, the living situation for this husband usually is not unlike that of the husband employing the martyrdom strategy. Although he keeps reiterating his plans to get a house and job, they never reach fruition.

Typically, this husband forces the dispute out of mediation and into the courtroom. Once in court, he presents his case aggressively, even though the odds are unmistakably against him. And he loses—but feeling that at least he gave it his best shot.

With both strategies, the husband more or less unconsciously sets up the situation so that his chances of losing are great. The real intent of his display is to prove that he at least tried to fulfill his role as a concerned father. His failure was not unintentional; rather, it served his need for freedom in a manner that allowed him a sense of self-respect and a temporary relief from guilt.

Strategies for Appeasing a New Spouse

While most strategies of spouses are motivated by the dynamics of the divorcing couple, there are some that are motivated by a new fiancee or spouse.

When a woman marries a recently divorced man who is still emotionally enmeshed with his previous wife over custody and visitation issues, she often suffers from a feeling of insecurity about her new husband's loyalty to her. A husband's emotional investment in his previous wife, even if it is primarily negative, is quite threatening to the new wife. Moreover, if the children, in playing out their own reuniting strategies, create conflict between their father and stepmother, she is likely to feel an even greater threat to the solidity of the new marriage. As a way of coping with these threats, the new wife may put subtle or overt pressure on her husband to resolve her insecurity either by pursuing sole custody or by pulling away.

Sole Custody for the New Spouse. The husband who attempts to claim sole custody of the children typically presents a very straightforward argument on his own behalf, such as being able to offer more resources for the children, a larger home, better schools, and someone who can be home for the children all day (that is, the stepmother). Occasionally, he may offer some mildly negative facts about his ex-wife, but usually he does not push his position beyond a simple presentation of facts.

When confronted by the outrage of his ex-wife over the threat of having her children taken from her, he usually remains rational and objective. The mediator's probe of his motives reveals a lack of any personal emotional commitment to the children. He is not really able to justify taking the children from their mother's primary emotional care. At this point, the mediator is often able to work out a compromise that includes more time for the children to be with their father.

Because it would be far too threatening for the husband to reveal his real motive—appeasing his new wife—he never offers a solid justification for pursuing sole custody. Over the course of the year following the signing of the mediation agreement, the husband typically reduces the frequency of his contacts with the children to less than it was before mediation. While this may be due to other factors as well, the primary reason usually appears to be his original lack of real commitment to involvement with the children.

With this strategy, the husband attempts to help his new wife satisfy her territorial needs and prove herself a better mother than the ex-wife. However, his efforts at gaining possession of the children typically are not fruitful. Unfortunately, all too often, the children are eventually disappointed by a dwindling relationship with their father.

Pulling Away. Sometimes, when ex-spouses have been grappling over custody and visitation for some time, the husband's new wife puts pressure on him to end the struggle by either getting sole custody or moving away. After the husband makes his bid in mediation for sole custody and his ex-wife refuses, he informs her that he will be moving away from the area (often out of state) very soon. He then settles for some minimal contact with the children, perhaps on a holiday or two and during a small portion of the summer.

The fact that he did not more actively pursue his original position is the key to recognizing this strategy. In probing, the mediator usually finds out that the husband feels caught between the ongoing struggle with his ex-wife and his new wife's intolerance for it. He then explains that he has been forced to make a choice. Once again, unfortunately, the children wind up with the loss of frequent contact with their father.

There usually is little that the mediator can do in these situations, since the only available solutions seem to be for the father either to lose his new wife and remain in the area to continue struggling with his ex-wife, or to keep his new wife, move, and lose significant contact with his children. It is a very difficult dilemma indeed for the father and for the mediator.

Although it is essential for the mediator to know the individual strategies of spouses as described in this chapter, the real challenge lies in working effectively with the complex matrix of *multiple strategies* that spouses actually present in mediation. Often there is a complementarity of strategies such that one spouse's strategy will elicit a complementary strategy on the part of the other spouse. For example, a husband's reuniting strategy is often complemented by a wife's emotionally disengaging strategy. A wife's strategy for emotional survival may be complemented by a husband's power assertion strategy. For the mediator, the challenge resides in the complexity of the multiple strategies used. In the next two chapters we turn to ways for meeting this challenge.

8

Strategies for Eliciting Cooperation Between Parents

This chapter will delineate the strategies for inducing cooperation between the spouses, and the next chapter will discuss strategies for handling conflict. Although many of the strategies can be used at numerous points in the mediation process, they generally are used sequentially, in the order presented here.

In the opening phase of negotiations, the mediator's central goal is to develop cooperation between the spouses. Because it is virtually impossible to begin negotiations that lead to resolution while overt conflict rages, the first step is to establish a cease-fire. The mediator can achieve this using strategies that are functionally incompatible with open conflict. It should be noted, though, that these strategies will not permanently prevent overt conflict, for such conflict will almost inevitably rear its head at some later point in the mediation process. However, a cooperative ambience at the beginning of mediation serves several functions: It optimizes the spouses' readiness to attend and listen to the mediator's opening presentation; it gives the spouses a period of relative calm in which to reflect on their struggle and defuse some of the angry feelings generated by the presence of the other spouse; and it gives the mediator a chance to observe the degree of each spouse's impulse control and the way the spouses relate to each other; and finally, it gives the mediator an opportunity to prove his or her positive intent by producing a beginning atmosphere of hope, cooperation, and interpersonal respect, which the mediator can anchor and refer to as needed in later, more conflict-laden phases of mediation.

By far the most important aspect of the mediator's interventions in eliciting cooperative efforts is maintaining control over every phase of the process. The mediation process needs to be carefully designed to yield just the right emotional and attitudinal climate, topic choice, and sequence and timing of topics. And the mediator needs to maintain a strategic flexibility, so as to sensitively and responsively direct the flow of events to the final resolution—the mediated agreement. Inefficiencies and blockages in the process occur if the mediator does not strictly adhere to the structure.

Some level of trust must be established between the spouses before any cooperative agreements can be developed. However, couples almost always begin mediation with little or no workable level of trust; moreover, from beginning to end of mediation they may be unable to believe that trust is possible. Even the most trusting couples experience intense mistrust during mediation. Trust requires letting go of the negative experiences of the past; however, the past is all there is on which to base predictions for the future. Because these couples have no maps for the future, their anxiety level tends to be very high. To cope with this anxiety, they seek some security by hanging on to the past.

Dealing with mistrust is a real challenge for the mediator because it is not something that can be argued against logically, and if challenged too forcefully, it will simply increase in intensity. One must deal with it indirectly. Acceptance of the mistrust by the mediator is an important start. The mediator should always assume that there is and will continue to be mistrust until the spouses have rebuilt trust by following through on their agreements. Paradoxically, by accepting the presence of mistrust within the sessions, the mediator facilitates trust building.

It is helpful for the mediator to initiate the growth of trust by offering a positive perspective. Often, the only trust that the spouses have in each other is the trust that they both love the children very much. Throughout the mediation process, the mediator can refer back to this basic area of agreement whenever the spouses begin to argue about issues based on their mistrust of each other. He or she may say, for example, "It would be a very loving gesture for you both to offer your children the possibility that the future might be better than the past. In spite of how you feel now and in spite of the past, just consider the possibility that people can change, and that by avoiding prejudging and by keeping as flexible and open-minded as you can allow yourselves to be, you can help your children to develop, emotionally, in healthier ways. With your help, they won't have to remain stuck at the point at which you two are now." If the spouses cannot even agree on their shared love for their children, then the mediator can request that they just *assume* it to be true for the time being, so that each can eventually give the other an opportunity to show his or her love.

From the very beginning of the process, the mediator should persistently affirm the fact that, in spite of their mistrust about each other as spouses, they can still develop sufficient trust to co-parent effectively. The mediator should search for even the smallest areas of trust regarding parenting, from the beginning of their relationship with their children until the present. He or she can then take whatever evidence is presented and elaborate upon it and refer to it repeatedly throughout the negotiations. The mediator might remind the couple that children typically can trust each parent more easily than the parents can trust each other.

The mediator should be aware that this alone will do little; the only way that trust can develop is if the spouses act in trusting ways with each other. The mediator can seed the beginnings of trust by establishing several minor agreements that *will* be kept. If mistrust is particularly high in the first session, then a structured task to which they both agree can be assigned. The task should be completed before the next session and should be similar to one they had already been able to carry out, although not without some conflict. However, the mediator's task should have a slightly different twist, designed to prevent conflict. For example, they could be asked to arrange two days and times of child transfer to take place at a new, agreed-upon place and time. This task can be presented as a challenge for each spouse to prove to the other that he or she can and will follow through as agreed. Usually this task has been successfully accomplished by the second mediation session, serving as the first step in trust building and perhaps also as a first item to include in the final parenting agreement. If the task is not carried out successfully, the details can be discussed, while still fresh in the minds of both spouses, as material for building time-sharing arrangements that *will* work. In the first case, the problem is solved, and in the second, a problem is objectively identified in such a way that solutions are more easily forthcoming.

There are, however, occasions when a mediator is confronted with a facsimile of trust between a couple. For example, one couple came into mediation requesting help in working out a joint custody arrangement that would be best for their young children. Both spouses were extremely pleasant, cooperative, and seemingly receptive to the ideas of the mediator. During the information-gathering phase, the husband said, "We still love each other very much." The wife agreed, adding, "We will probably get back together in the near future." When asked why they were getting a divorce, the husband replied, "Well, we both definitely want a divorce now, so that we can do our own things for a while." He then added, "We both have done really well in sharing the kids." To the mediator, this case looked like a piece of cake. However, their apparent trust and respect was revealed as false as soon as they got down to discussing details of the joint custody plan. At that point, the husband utilized a 50-50 percent power assertion strategy, the wife utilized a 51-49 percent power assertion strategy, and the negotiations broke down into accusations and assertions of mistrust. It was as if the mediator had been walking through a hall of mirrors, cautiously at first, and then, seeming to see the clear path through, had forged ahead to the exit only to be confronted harshly and suddenly by a solid mirror. Such an unexpected event can be quite disorienting and frustrating, and if the mediator pushes on the mirror, it may well shatter and destroy the possibility of mediated settlement.

Had the mediator been more skeptical about the couple's initial display of trust and respect, he might have been able to reveal their underlying agenda before attempting to solidify a final agreement. However, because the display was so unusual and refreshing, he was taken off guard and succumbed to it. In order to avoid such traps, the mediator must be wary of any situation that appears too easy.

Specific Strategies

The process of eliciting cooperation from the couple requires the mediator to have a set of versatile and effective strategies at his or her disposal.

Pre-empting. Certainly the best strategy for dealing with undesirable conflict is to prevent it in the first place. Effective pre-empting of conflict depends heavily on information gleaned by the mediator before negotiations begin. For example, suppose that in the first phone call a husband tells the mediator that he is furious with his ex-wife, and elaborates on all the terrible things that she has done, but then subtly adds that he still loves her and will do anything to get back together with her. He then proceeds to tell of his goal to "keep the children from seeing her, because she is too unsettled." Armed with the knowledge that this husband really wants a reconciliation and that he is prepared to utilize *reuniting* and *retaliation* strategies, the mediator can pre-empt some of these moves in the first mediation session. He or she can emphasize that it is very difficult for spouses to think about their children objectively and to make plans for sharing them if they are not yet emotionally divorced from each other and point out that while it is perfectly natural and common for a spouse who does not want a divorce to punish the other spouse by wanting to withhold the children from him or her, actually doing it will only hurt the children. The mediator can then inquire about the degree of certainty of the divorce decision and explore the feelings and expectations around the divorce decision. It is important that the mediator address these comments to both spouses equally (turning toward and making eye contact with them for equal periods of time) so that the comments do not appear to criticize either spouse singly (of course, both spouses are aware that the comments are more appropriate to one of them—in this case, the husband). In this way the mediator pre-empts the *reuniting* and *retaliation* strategies of the husband in a way that allows face-saving but clarifies the couple's differing expectations regarding the divorce decision.

To take another example, suppose that in the first phone call the wife informs the mediator that she is not going to allow the husband to have any further contact with the children because he is irresponsible, does not discipline the children, and returns them home dirty. She rants about all the years that she had to put up with his antics. On calling the wife's attorney, the mediator then hears that the wife has said that she really feels the husband is a good father, and that even though he makes many mistakes, the children need contact with him and she wants him to be more involved with them. However, she has filed a petition to restrict visitations in order to get him to listen to her. Having determined that the attorney's information is probably valid, the mediator then sets out to pre-empt conflict.

In the first session, the mediator can elaborate on the benefits of mediation as follows: "This format gives each of you an opportunity to clarify what you expect of the other in sharing your children. Sometimes it's hard to make clear to each other the things that get in the way of sharing your children. Sometimes it might even feel easier not to have to deal with each other at all, but you both know that your children need both of you." Then the mediator can ask, "What things do you each need the other person to do to make sharing your children easier for you?"

Here the mediator cuts right through the conflict that would probably arise if he dealt directly with the wife's initiating a petition for restricting visitation. Had he instead asked the wife why she wanted to cut off her ex-husband's visitation rights, she would likely have uttered her list of accusations in such a manner as to justify her action, which would doubtless elicit defensive retaliation from the husband, who would perceive her actions as an insult and a power play. Instead, the mediator simply refuses to deal with the superficial legal threat and proceeds as if it were clearly understood that the husband would continue sharing time with the children. Typically in such cases the couple immediately begin to make constructive requests of each other to facilitate sharing of their children.

Pre-empting, then, is a rather sophisticated tool for circumventing polarized conflict and saving face for both parties simply by going directly to a level where a concordance of opinion is likely to exist.

Giving Information and Hope. Much of what underlies conflict between people is a lack of information about their situations. When people pass through a major life crisis such as a divorce or a custody dispute for the first time, they find that there are few road maps with any guarantees of reliability. As a result, they feel scared, insecure, and vulnerable. It is comforting at such times to be offered an authoritative description of what they are going through and what others in similar situations have gone through, and a perspective on how these crises are most effectively resolved. Just knowing that it is possible to come out of such a crisis relatively intact and rational can bring great comfort—and out of such comfort come reductions in acrimony and defensive maneuvering.

Oftentimes, in a first phone call, a spouse will tell the mediator, "I don't know about mediation. I'm sure that there's no way it could work or that you could help. You don't *know* my ex-wife; she's totally irrational and unpredictable and she won't stick to *any* agreements—you can't even talk to her." In response, the mediator can say, "I know that it may seem impossible for you to imagine your ex-wife being reasonable, but every couple that comes into mediation starts off feeling that way about each other. That's our usual starting point, but we have a pretty good track record. In fact, I've even had some couples physically assault each other, but they still came to agreements about sharing their children." This tactic invariably elicits a comment like "Really? Well, *our* situation isn't *that* bad." The information that people whose mutual animosity is greater than theirs have successfully worked out parenting agreements in mediation provides a gleam of hope as well as a challenge for them to give mediation a try.

The mediator also needs to offer information about the stages that people typically go through from the time of separation until at least several years later, about the normal reactions of children following divorce, and about the new forms that family dynamics take when parents in two different homes share their children, as well as the hopeful message that things typically improve and negative feelings subside over time. Once couples develop a new structure for relating to each other as *ex*-spouses, they typically start to get along better, with less conflict and less anger over sharing their children.

It was recently suggested by one attorney that "child custody mediation is just a disguised form of divorce counseling." Her observation has some truth to it but is clearly overgeneralized. The information that a mediator gives a couple about the nature of divorce is certainly helpful in reducing their anxiety and anger and, consequently, in eliciting more cooperation. However, this is only one aspect of the mediation process and although it is not unlike divorce counseling, the in-depth discussion of these points that takes place in divorce counseling is mostly inappropriate to mediation. Giving information and hope is a useful strategy for anchoring out-of-control feelings, but it should not be used by the mediator as an opening to the process of divorce counseling. Unless both parties request it, an unsolicited imposition of such counseling will probably backfire, as one spouse asserts, "I don't want to dwell on the divorce, I just want to settle the custody problem—so let's get on with it."

Complimenting. When praise is given, most people feel disarmed and even somewhat embarrassed. It is a very rare individual who can feel angry and defensive while being flattered. This makes the use of praise particularly effective in mediation. Because spouses entering mediation frequently have been devalued and humiliated by each other, favorable and even flattering words coming from the mediator tend to disarm them.

Moreover, to have complimentary things said about them in the presence of the other spouse further enhances their self-esteem. Indeed, this may be the first time anything positive has been said about either spouse since well before the separation.

Because of the sensitivity of both spouses to evaluative comments, any praise or flattery needs to be carefully chosen. Avoidance of all areas of contention is essential. Taboo areas may include parenting skills, availability to and emotional involvement with the children, resources available to the children, and personal qualities that may be linked up with areas of contention, such as flexibility, self-control, spontaneity, or honesty. Safe areas generally include the competencies and positive traits of the children ("Your five-year-old is already reading? Gosh, what a bright child!"), physical attractiveness of the children (the mediator can ask to see wallet pictures if the children are not present and then volunteer, for example, "Gee, what beautiful blond hair—looks like she got it from *both* of you"), and the competencies of each spouse in areas unrelated to their relationship, such as work, sports, or hobbies ("What's it like to fly a plane? I understand it takes a great deal of *skill*—how did you *master* the natural fear of heights that most of us earthbound folks have? I've always dreamed of flying my own plane, but I was always too terrified to try it"; "How do you carry all those meals on one arm without dropping them? It must take a lot of skill. I've always admired how many things a waiter/waitress can handle all at once. I think *I* would forget all the things I needed to do. You must have a fine memory"; "You've run several marathons? Gee, you must be in great shape—how long did you have to train to achieve such an admirable goal?").

Particularly helpful are compliments to both spouses for jointly contributing to their children—for example, "I think your children are really lucky to have you two as parents. It's a valuable gift to your children that you decided to remain living in the same area so that they could continue to enjoy their relationships with both of you, uninterrupted."

In offering compliments, the mediator must remain within the bounds of sincerity and moderation. Insincerity can backfire on the mediator, resulting in greater resistance and mistrust and a loss of the mediator's credibility in the eyes of the flattered spouse. Moreover, flattery of one spouse can result in a perception of mediator bias on the part of the other spouse ("You were taken in by my ex-, you were conned and blinded by him, just like so many people who don't know him very well") and in a loss of the neutrality necessary for the mediator to be effective.

For some mediators, complimenting other people with sincerity is a natural behavior. For other mediators, who are not used to offering compliments, this strategy will require some practice. If one has good intentions, then practicing giving compliments will soon yield sincerity. Furthermore, the practice of finding good in other people can only enhance one as a person. Finally, complimenting one's clients functions not least as a corrective for therapists and lawyers, who all too often are judgmental, critical, and cynical.

Reframing. Another powerful strategy is to redefine a particular concept so as to give it a more constructive interpretation. The process by which we label feelings, thoughts, attitudes, behaviors, and events, has in recent years been recognized by cognitive psychologists to have a great influence on the way we perceive reality. In essence, it appears that to a large extent we construct our own reality on the basis of the frames, or points of view, that we impose on the world of our experiences (Watzlawick, 1976, 1978; Watzlawick, Weakland, and Fisch, 1974). Moreover, these frames guide our behavior and persist even when they result in self-defeating or even destructive behavior patterns. When such perspectives are altered, we have the opportunity to get unstuck from old behavior patterns and to try new behaviors.

Reframing is especially useful in mediation for changing adversarial perspectives into cooperative ones, particularly when the couple are talking about their child-sharing plans. For example, when one spouse says, "I want to keep custody of my children," the mediator can reframe it as "You would like the children to share a significant amount of time with you." When one spouse says to the other, "You can visit the children every other weekend," the mediator can reframe it as "The children will be able to share time with their father for two weekends every month." Finally, if a spouse says, "I don't care if we live three blocks away from each other, I want custody of the children and you can see them once a week," the mediator can reframe it as "So it would be hard for you to give your children the opportunity to share lots of time with both of you." Even though these word and syntax changes are subtle, the differences in connotation are profound and can set the stage for more cooperative negotiations. The rephrasing effectively shifts the perspective from that of the parent to that of the children, which helps keep the children's needs foremost in the awareness of the parents. Moreover, after the mediator reframes their language a few times, it is not uncommon for the spouses to begin imitating the mediator's language.

Anecdote Telling. Telling stories is a powerful way of conveying information. Because the story typically involves someone else, and the situation happened some time ago, and the content may be only tangentially related to the couple's present situation, it is relatively easy for angry and suspicious spouses to accept the message.

For example, to a very mistrustful couple the mediator might say, "I saw a couple, way back about a year ago, who were so suspicious of each other that they had developed many tactics for spying on each other. The husband secretly taped all his wife's phone conversations with her mother, and the wife drove to his place of work every day to make sure he wasn't running around with other women. When they got divorced, they each called me to warn me of the lies that the other would doubtless tell me in mediation. Well, when they got here, they were still paranoid about each other's every word and move. They fought over every single issue until suddenly one of them stopped and began to laugh. When the other asked what the laughing was about, that spouse was told, 'I'm laughing because I realize how absurd this all is. We both love our children and hate each other. So we should just work it out for them—let's not make them miserable too.' And you know, after that they worked out a parenting agreement that's still working very well a year later . . . and they still hate each other."

When stories are told in a more allegorical fashion, the message speaks directly to their unconscious minds (Haley, 1973; Zeig, 1980). This way, both the threat of the message and the resistance to it are practically nonexistent. An example of this form of anecdote was told by a mediator to a couple who were extremely hostile to each other. The mediator said, "My daughter came crying to my wife and me last night. It seems that she had a nightmare about some rabbits, and she was very upset by it. She dreamed of three rabbits who lived in a small bush by a meadow. Whenever the baby rabbit started to go out and play, the mother rabbit would pull it back into the bushes by its rear legs. The father rabbit, though, didn't like the way the mother rabbit made the baby stay around the nest, so he would pull on the baby rabbit's ears to get it away from the mother's grip. The baby rabbit would squeal and cry and the mother and father rabbit would drop the baby rabbit and start biting each other. The next day the same thing happened—and then it began to happen more and more frequently. After some time, the baby rabbit's ears were very long from being pulled at, and its rear legs were very long from being pulled at too. And the baby rabbit's fur was pulled out in patches and its body was all bloody and scarred. The baby rabbit cried and cried, because now that its ears were so long, it was supersensitive to noise and it could not help but hear every sound of every argument of its mother and father. And now that its legs were so long, it could only move awkwardly, and now that its fur was so bloody and blotchy, it looked very ugly. The baby rabbit felt awkward, and ugly, and worthless, and unloved, and the saddest thing of all was that its mother and father did not even notice because they were too busy biting each other. The baby rabbit cried and cried."

After telling such an anecdote, the mediator can simply move on to another subject, letting the metaphoric impact of the story sink quietly into the unconscious minds of the spouses.

Resisting a "Time Squeeze." As has been discussed earlier, there seems to be an optimal time frame for each couple within which the mediation process is most successful. When this time frame is compromised, mediation efforts can be sabotaged.

There are two situations in which a mediator may have to resist pressure to complete mediation too rapidly. One arises, usually in the first mediation session, when one spouse demands that the other decide about co-parenting arrangements on the spot. The spouse may add, "I want your decision *right now,* so I can sell the house (get a loan, take my new job, move out, plan to rent a house)." In response to this time squeeze, the other spouse freezes up. The mediator must persuade the demanding spouse to back off and give more time so that a workable decision can be made. Usually this spouse is pushing to get things settled because of the pain suffered in the divorce. If the mediator gives encouragement to slow down, the spouse will usually do so.

The second such situation arises when one spouse's attorney responds to threats made by the other spouse as a challenge to be dealt with aggressively and immediately, rather than gently over time. In one case, for example, a couple had just separated and filed for divorce; both were distraught. The wife, who was in shock after her husband suddenly left her for another woman, threatened that the husband would never see their children again. Challenged by the wife's threats, the husband's attorney tried to gain leverage to establish the husband's visitation rights by attempting to arrange for an *immediate* mediation session. When the mediator talked on the phone to the spouses, it was clear that neither of them was ready to mediate. The wife had sought counseling on her own to help put herself back together, and the husband wanted to wait to start mediation because he was afraid his wife's state would prevent rational agreements. When the mediator informed the attorney that mediation would not begin for a month, the attorney threatened to file a petition ordering immediate visitation. Even after the mediator explained the marital dynamics, the attorney had difficulty seeing beyond the fact that his client's legal rights were being threatened. After the month had passed mediation was, in fact, not even necessary, as the wife voluntarily arranged a workable visitation plan directly with the husband. She told the mediator that it just took her some time to realize that she did not want her anger at her husband getting in the way of the children's positive relationship with their father.

Clearly, if the mediator had succumbed to the attorney's time squeeze, the marital conflict would have been further aggravated, perhaps forcing the spouses into a standoff. Many times attorneys operate out of a sincere interest in asserting the legal rights of their clients. However, on occasion an attorney may take a wife's threat as a personal challenge to prove her weak or call her bluff. Either way, the attorney can benefit by learning to appreciate the psychological aspects of such matters. Respecting the natural course of emotional changes after a separation can facilitate cooperative settlements, while ignoring it and working with legal sledgehammers will only create problems that did not exist before.

9

Skills and Techniques for Managing Conflict

In spite of the mediator's best efforts at preventing conflict and setting an atmosphere of cooperation, there are almost always some points in the mediation process where overt conflict erupts. In order for mediation to proceed, the mediator must have a set of tools for dealing with such disruptions. In general, from the first phone call on, the mediator must establish his or her authority. This comes across in the firmness of the mediator's words and tone of voice, in the confidence of his or her bearing, and in the ground rules as to what the spouses can and cannot say or do in the mediation sessions. When the mediator projects confidence and authority, the spouses will show respect. When the mediator projects ambivalence and weakness, the spouses will make more than the usual number of attempts at power assertion and intimidation. In many ways, the mediator must act as a parent figure to the parents, since their struggles are often not unlike those of siblings squabbling over joint possessions.

General Aspects of Conflict-Management Strategies

Questions Asked. Unlike traditional psychotherapy, in which the process is guided largely by the client, the mediation process depends on the structure set out by the mediator. The mediator delineates this structure both by making statements and by asking questions. The questions themselves have at least two primary functions: seeking information and giving it. That is, asking a question lets the responder know what information is of importance to the asker.

Rather than asking questions that lead nowhere constructive for the mediation task, such as "Why do you feel so angry when he returns the children a half-hour late?" or "What do you think makes him drink so much and act so violently when he picks up the children?," the mediator can ask more appropriate questions, such as "What specific time would you like the children returned from being with their father, and what needs to happen for that time to work out for each of you?" or "What specifically do each of you need to do in order for the transfer of the children to go smoothly and uneventfully for both of you?" These questions imply the following: (1) Elaboration of your feelings during conflicts with each other is irrelevant and counterproductive; (2) I am interested in your ideas for solutions to these problems.

Scheduling of Sessions. Another way in which the process of mediation is a function of the structure is the mediator's use of scheduling to regulate conflict and create an opening for solutions to develop naturally. A large part of the mediator's task is to apply a brake (or break) to the couple's conflict so that intervening life events can influence the mediation process.

This awareness that daily life events tend to change people's attitudes, feelings, and behaviors far more frequently and fully than therapy can is the basis of the contemporary practice of brief strategic therapy (Haley, 1973, 1976; Watzlawick, Weakland, and Fisch, 1974; Zeig, 1980; Saposnek, 1980, in press; Fisch, Weakland, and Segal, 1982). In this therapy approach, clients are given behavioral tasks intended to hasten the natural resolution of their problems. The client is sent out with a slightly new perspective that is reinforced by the events that occur between sessions, typically resulting in changed behaviors by the next session. The goal of this approach is to change unproductive behavior patterns. By strategically utilizing interim periods of time—from a week to a month (Selvini Palazzolli, Boscolo, Cecchin, and Prata, 1978) between sessions—the goal is more easily attainable.

Behavior Change First. From the mediator's perspective, the emotional conflicts of a couple, whether married or divorced, are dilemmas, that is, inherently unsolvable problems. If the mediator views them as solvable, he or she is courting frustration. Resolutions to the emotional problems presented in mediation may be forthcoming *after* an agreement is reached, but not before. It is only when couples begin to behave in trustworthy and trusting ways that they can begin to develop insight about themselves and each other.

Maintaining Neutrality. A mediator must always maintain neutrality with respect to both spouses. This is often difficult to achieve, because being neutral with respect to each spouse is more a function of their respective *perceptions* of the mediator's neutrality than of any objective reality. A spouse may feel that if the mediator is of the same (or opposite) sex, then he or she is not neutral. Another spouse may feel that if the mediator ever previously met or talked to one of the spouses, then he or she is not neutral. Still another spouse may fully accept the mediator as neutral by her mere verbal declaration of neutrality, even if she is known to be an acquaintance of the other spouse. Each spouse's perception of the mediator's neutrality must be assessed before proceeding, for if one spouse perceives partiality and this is not revealed until late in mediation, a gradual buildup of resistance may already have jeopardized the mediation process.

Sometimes what may seem to the mediator a neutral perspective appears to one spouse as clear evidence of partiality toward the other spouse. As noted in Chapter Four, a mediator who advocates joint custody when only one spouse wants it may appear biased to the spouse who does not desire joint custody. Similarly, a mediator might in good conscience emphasize the necessity of predictability and regularity for the healthy development of young children in a case where one spouse has been accusing the other of unpredictable and irregular behavior. Such advice ordinarily makes much sense; however, within the context of custody or visitation negotiations it creates an impression of partiality. In one such case, a husband had been accusing his ex-wife of changing her life-style too much and not being predictable or structured enough during her time with the children. The mediator then gave a lecture, addressed to *both* spouses, on the importance of predictability for the emotional security of young children. Upon hearing this, the husband overtly agreed, nodding repeatedly and showing overt signs of approval. The wife became very defensive and accused the mediator of siding with the husband against her. She insisted that she was not unpredictable and that the husband's perception was faulty. Each time thereafter when the topic of predictability came up, the wife would attack both the husband and the mediator, bringing the mediation to a standstill. Even though the mediator eventually recognized the pattern and tried to divert the discussion to another topic, it was too late. The wife had already deemed the mediator biased and further mediation efforts were futile.

In order to help maintain a position of neutrality, the mediator must early on learn an important lesson; that is, to forgo the search for truth and adopt a relativistic perspective. By focusing on truth, the mediator will slip into judging the spouses and will soon experience a bias in favor of one spouse and against the other that will sabotage effective mediation efforts.

The Dilemma of Relativity. If we consider how a mediator might deem a particular spouse's behavior reasonable or unreasonable, we find that there are at least three different perspectives on what constitutes reasonable and unreasonable actions: the view of one spouse (for example, the wife) about the other spouse's (the husband's) behavior; the view of the mediator about the husband's behavior; and the view of the mediator about the marital system. The wife may view the husband's actions as unreasonable, while the mediator views them as quite reasonable. Or the wife may view the husband's behavior as reasonable, while the mediator views it as very unreasonable. By the same token, the mediator can view the interactional system between the husband and wife in such a way that each spouse's behavior appears perfectly complementary to that of the other spouse and the concepts of reasonable and unreasonable no longer apply.

It is the first two standards that are used by lawyers and judges in court custody battles, and the third standard that is used by family therapists. The mediator must use both but lean toward the third, so that neutrality is maintained while the interests of the children are always safeguarded. With very few exceptions, there are no angels and no devils in custody/visitation disputes, but only "double conspiracies," in which both parties play their complementary parts in the ongoing conflicts. In this systems perspective, there are no better *sides,* only better *balances.*

Specific Strategies

The specific strategies the mediator uses to deal with conflict fall into three categories: conflict-reducing strategies, conflict-diverting strategies, and impasse-breaking strategies. In the following section, we will discuss the variety of these strategies. The strategies are generally arranged sequentially, from the most mild to the most potent ones. The mediator should utilize them in a similar fashion, always beginning with the mildest strategies that are likely to effect results for a particular couple and using more potent strategies as needed, until one is found that achieves the desired results. Obviously, there are cases in which none of the strategies is helpful for reaching agreements (see Chapter Eleven). In such cases, the couple should be referred back to their attorneys or to court for resolution of their disputes.

Conflict-Reducing Strategies

Reflective Listening. By reflecting back to the spouses the feelings behind their words, the mediator attempts to take the emotional charge out of the conflict. If, for example, a wife begins a tirade about how the husband is completely uncooperative and never listens to or follows through on any request she makes, the mediator can cut through the content and address the feelings directly. He or she can say, "It sounds like when you've got something important to say to him and he does not seem to listen, you feel really angry and frustrated." Then, if the husband says, "But she always tries to talk to me when I'm furious about something," the mediator can say, "It sounds to me like you have a hard time hearing her when you are angry but could probably listen much better when you are calmer."

This strategy will work if many of the conflicts of the spouses are grounded simply in poor communication skills. If these skills are underdeveloped, reflective listening can at least build enough clarity of communication for a parenting agreement to be negotiated. Surprisingly enough, this is all that some couples need to reach workable agreements.

Absorbing. Sometimes when a spouse is expressing anger and frustration, reflective listening does not help and may even act as an irritant. In such cases, the mediator can simply listen and try to absorb that anger. This is much easier to do if only one spouse speaks while the other spouse listens. The mediator can safely allow the venting of feelings by the angrier spouse because steering those feelings away from the other spouse and onto the mediator reduces the need for that spouse to defend himself or herself. And when that spouse maintains a quiet, nondefensive demeanor and appears to be sincerely listening, whether out of guilt or a real willingness to cooperate, then the mediator can often successfully absorb the rage from the angry spouse. This can be followed by rational negotiation.

There is a risk to using this strategy, however. If the other spouse actively challenges the assertions uttered by the angrier spouse, then an escalation of the conflict may well ensue. Or, if the angry spouse is just manifesting a habitual hysterical behavior pattern, then the venting may continue indefinitely. In either case, if the mediator allows the venting to continue, the conflict that is likely to ensue will either sabotage the mediation efforts or necessitate that the mediator change strategies.

Blocking and Soothing. When conflict escalates to the

point where milder strategies are unsuccessful, the mediator can block it by interrupting and taking charge of the discussion, converting the dialogue to a monologue, and slowing the pace. If done skillfully, this technique allows the mediator to maintain sole control by delivering, in an almost trancelike monotone, a monologue about *anything* that will keep the conflict quelled. This gives the couple a chance to cool off, since the more the mediator talks, the less opportunity the spouses will have to talk. In such cases, the mediator should allow the spouses to talk only insofar as their talk is productive.

Taking an Assertive Stance. If the conflict does not respond to more indirect efforts, the mediator can assertively request that the spouses stop their verbal assaults. This may mean raising his voice and saying, "Stop," or it may mean standing up between their chairs and blocking their view of each other, or it may mean engaging in some other unexpected behavior, such as jingling a string of bells (some mediators keep a set of bells in their office for this purpose).

If the couple responds to this, the mediator needs to follow up with a lecture about the ground rules of no talking about the past, and speaking about one's own feelings only in the form of "I" statements rather than "you" statements. The couple can also be advised that if they are unable to conduct themselves civilly, the present session will end immediately and their attorneys will be required to be present in the next session to assist them in remaining rational. It should be added that they each will be responsible for paying their attorneys' hourly fees to sit in the session with them.

If these efforts do not reduce the conflict, the mediator can admonish the couple that he will refer them back to court if they want to continue arguing. Such an admonishment can work strategically only if one or both spouses dread court.

Leaving the Room. As a last strategy, the mediator can simply get up out of his or her chair and announce to the couple, "I am not interested in listening to you two argue—that behavior is for the courtroom, not for mediation. Please continue your argument until you are finished. I will be in the waiting room; when you are done arguing and are ready to mediate, please let me know." The mediator then walks out of the room, closes the door, and reads an entertaining magazine. Usually within five minutes or so, one of the spouses sheepishly opens the door and announces that they are finished arguing and are ready to resume mediation.

Most mediators have a difficult time carrying out this bold strategy the first time, but after doing so once, each occasion thereafter is much simpler. The unexpectedness of the action throws the spouses off balance and startles them into realizing how unproductive their behavior has become. It is an effective message to the sparring spouses and, at the same time, a self-preservation tactic for the mediator, who may welcome a short break from the argument.

Conflict-Diverting Strategies

After talking with a couple for some time, the mediator gets a sense of the degree of conflict that is likely and of the specific topics most likely to trigger it off. Once the mediator has a sense of these factors, he or she can use one of several strategies to divert conflict at the first warning of its presence.

Converting Accusations to Requests. A useful technique to use when one spouse begins to make accusations about the past behavior of the other is to turn the accusations into requests for the future. For example, if one spouse accuses the other of never cleaning or bathing their child and of returning her dirty, the mediator can instruct the spouse to put her accusation in the form of a request: "I would like you to bathe our daughter once a day and return her with clean skin and clean clothes." Only rarely will the other spouse refuse to agree to such a straightforward, unthreatening request, and this can then be an item to include in the written parenting agreement.

If, however, the accused spouse springs to defend himself, the mediator can say, "Whether or not it happened that way in the past is not important, and I would have no way of knowing for sure anyway, but will you agree to respect this request for the future?" The spouse will only rarely not agree to this.

Diversion Problem Solving. Another technique for diverting conflict is for the mediator to lead the couple off the topic of contention onto a topic of common concern, which would bring them on the same side of the issue. For example, one couple had two younger children over whom they both vied for primary physical custody, and their negotiations would regularly escalate into heated argument whenever they discussed these children. However, they also had an older teenager who had developed some problems as a result of the divorce. Since both parents were equally concerned about that child and had no contention over his primary residence, the mediator steered the discussion away from the younger children and onto the older child. The spouses discussed this child for about forty-five minutes, until they had formulated plans to seek counseling for that child. Having made this joint decision, they were then able to cooperate enough to develop a satisfactory co-parenting agreement for the younger children. This diversion strategy can be used to detour the couple onto any nonconflictual topic—Grandma, the family house, the family pet, or any other topic about which the parents have similar and concordant concerns.

Sudden Positive Shifting. When spouses become entangled in arguments, they often rigidly persist in discussing more of the same while knowing full well that their conflict will merely escalate. A useful strategy for getting them unlocked from their negative pattern is to suddenly shift the topic to a positive one. One way is to shift the couple's focus in time to past, present, or future, depending on where they seem stuck. For example, if spouses are arguing about present co-parenting arrangements, the mediator can shift them to the past by suddenly asking, "When you two were first married, how did you make decisions?" After they respond, the mediator can follow through by asking, "Do you remember how you felt about each other at that time?" It is assumed that the mediator would shift the conversation to the early marital relationship only if he or she had evidence that it was a positive period for both spouses.

Alternatively, with a couple who keep slipping into arguing about the past, the mediator can suddenly shift the focus to the future by asking: "When your children are teenagers five or six years from now, and you two are well past your divorce and your present angry feelings and are each settled into new relationships, how would you like your children to feel about their parents?" The mediator can also shift to other topics. If, for example, the spouses begin to argue about finances, the mediator can suddenly ask, "Tell me, what do you like most about your children?"

In each of these examples, the shift is effective because its suddenness is disorienting. As one observer noted, these shifts are like pulling the carpet suddenly out from under the parents. When the mediator's moves are more unpredictable than those of the spouses, the mediator is able to control the direction of the sessions.

Deflecting. Part of the mediator's task is to prevent the spouses from saying things to each other that are so hurtful that irreparable harm is done to whatever trust each may have had in the other. Contrary to the prevalent belief of beginning psychotherapists, it is not useful to allow conflicting spouses to share all their feelings. For example, it sometimes happens that one damaging remark uttered at the wrong time will permanently close communications between a couple. No matter what the reasons were or how apologetic the attacking spouse later appears, the other spouse will never forgive him or her.

Hence, there are times when the mediator must deflect one spouse's words from the other before such harm can occur. The mediator's intervention could be in the form of a clarification or rationalization that helps the attacked spouse interpret the other spouse's comment. The other spouse may pick up the mediator's cue and phrase the comment in a less provocative way. For example, in the middle of a heated exchange, a wife said to her ex-husband, "You never paid any attention to the children, then you left me, and you're *not* getting the children now or ever." Before the husband had a chance to respond, the mediator deflected the comment by saying to the wife: "The anger and hurt that you feel right now is not unusual, and it is very understandable. And it's also not unusual for a parent who was not involved with the children before a divorce to decide to become sincerely involved after the divorce. Allowing that opportunity will give your children a chance to get to know their father in the future in the way that you wanted it in the past. But give yourself plenty of time to get through those difficult feelings."

On hearing this the husband kept quiet, for he knew that the mediator's remark implied support for his continuing relationship with the children, yet presented in a way that allowed both him and his wife to save face. He then tearfully expressed his sincerity in wanting to become more involved with the children. The wife cried and was able to constructively express her hurt feelings at being left by the husband. Negotiations then became possible.

Sidestepping. Sometimes the conflict that needs diverting arises between a spouse and the mediator. Typically, one spouse presents a rigid position that is not in the best interests of the children. This spouse's manner is self-righteous and provocative, and the other spouse appeals to the mediator to intervene. Because the mediator feels a compelling urge to argue the challenging spouse out of the inappropriate position, her response is critical at this point. If the mediator gets pulled into debate with the spouse, she loses her neutral stance and will thereafter be viewed by that spouse as one-sided. If she restrains herself, she can continue to be neutral.

The strategy of sidestepping is intended to help prevent the mediator from succumbing to such provocation. Instead of responding to a challenge, the mediator simply lets the issue drop and goes on to another topic. For example, in one case a husband said to the wife and mediator, "*My* children do not have to follow any rigid rules. Children need to be free; *they* know what's best for them. They've *already* been harmed by your rules and I'm not going to impose any more on them. They are almost six and five years old and they can go to sleep whenever they are tired, and eat whatever they like whenever they are hungry, and wear whatever they want to wear." The wife looked at the mediator incredulously and said, "Would you tell him what children *really* need?" The mediator, sensing a trap if he were to debate the point, sidestepped the issue by saying: "The differences the two of you may have about ways to raise children are important to consider, but let's put that off for now because I want to ask you about the kinds of things that your children enjoy doing together with each of you."

In this way the topic of contention is labeled in a neutral fashion, its importance acknowledged, and a transition made to a topic that is not emotionally charged. Later the mediator may return to the issue of child-rearing differences, but from a perspective that is within his or her control.

Impasse-Breaking Strategies

During the period of negotiations over workable agreements, there are often points where the couple reach an impasse and are unable to negotiate any further. The problem at these points is not overt conflict but rather resistance to workable compromises. Unless the mediator actively initiates some strategy to overcome the impasse, it may eventually force the couple into court.

The strategies used by the mediator in this particular phase of mediation are somewhat controversial; because they are expedient, there are certain risks involved in using them. The central risk is that they could backfire, making the situation worse for both parents and children. It appears, however, that the risks are usually outweighed by the potential gains in reaching compromised agreements.

Offering Suggestions. Certainly the least risky of these strategies is the straightforward offering of suggestions for a compromised agreement. However, the term *straightforward* must be qualified; because the mediator must maintain a balance between the spouses, suggestions can be offered only if they support each spouse equally. If the mediator suggests that one spouse compromise more than the other, that spouse may then feel as if he or she must resist the mediator as well as the other spouse.

Offering suggestions is helpful because spouses typically are aware of few alternatives to the usual time-sharing formula —every other weekend, alternate holidays, and a month in the summer—or the fifty-fifty joint custody formulas portrayed in the popular media. Moreover, even if a spouse does have alternatives in mind, he or she often is reluctant to be the first to suggest a compromise. In other cases, spouses are so angry that they are locked into defending narrow positions. In both situations, the spouses can much more easily agree to a third person's suggestions for compromise if such suggestions are indeed balanced.

Suggestions can be offered in a very direct form or through examples from other couples' creative solutions to similar problems. For example, one couple could not come to an agreement on how to share time with their two children. The husband said the children should not be separated, and the wife said she would like to have at least one child living with her. At this, the mediator said: "Some couples with two children have worked out this kind of situation by having each child spend some time with each parent alone, and some time with each parent together with the sibling. That way, the children are together for significant amounts of time, and each parent also gets the chance to know each child as a separate person—and the children usually love the special attention they receive from each parent when they get to spend time alone with him or her."

In another case, the mediator offered a direct suggestion to a couple in which the wife was leery of trusting the husband enough to share physical custody with him. He had not been very involved with the children before the divorce, and the wife wanted him to prove his intentions before allowing the child to share equal time with him. The mediator offered this suggestion: "Since the two of you are fresh from a divorce, and we know that it takes some time to rebuild trust in each other, how about setting up a plan in which over the next six months you gradually increase the amount of time that the children spend with their father. This will give the children and you, Phil, a chance to build a stronger relationship, which does take time for most children, and it will give you, Sarah, time to build more trust in Phil."

Such suggestions are, of course, offered only when the mediator has prior evidence that they will be feasible for the couple. Offering unfeasible suggestions can destroy any hope for future cooperation, since the couple may well feel: If the expert cannot think of a workable alternative, how can *we*?

Leveraging the Children. When a couple reach an impasse, the mediator can utilize the children's input and impact to unlock the negotiations. This is an extremely sensitive maneuver because of the potential for emotional trauma to the children. If it is handled skillfully, however, the children can teach their parents an important lesson.

When children are brought into the mediation session at a point of impasse, they are always uncomfortable. They may look and feel sad and scared, they may verbalize their discomfort, and they may even cry. It is rare for a parent not to react to this in some fashion. When the children's main contribution is simply an express desire for the parents to stop fighting and settle the custody battle, the parents are confronted with a powerful challenge. One exceptionally mature four-year-old said poignantly, with tears in his eyes, "Mommy and daddy, I wish you would just stop fighting; you act more babyish than me!" When the child left the room, the father, who was the more resistant of the parents, said, "I care enough about Billy and the pain that he is going through that I will make a sacrifice for *him*. I'll agree to having him live for the school year at his mother's house."

The risks in bringing children into a mediation session at a point of impasse are several. For one thing, the discomfort manifested by the children can be interpreted by one of the spouses as evidence of the destructive effects of the other spouse's presence on the child. Second, a spouse may take the children's upset state as evidence of callousness on the part of the mediator. One such spouse said to the mediator, "You are torturing my children. I can't stand to see them tortured and I don't think it's fair or necessary for them to have to be here." Such an interpretation is difficult to counter and can alienate the spouse from the mediator and also build up resistance to the other spouse.

Before using this strategy, the mediator must seriously consider whether the risks are too great for the children or the ongoing negotiations. If the mediator decides to go ahead, he or she must carefully guide the session to protect the children from excessive pain while making sure that the parents hear the children's feelings about the issue.

Persuading with Dramatic Anecdotes. If the mediator has evidence that one or both of the spouses are worried about some particular aspect of an unsuccessful mediation outcome, then the mediator may be able to use this as leverage to overcome an impasse. For example, a mediator may be able to facilitate an agreement by supplying vivid stories of other couples' traumatic experiences of court custody battles, of their near financial ruin from lawyers' fees and court-related expenses, of the damaging psychological effects to children of testifying in court, and of the endless cycle of court battles, which typically repeat year after year.

The anecdotes selected should be related directly to the areas of most psychological concern to at least one of the parents. For example, before telling of traumatic court battles, the mediator should already have determined how badly each spouse wants to stay out of court. Some spouses are very willing to compromise if they know that court will be the next step, and traumatic stories of court battles will enhance that willingness. Other spouses are so driven by power assertion and revenge motives that they would love to have their day in court, and the mediator's intended warnings function instead as incitement to go to court. Naturally, it is important that the particular story selected by the mediator be presented in a balanced manner so that neither spouse feels unduly pressured. The mediator must modulate the degree of vividness and pointedness in content, so that the intent of the story is not perceived as a biased persuasion of just one spouse. Addressing the stories to both spouses also allows a face-saving format for the target spouse (if any) to hear the message. With sensitivity, tact, and professional and personal clarity and judgment of its ultimate good, a mediator can often leverage spousal concerns into constructive agreements.

Leveraging with Attorneys. There are several ways in which attorneys can be useful if a couple reach an impasse. For example, it can be useful to consult with an attorney by phone if the mediator knows the attorney to be supportive of the mediation approach or suspects the attorney to be discouraging a mediated settlement. As previously noted, attorneys may have difficulties with the concept of mediation because it is a relatively new and unfamiliar approach and because the nonadversarial approach of mediation may seem to conflict with the legal canon of ethics.

If the attorney is supportive of mediation, the mediator can suggest that he discuss with his client the likely outcomes of a court-rendered decision and the advantages of mediation over court. Oftentimes, the support offered by such an attorney to his client can be just the event that unlocks the impasse. If, however, the attorney is skeptical of the mediation approach, then the mediator can discuss with the attorney the long-range benefits to the children of a mediated settlement. If he still seems unpersuaded, then the mediator had best not request his direct assistance in the mediation efforts.

Sometimes requests for assistance by an attorney who appears to be supportive of mediation can backfire. In one case, for example, the mediator called the husband's attorney, with the client's permission, and explained that mediation was at a stalemate because his client was not yet willing to accept the fact that his wife was really divorcing him, even though she had filed the papers, followed through on every step, and gave no evidence to the contrary. The attorney was requested to talk with his client and help him realize that the divorce was really happening. He agreed to assist the mediator in this way. However, the husband came to the next session enraged at the mediator. He explained that his attorney had met with him after talking with the mediator, adding, "My attorney made fun of me. He laughed and criticized me for hanging onto my child to keep my wife. I was humiliated and insulted. That is *not* what I'm doing." The upshot was that the husband was even more resistant than before.

Hence, the mediator needs to be extremely careful about the specific type of assistance requested of attorneys, since the mediator has no control over how the request will be carried out. When a mediator requests help from an attorney who is not cognizant of the family systems perspective of the mediator, the request may get translated from a psychological to a legal framework and become distorted in the translation.

Another way the mediator can seek assistance from attorneys for breaking through an impasse is to arrange for them to be present in the next mediation session. Again, this can be helpful only if the mediator is assured that the attorneys are supportive of mediation. Before the session, the mediator meets briefly with the attorneys without their clients. She discusses the expectations of each concerning what would constitute an acceptable agreement, and she explains the ground rules for mediation, focusing on how they differ from legal methods. Each attorney's purpose in the session is to be the link between his or her client and the other spouse, and they are encouraged to stress compromise and to temporarily suspend advocacy for their own clients.

When the attorneys carry out their task, an agreement is almost always reached within the session. If one attorney slips into an adversarial position, the task is made more difficult but it may still be possible to salvage an agreement. Either way, the extra effort required to steer the attorneys away from adversarial positions usually pays off, since such sessions usually produce workable agreements.

Because of the added expense to the spouses in having their attorneys present, this strategy should be saved as a last step, to be used only if absolutely necessary. However, this strategy is still less expensive than a court appearance. It is highly unusual for a spouse to refuse to continue mediation just because of the extra expense.

10

Reaching Lasting Agreements:

Successful Cases

Couples contribute certain elements to the mediation process that are essential for a successful outcome. These include trust in each other's parenting intentions and skill, a willingness to compromise, relatively consistent and predictable behavior patterns, some ongoing communication about co-parenting, and general agreement about basic child-rearing values. Interestingly, it is these same elements that generally are important for effective parenting within intact families. Moreover, it appears that if most or all of these elements are missing, the mediation effort is destined to fail despite anything the mediator can do.

Success may have two meanings with respect to mediation. One definition of success is the development of a written and signed mediation agreement. A second, more rigorous definition is *the development of a workable, written and signed mediation agreement and plan for future self-determined modifications that hold up over time.* Recent follow-up research of voluntary mediation (Pearson and Thoennes, 1982a) and of involuntary mediation (Saposnek and others, 1983) has shown that within the first year after mediation approximately one third of parents who had successfully reached agreements in mediation reported that the other parent was, to varying degrees, not in compliance with the agreement. This suggests a need to apply the second, more rigorous definition of success in mediation.

Let us now explore five cases in which the elements of success just cited played a central role in the sustained resolution of the custody and visitation disputes.

Paul and Florence

Paul and Florence had been married for almost twenty years and had six children when they entered mediation. The two oldest children were away at college; three teenagers and an eight-year-old girl, Christine, remained at home.

During the early years of their marriage, Paul and Florence were a traditional, conservative, church-going couple. Paul worked as a certified public accountant, and Florence stayed home and raised the children. After their fifth child, Florence went back to school to get a degree in nursing but became pregnant with Christine after working only one year.

Although the earlier years of their marriage reportedly were quite satisfactory for both spouses, the years following Christine's birth had been unsettling. Florence grew bored with her role as a mother and homemaker, while Paul became increasingly involved in his work. By this time, he had become a consultant to several national corporations, which gave him many opportunities for travel and for personal and professional contacts away from home. Because Florence felt intimidated by her husband's success, she never expressed the tremendous loneliness, emptiness, and boredom that she felt at being "just a housewife."

One weekend, when Christine was about seven years old and Paul was away on a business trip, Florence decided to take a weekend course in holistic health practices, a field that had fascinated her for several years. Paul returned from the business trip and found that Florence had left Christine at a friend's house for the weekend while she took some "offbeat" class. He then proceeded to lecture her about her duties and responsibilities as a mother. Florence apologized but was unable to shake her interest in holistic health practices.

Over the next few months, their increasing conflicts led them to seek marital counseling. After several months, Paul terminated the counseling because he thought the counselor was biased toward Florence: "She told me that Florence should be able to express her independence as a woman, which I think gave her a license to be selfish and irresponsible to her family." Moreover, Paul felt threatened by the nontraditional values expressed in the doctrines of holistic health. He was alarmed that those values would negatively influence the Christian values which they had instilled in their children up to that point. In fact, Paul attributed the older children's declining interest in church attendance to Florence's "kooky ideas."

Because she wanted to pursue her studies in holistic health and knew that Paul would never consent to it, Florence left home one day with Christine. She left behind a lengthy, sensitive farewell note for Paul which expressed her dilemma, the reasons for her leaving, a request to pursue a peaceful divorce without lawyers, and a request to share joint custody of the children. She added that she had taken Christine to live with her because she felt that Christine, being only eight, still needed her mother's daily influence.

During the next three months, Florence lived in an apartment about a mile from Paul and the family house. She and Paul attempted to negotiate a divorce agreement, but Paul continued to resist it. After much struggle, Florence took Christine and moved out of the neighborhood and unilaterally consulted an attorney, who served Paul with divorce papers. Paul was shocked to receive these and immediately hired an attorney and petitioned for sole legal and physical custody of Christine. At their first court hearing, Paul and Florence were referred to mediation, with Florence receiving temporary custody of Christine.

In the first mediation session, the mediator explored the marital relationship. When the subject of the degree of certainty of divorce was brought up, Paul made a striking comment. He said, "Although my wife wants a divorce, there will be no divorce. First of all, I do not believe there are irreconcilable differences and secondly, I am a Catholic, and our religion does not permit divorce." When the mediator further probed the solidity of Paul's position, he said "There may be a civil divorce, but there will *never* be a divorce under God. I love my wife, and I will *never* stop loving her—and my family will not be split up."

On hearing this, Florence remained quiet and appeared hesitant to respond. With some encouragement from the mediator, she gently told Paul that she still loved him but needed to do certain things with her life, things that he had said he could not accept. Paul then said that she hadn't given him a chance and that in retrospect he regretted not having helped her with the dishes. Florence was quiet and tearful on hearing this.

At this point, the mediator was able to assess Paul's court petition as a combination of a *retaliation* and a *reuniting* strategy. Moreover, it was clear that the couple had the potential to work out a reasonable child-sharing plan if Paul could come to accept the divorce. It was unclear to the mediator, however, to what degree Florence was actually ambivalent about the divorce and to what degree she was simply trying to protect Paul from hurt. In order to clarify the couple's actual probability of divorce, the mediator assigned them a task. They were requested to meet at a restaurant for coffee before the second mediation session two weeks later, to discuss their respective plans for the future. This gave them both an opportunity to talk with each other further and time to digest the discussions from the first mediation session.

At the second mediation session, Paul and Florence explained how they had met for coffee and talked. Florence said that until they talked she had not realized how uncomfortable she had been in telling Paul that she definitely intended to go through with the divorce. Now she could understand his reluctance to accept it, since she had been trying to protect him by softening her intent, and he had interpreted her attitude as offering hope for reconciliation.

However, Paul still was not ready to accept the divorce. During the second session, he continued his attempts to persuade Florence to reconsider, alternately preaching his religious, family-oriented values and criticizing her for her waywardness. He also accused her of confusing Christine to the point that she did not want to talk with or be around him very much. However, Florence's response clarified for the mediator that Christine had been utilizing a *self-esteem protecting strategy* in subtly resisting contact with her father. Florence said that Christine felt pressured by Paul to stay with him and also felt criticized for wanting to spend so much time with her mother. Because these messages were conveyed in a context of loving support, which left Christine feeling double-bound and guilty, her way of coping was to pull away from her father's psychological grip.

The mediator then offered further clarification of Christine's strategic behavior and *complimented* Paul for his obviously loving concern for Christine. Because Florence remained quiet and noncombative, the mediator felt that he could safely focus on Paul's feelings about the divorce. The discussion returned to religious values and the mediator asked Paul whether he had talked with his priest about the divorce. Paul said that he had not but was considering attending a group meeting for divorced Catholics, sponsored by his church. The mediator gave much encouragement to Paul to follow through with this idea. The mediator then assigned Paul the task of going to several meetings before the next mediation session, and requested that both Paul and Florence consider some plans for sharing time with their children. The third and last mediation session was scheduled for six weeks later, giving Paul ample time to work on accepting the divorce.

In the third and last session, Paul declared that he was finally ready to accept the divorce. He also said that he had engaged Christine in several good talks in the interim since the previous session. Paul then questioned the effect that Florence's new values would have on Christine, and the mediator requested both Paul and Florence to write out their respective values in raising Christine. In comparing their lists, the mediator found that they were very similar. Paul and Florence both valued the teaching of loving relationships, responsibility, and morality. Paul also had religion on his list, while Florence had respect, honesty, and empathy on hers. The mediator then attempted to elicit cooperation by insulating trust. He repeatedly highlighted the unusually high degree of agreement on what they both felt were important spiritual values for Christine. Each time Paul looked for a difference, the mediator persistently talked about the congruence in their basic spiritual values. Florence repeatedly concurred with the mediator in this. The mediator also repeatedly *complimented* both parents for maintaining such a solid foundation of values for their daughter.

At this point, the mediator requested their proposals for sharing time with Christine. They were able to work out a joint legal custody agreement, with time-sharing based flexibly around Paul's travel schedule and Florence's class time. They both agreed that Christine needed extended time with each parent and that each had important things to offer her, as they had done with their older children.

One year later, Paul, Florence, and Christine were still sharing time quite well. Although Christine had some difficulty adjusting to alternating households, she felt it was worth it so that she could be with both parents. After Paul became engaged to another woman, he was much friendlier and more accepting of Florence. He finally was able to let go of her, and he said that he had learned a lot about himself in the preceding year.

In spite of the apparent differences in their new lifestyles, it was clear to the mediator that after twenty years of successfully raising six children, the differences in Paul's and Florence's child-rearing values were negligible and would dissolve once the spousal strategies for retaliation and reuniting were deactivated. Florence had become more independent, which imbalanced the marital system, and Paul was unable to accommodate to this change. In the midst of the resulting tension, Christine's *self-esteem protection strategy* scared Paul even more, for he felt that he was not only losing the love of his wife but now also the love of his daughter.

The mediator's overall task was to support Paul with lots of time and adjunct resources (such as the church) so that he could accept the reality of the divorce, while making sure that Florence would not escalate the conflict before Paul was ready to negotiate. The mediator was able to find leverage in their basic respect for each other's parenting, in the consistency of their behavior as co-parents for so many years, and in their long-established pattern of effective communication about their children. Out of these elements came compromise for a very constructive and flexible agreement.

James and Carol

James and Carol had been married for thirteen years and had three children, who at the time of mediation were nine, eight, and six years old. Carol felt that their marriage had been fine up until the time that James left. James felt that the first part of the marriage was good but said he felt trapped later in the marriage. This culminated in his having an affair with a good friend of Carol's, as a result of his self-labeled "mid-life crisis." Carol tolerated the affair but became increasingly depressed over James's frequent absences. When he was not making travel plans, he spent most of his free time with his parents and siblings. Carol felt isolated and left out of these activities.

Increasingly, James began to explore new life-styles for himself. Carol, in contrast, became more and more conservative and began attending church. Because she had been raised to be family oriented, she tolerated all the changes through which James was going, while secretly hoping for more attention from him.

One day, James told Carol that he wanted a divorce, and he left. The decision took Carol by surprise, and she became angry and then depressed. Over the next several years, Carol became financially independent from James by pursuing her own professional career. She worked hard and was quite successful, eventually making more money than James, who worked at a management-level job.

Neither parent remarried, and for three years following the divorce James and Carol communicated very little. Through attorneys they were able to arrange joint legal custody for all three children, with physical custody retained by Carol. James spent time with the children one day and night per week, one month in the summer, and on alternate holidays.

After three years of this arrangement, James began attending a men's consciousness-raising group, from which he received peer support for requesting joint physical custody of his children. He filed a petition for modification of custody, and he and Carol were ordered to mediation by the court.

When Carol found out about this petition, she panicked and cut off all contact with James. She refused to let the children see him and said to the mediator over the phone, "He's not taking my kids from me." She explained that she did not want mediation and that if she just knew what he wanted, they could settle it themselves. She added that James had indicated through his lawyer that he wanted mediation in order "to chat" but that she had nothing to chat with him about. There was a very tight, scared, and rageful quality to her voice.

At the first mediation session, Carol walked in carrying a two-inch-thick folder containing details of every transaction that had taken place over the previous three years between James, herself, and the children. These included phone calls, notes, and letters. She maintained a very defensive posture and responded with short, sarcastic, biting retorts to the mediator's attempts to put her at ease. Clearly, she did not want to be there. In contrast, James appeared friendly, open, good-humored, and very receptive to the mediator.

The mediator took a great deal of time setting the context and *pre-empting* all the concerns that he imagined Carol might have. He especially emphasized the benefits to children of frequent access to both parents. He looked for things to *compliment* Carol about, such as her loving care of the children, her managing to develop a career for herself when so many women in her situation do not, and the excellent way she had taken care of herself.

Soon Carol began to loosen up and talk about how painful the abruptness of the divorce was for her. This was the first time she had let James know about these feelings, and he listened sensitively. Carol related how she had always wanted to be just a housewife but was forced to go to work after James left. Consequently, she felt very angry at James for "suddenly coming into my life again and threatening to take my children away."

The mediator quickly *deflected* this comment and asked James to clarify his intent. James told Carol that he did not want to take the children away from her but just wanted to share them equally. This comment elicited much anger from Carol, which the mediator *absorbed* by continually asking her for further clarification. She continued to express her anger at James, fuming that he was "not around when I needed him to help with the kids, but now when he wants to, he just steps in." After absorbing a large part of this anger, the mediator used a *sudden positive shifting* strategy to direct the conversation to the children by suddenly asking both parents to describe their children. This got them onto neutral ground and rapidly defused the tension.

It became clear that neither parent had any real qualms about the other's parenting skills and that Carol's resistance was based largely in a combination of *retaliation* and *emotional survival* strategies. She was still furious at James for leaving her and wanted him duly punished. Moreover, she still defined her primary role as that of a mother and felt very threatened by the thought of "giving up" any part of her time with the children. At one point she even said, "I do not want to share the children."

The mediator, sensing an impasse if he were to push for proposals at this point, ended the first session and requested that they not attempt to talk with each other about time-sharing plans until the next mediation session. The mediator then scheduled the next session for three weeks later, allowing ample time for Carol to reorganize her defenses after exposing her vulnerability and for James to think about Carol's feelings.

In the second session, Carol continued to be angry at James and generally was more expressive of her feelings. She felt pressured to give in to his demands, just as she always had, and she was concerned about saying no to him for fear that he would get even more angry and intrusive. At this point, the mediator needed to encourage Carol to consider more time-sharing while giving her a face-saving way to lower her resistance without feeling that she merely gave in. So he offered her support and empathy for her angry feelings and *reframed* her expression "giving in" as "allowing your children the contact with their father that they unfortunately missed out on earlier in their lives." She was further told anecdotes about several other men who did not start feeling like fathers until many years after their divorces. While implicitly criticizing James's neglectful behavior, the mediator supported his current intent in a way that also allowed Carol to concede to more time-sharing and still save face.

Carol, however, was still too resistant to even consider equal sharing. So the mediator decided that he would have to escalate the pressure on Carol in an attempt to dislodge the imbalance in attitudes toward time-sharing. In a supportive way, he explained that if this case were to go to court, it was very likely that a judge would consider the standard plan (every other weekend, a month in the summer, and alternate holidays) as fully appropriate for James's contact with the children, and likely also that it could be even more, considering the court in question's presumption of joint custody (the case was set in California). In addition, he told some *dramatic anecdotes* about court custody battles, in an indirect attempt to persuade her to reconsider her position. Before she could respond, however, he once again offered empathic support for her difficulty in deciding to make the sacrifice and offer her children more time with their father. At that point, James gently asked Carol whether he could take the children to a special ball game the next weekend. Carol agreed reluctantly, and the mediator then ended the session and scheduled a final session, to take place three weeks later.

In the final session, James and Carol were able to work out a very detailed plan for increasing James's time with the children, but only after much struggle. Carol still refused to agree to an equal split but was willing to concede to alternate full weekends (Friday after school until Sunday evening) and one full day on the other weekends. She also agreed to expand summer time with James to five weeks and to add several extra ten-day stretches during the school year. Holidays were divided up by respective preferences, and school vacation times split in half for each parent.

In order to maintain a sense of control, Carol insisted on

including many specific details about exact dates, times, and conditions in the agreement. James tolerated these details nicely. Carol said that the changes were extremely hard for her to make, but since she had talked with the children and got their consent, she was willing to try it out. Hence, the children offered her another face-saving way to concede.

The mediator then asked Carol, "How long do you think you will need before you could feel comfortable in allowing your children to share even more time with their dad?" Carol responded tearfully, "I don't know, but I do know that I need more time." James responded supportively and said that he was willing to allow all the time she needed, since he now felt that they were at least working toward equalizing time spent with the children.

A year later, James reported that the agreement continued to work and the children were doing well, but that Carol still insisted on sticking rigidly to every detail of the agreement. While this irritated and frustrated him, he understood that it was going to take quite a while for Carol to feel more comfortable about letting go.

In this case, the mediator needed to be extremely sensitive to the feelings and strategies of Carol. Clearly, she had the most to lose, while the children and James had the most to gain. If the mediator offered too much support to Carol, it might have further reinforced her rigid stance and alienated James. If the mediator offered too little support, he would have been cast as insensitive and as a threat, and she would likely have refused to go on with the mediation process. Just the right balance between support for her feelings and leveraging for change was needed and was achieved. Had James not been patient and supportive, the mediator would have had to reprove him firmly but supportively, in front of Carol, for his "insensitivity." Fortunately, he remained patient and helpful in seeing Carol through her difficulty in compromising.

Because the mediator felt that Carol did trust that he understood her feelings, he decided that it would be safe to leverage the impasse with *dramatic anecdotes* and a discussion of the likely outcome of a court decree. By supportively persuading Carol that she had more to lose than gain in going to court, the mediator got her to negotiate directly with James.

This couple had much difficulty with compromise and with communication, but they basically had no problems in trusting and respecting each other's parenting skills or intents and no significant disagreements about basic child-rearing values.

Harvey and Judith

Harvey and Judith had been married for nine years and had two children, Susan, aged ten, and David, nine. Judith felt that for the first half of their marriage they had been "best friends" and that over the last part of the marriage, Harvey had become more controlling, jealous, and temper-prone. Harvey agreed, saying that he had become quite critical of himself and of others and that he was indeed hard to be around. He also admitted that he had been a neglectful father in the past and that his energy was increasingly absorbed by his work as a pharmacist. He further admitted that he had never fully committed himself to Judith.

Judith's response to Harvey was to argue with him over every point until he would intimidate her, whereupon she would appease him and then change subjects and argue further. Their conflicts had finally become so overwhelming that Judith decided to leave. Owning her own dress shop, she was financially able to survive quite comfortably. Moreover, within six months she began to live with another man, and within another six months she married him. Over the first year after their separation, Harvey and Judith had many fights over money and property, and they enlisted two attorneys in their messy battle. Because they had accumulated a considerable estate through their marriage, the legal negotiations became quite complicated and were frequently heated. Soon the children were also subtly enlisted in the battle. Each parent criticized the other parent to the children, and each withheld the children from the other. The children soon developed behavior problems in response to this setup. At one of the many court hearings over their complicated marital dissolution, a judge ordered them to seek private mediation in order to make a plan for sharing the children more constructively.

Both parents attended mediation willingly, for they were quite aware of the effects their conflicts were having on the children. In the first session, after saying hello, both Harvey and Judith hurriedly started telling the mediator all the horrible things about each other's parenting abilities and behavior. Without even having had an opportunity to set the context, the mediator had to use an *assertive stance* strategy and firmly tell them both to stop talking, that each would get a chance to talk. The conflict again got well out of hand, so the mediator *left the room* and told them to invite him in when they were finished arguing and were ready to mediate. Very shortly, they called the mediator back in and apologized sheepishly. Harvey explained that they both tended to lose control but could get along fine if they tried.

Up to this point, it had seemed to the mediator that there was little hope for this couple to reach an agreement. However, their insights into their marital argument game ("we've always argued but have always been good friends") gave the mediator some hope for a settlement. He then requested information about their backgrounds, their marital relationship, and their children.

When the subject of their children was raised, Harvey and Judith suddenly began to throw accusations at each other once again. The mediator *blocked and soothed* this conflict, *told anecdotes,* and *gave information* about the nature of children's strategies. Both parents were apparently stunned by the idea of children's strategies. They turned to each other and said, "*That's* what they're doing." It seemed that in their efforts to create some peace, Susan and David had been desperately utilizing *tension-detonating* strategies and strategies for *protecting* their *parents' self-esteem.* Both children were regularly telling one parent the opposite of what they told the other. For example, Susan would tell her father that she wanted to stay at his house all the time because her mother had been hitting her and forcing her to eat food she did not like. Then Susan would go to her mother and say that she wanted to stay at her house because her dad got angry easily, was never home, and left her and David home alone all the time. Predictably, such words had triggered off major fights between Harvey and Judith and had brought them to court each charging the other with being unfit. Never had either parent checked out the children's report with the other, nor had they ever questioned the validity of the children's complaints.

After some time, the children had each taken sides with the parent of the same sex, in an effort to *prove loyalty* and keep at least one parent loving each of them. Each parent had concluded that these choices represented the children's clear preferences for place of residence. They had then gone back to court again to legalize these preferences, only to have the children change their minds once again. Needless to say, both parents were quite confused by all this and were intrigued and enlightened by the mediator's perspective on their children's strategies.

The mediator ended the session with a request to bring the children to the second session two weeks later. He felt that he needed to know the children's feelings about their parents' situation, and he also tentatively planned to *leverage the children* as a way to encourage a settlement.

At the beginning of the second session, the mediator talked with Susan and David together without their parents present. They were both perceptive, intelligent, and at ease in talking. Moreover, they were both clearly quite skilled in manipulating their parents, and they shared their "secrets" for getting their parents to stop fighting. Susan said, "I tell one of them a big story about the other one—you know, sort of like something that really happened, only way worse. Then they yell at each other and then they don't talk to each other any more for a while." When the mediator asked whether that worked, Susan replied, "Not really, they actually just fight worse later when they talk to each other again." Both Susan and David then told the mediator how much they hated it when their parents argued. David added, "Sometimes I tell dad that I want to stay with him only 'cause I know he doesn't want me staying with mom—it makes him feel better and less like fighting." Susan said that she did the same with their mother. Both children discussed the negative and positive aspects of living at each parent's home and concluded that they really had no preferences either way, since they loved both parents.

With the consent of the children, the mediator then invited both parents in and helped Susan and David share their feelings and their request that their parents stop fighting and share their time with both of them. On hearing this, Harvey and Judith were both surprised and relieved. They each felt once again on equal footing and were fully supportive of the idea of equal sharing. Because time for the second session had run out, the mediator requested Harvey and Judith to go home and consider ways to share time with their children.

In the third session, Harvey and Judith said that they had done a lot of soul searching and had decided to call a truce to their fighting. However, very soon after they agreed to this, they began another argument over money and property. As part of this argument, Harvey mentioned his concern about Matthew, Judith's teenage son from her earlier marriage. Judith agreed that she too was concerned about Matthew's depression and poor school performance. On hearing this, the mediator saw an opportunity for *diversion problem solving* and began to pursue a line of questioning aimed at the area of shared concern. After they had discussed Matthew's problems for about twenty minutes and agreed to get him some counseling, the mediator then shifted the focus to Susan and David. He emphasized the obvious love that the children had for both of them and underlined the fact that the children were even willing to sacrifice their own comfort and emotional stability to get their parents to stop fighting. Immediately, Harvey said tearfully, "We've just got to stop this arguing—our kids are getting destroyed." Judith agreed, and the mediator immediately requested their proposals for time-sharing. Over the next hour, Harvey and Judith worked out an agreement for a one-year plan. They set up temporary time-sharing arrangements until the family house was sold and agreed to establish two separate residences within the same school district so that the children would be able to spend alternate two weeks at each parent's home. They divided up holiday times by preference and made an explicit agreement to give each other plenty of advance notice if the plans of either were to change. They also explicitly agreed to keep the financial aspects of their divorce settlement independent of their time-sharing plan with the children. Finally, they agreed to meet again in mediation in one year's time to reassess their plan.

After nine months, the mediator received a call from Harvey requesting another session. He also requested the mediator to contact David's teacher, as David had been having problems in school. On calling the teacher, the mediator was informed that David had had a hard time adjusting to the frequent residence changes back and forth, and that he had cried about his parents' frequent arguments. David felt that if he did not go along with frequent and equal time-sharing, then one of his parents might feel betrayed.

In the mediation session, Harvey informed the mediator that about two months after the previous mediation agreement had been completed, he and Judith had changed the time-sharing plan between themselves from biweekly to weekly alternations. Also, the parents once again had been fighting about the complicated property settlement. As a matter of fact, the attorneys had got involved to the point of sending personally deprecating letters back and forth, with copies to the mediator, as each attempted to gain his alliance against the other spouse. In the midst of this circuslike atmosphere, the children had been playing out their *tension-detonating* strategies once again and were more recently utilizing *loyalty-proving* strategies by resisting going over to the opposite-sex parent's house.

On hearing the mediator's report from school and analysis of the status of their conflict, the parents acknowledged the problems and proceeded to develop a modified plan, in which the children alternated houses every three weeks. Moreover, both parents explicitly agreed to check out any future complaints of the children with each other before getting angry and escalating their threats.

Five months later, Judith called the mediator and requested another session because the children were acting up again with both parents. She also said that the property settlement was nearing its conclusion, and the tension had been rising rapidly. Hearing this, the mediator decided that it was time to bring in the attorneys. He reasoned that he needed more leverage to encourage Harvey and Judith to stop fighting, and to effect a clear separation between child-sharing issues and property settlement issues, and he wanted to assist both the parents and the attorneys in doing this.

In this session with Harvey and Judith, their attorneys, and the children, all were able to hear the children's pleas for a cease-fire. There was no excuse to discount or ignore the children's needs. The attorneys agreed to settle the property issues swiftly and smoothly, and each sincerely emphasized to his client the importance of keeping the children out of their battle.

This session seemed to be a turning point, for a week after the new agreements were made, the property issues were settled and the children's behavior calmed down both at school and at home. The new mediation agreement included a reiteration of previous clauses for restraint from overreaction to the children's words and to each other, and a return to the scarcely tried alternating two-week plan for time-sharing.

Ten months later, the mediator received a call from Judith requesting another mediation session, because she and her new husband were moving out of state for several years, and she and Harvey needed to make new plans for sharing the children.

In this last session, the parents reported that the previous ten months had worked quite well. The children had adjusted, and Harvey and Judith had minimized their conflicts. After much calm and refreshingly rational discussion of the many possibilities for sharing the children, they came up with a plan that involved each child living with one parent through the school year, alternating parents every other school year, and both children living with one parent during the summers, alternating parents every other summer. Any future modifications would be made by the parents and with the assistance of a mediator, if necessary.

Although neither parent was completely satisfied with this plan, the children found it acceptable, and Harvey and

Judith could live with the compromise, since it was perfectly equal for both of them.

This case involved two parents whose argumentative and competitive style preceded their battles for custody and had the power of a whirlwind to draw into the battle anyone—children, attorneys, mediators—interested or concerned. It is exemplary of cases that have the elements for resolution but need *repeated* firm outside structure to control the conflicts. Within such a structure, the spouses can come to their senses and use reason to resolve their differences amicably rather than thwart each other. The mediator's task in this case was to offer a structure for communication and clarification of the children's needs and strategies; to help the attorneys cease encouraging the couple's antagonism; and to continuously refuse to ally with either side against the other.

Although Harvey and Judith both acknowledged each other's love for the children, they had some differences in parenting styles and child-rearing values which the children were quick to pick up on and use in their *tension-detonating* strategies. Harvey and Judith both acknowledged having difficulty being consistent in parenting, and they had much difficulty in communicating on their own, but with the structured guidance of a third party they were able to communicate quite well. Finally, compromise was always possible for them so long as they each achieved an exactly equal share of any resolution. And indeed, it was this style of compromise that allowed them to resolve each impasse in their custody fight.

This need for equality, however, had an unfortunate consequence for the children. In spite of the children's emotional closeness with each other, they had to agree to live separately through the school year in order to keep peace between their parents. The children's sacrifice was effective in resolving the parental dispute but questionably fair to the children.

Warren and Lorraine

Warren and Lorraine were married for five years and had been separated for two years at the time of mediation. Warren had three adopted children (aged eight, nine, and eleven at the time of mediation) from a previous marriage when he met Lorraine. They lived together for a year and then got married. Lorraine also had been previously married for a short time but had been unable to conceive a child. When Warren and Lorraine finally conceived Jill Ann (aged four at mediation), both were elated. Warren, a muscle-bound athlete who had been very worried about his virility, took this birth as evidence of his worthiness as a man. Lorraine, however, became increasingly disenchanted with Warren and with motherhood. She began to withdraw, feeling isolated and depressed. She claimed that Warren never paid any positive attention to her and that he controlled and intimidated her. Warren, by contrast, felt that he had no control over her. At the same time, however, he stated, "I allowed her to have her freedom."

Lorraine quietly left one day with Jill Ann. She left Jill Ann at her mother's house, filed divorce papers, and went on a three-week vacation with a man she had just met. Warren, who was quite distraught, immediately filed a petition for modification of custody and was awarded temporary custody of Jill Ann.

For the next two years, Jill Ann lived with Warren and his three children from the previous marriage and spent every weekend with Lorraine. During this period, Lorraine had two love affairs, with the second turning into a permanent relationship. Lorraine's new boyfriend, Gerry, had one child from a previous marriage who was two years older than Jill Ann. Lorraine, Gerry, and Gerry's child moved out of the area, about 130 miles away. Lorraine then requested that Jill Ann live with her and her new family and visit Warren on the weekends. Warren refused, Lorraine filed a petition for modification of custody, and the couple were referred to mediation.

In the first phone call with Warren, it became apparent that he had no concerns about Lorraine's parental competence and was not completely against Jill Ann living with her but was not about to let go of control too easily. As he put it, "Lorraine is not a bad mother, but she needs to settle down a bit more."

In the first phone call with Lorraine, the mediator was informed that Warren had told her that *she* should be raising her daughter because he was having a hard enough time raising his other three children. "But," she added, "he always has to be in control." She also indicated that Warren probably felt threatened by Gerry, because Warren felt that Gerry had taken her away from him.

Given this information, the mediator began the first session by presenting a long monologue in an attempt to *pre-empt* Warren's resistance to Jill Ann's moving to her mother's house. The reason for this was that it seemed to the mediator that both Warren and Lorraine were more inclined to have Jill Ann live with Lorraine than with Warren, but that both needed a gracious way out of the power struggle. Emphasis was placed on the need for young children to get to know *both* parents by spending lots of time with each. The mediator also talked about the difficulties of raising three children, the commendability of parental sacrifice in the best interests of a young child, and the importance of a child's settling into one area when he or she first enters school.

After the mediator gathered the marital history, Warren expressed his anger about Gerry. He felt that Gerry had interfered with every aspect of the divorce settlement, from meddling in their financial affairs to blocking communication between him and Lorraine. He said that until this day he had not been able to talk alone and freely with Lorraine because Gerry was always around "to put in his two cents!" As the discussion unfolded, it became clear that Lorraine had been using a *buffering* strategy and had orchestrated Gerry to block communications between her and Warren. She expressed again that she had always felt intimidated by Warren.

Warren's response to this was a power-assertion strategy of acting *holier than thou.* He went on to express more anger at Gerry and to declare that he was not about to let his daughter live with a woman who was unmarried and living with a man "in sin." In the same breath, he expressed rage about Gerry and smoothly adopted this holier-than-thou stance, and thus seemed immovable. Attempts by the mediator to deflect this comment were unsuccessful because Warren took a hard line on this point. However, because the mediator had prior knowledge that Warren might be open to Jill Ann's living with her mother, he returned the discussion to the apparently more central topic of Gerry. The mediator suggested that Warren and Gerry needed to get some financial issues cleared up so that Warren and Lorraine could talk more directly with one another. The session ended with a request for Warren, Lorraine, *and Gerry* to attend the second session.

In the first half of the second mediation session, Warren and Gerry talked out their financial difficulties and called a truce to their malice toward each other. However, still needing a sense of control over the pending child-sharing plans, Warren reasserted that he would not allow Jill Ann to live with an unmarried couple. At that point, Gerry and Lorraine announced that they were getting married within six months. With this face-saving news, Warren was given the opportunity to express his support for Lorraine's parenting of Jill Ann. He said, "Well, I'm greatly relieved to know this, and I think we can work out a plan now."

An agreement was then drawn up whereby both parents would share joint legal custody of Jill Ann and, until the following year when she was to begin school, Jill Ann would alternate living at each parent's house for two weeks at a time. It was not necessary to specify any further details, since both parents agreed that they would now be able to work out the details between themselves, including plans for the living situation during the school year.

One year later, three months before Jill Ann was to begin school, Warren informed the mediator that Jill Ann was doing fine but that Lorraine and Gerry had not yet married. At the suggestion of the mediator, Warren and Lorraine drew up and signed an agreement between themselves to the effect that at the time Jill Ann began school, she would live with Warren if Lorraine was still not married and with Lorraine if she was married. Included was a visitation schedule for weekends, holidays, and school vacations for the parent with whom Jill Ann was not residing. Three months later, one week before school was to begin, Warren happily informed the mediator that Lorraine and Gerry had finally married and Jill Ann would begin school at her mother's house.

Because from the first phone calls the mediator had implicit knowledge of both parents' desired resolution to this custody conflict, he was able to steer the negotiations directly to the real issue—the relationship between Warren and Gerry. Because of Lorraine's *buffering* strategy, Warren and Lorraine were unable to communicate directly and resolve their issues between themselves. Hence, Warren's need to save face and maintain control over Gerry's involvement focused inappropriately on Jill Ann.

Warren and Lorraine had basic respect for each others' parenting even though Warren had some minor concerns about Lorraine's parenting skills. They had no real disagreements about child-rearing values, except for Warren's face-saving concern over Lorraine's unmarried state. Moreover, because they had not been too inconsistent in their actions toward each other, they could communicate and compromise as long as nobody interfered, and as long as Warren felt some sense of control over the direction of such interactions.

Rod and Tanya

Rod and Tanya had been married for fifteen years and had two daughters who, at the time of mediation, were fifteen and twelve years of age. Tanya described how she and Rod had met on a blind date and she had got pregnant, so they married three months later. Tanya claimed that she had never wanted to be married to Rod and that she had felt unfulfilled and unhappy throughout the marriage. Rod, by contrast, said that he felt they had a very close relationship for the first four years, which then steadily declined in quality until the end.

When asked how they stayed together so long, Tanya replied that both of their families were strongly against divorce and that they wanted to stay together "for the children." They were able to tolerate each other because Rod, a university professor, was at his office and away from home much of the time. Rod added that he stayed away because whenever he tried to talk with Tanya, she would berate him. He felt that she had always resented him for her having to get married prematurely.

Tanya concurred and said that she never really wanted children, but that over time she grew to love her two girls. After three minor separations in the last two years of their marriage, Tanya asked Rod to leave permanently. It was a peaceful final separation and a relief to both of them. They mutually agreed to have the girls live with Tanya at the family residence through the school year and spend every weekend, vacation, and summer with Rod at his small rented house. One year later, Rod filed for divorce, and as part of their divorce settlement, Rod and Tanya agreed to seek mediation to work out a more permanent plan for sharing the children.

In the first phone call to each parent, the mediator learned that both parents had already talked with the girls and could represent their desires quite well. Moreover, both Rod and Tanya said that they had basically worked out a plan since agreeing to seek mediation, but that they needed assistance with several details and with an effective way to word their agreement.

In the first and only mediation session needed, the mediator very briefly set the context since it was apparent that the couple had already done most of the necessary preliminary work for reaching an agreement. He then got a brief background on their marital relationship and the circumstances of their divorce. It appeared that although they had had hostile interactions through the last few years of their marriage, they had since worked through most of these feelings and viewed their co-parenting relationship from a fairly positive perspective.

The mediator then asked them to describe their two children. Their descriptions were very realistic, with both positive and negative characteristics presented in a balanced way. Tanya then told how both their daughters had expressed a preference to live with their father for a while, because they had just spent a year living with their mother and wanted to "give dad a turn." Tanya accepted the girls' *fairness-seeking* strategy without much resistance, since she felt good about their relationship with her.

During negotiations between Rod and Tanya over living arrangements, Rod said that he would like to move into the family home with the girls, since that is where they would be most comfortable. Tanya agreed to this and also agreed to move into a house that was just a mile away from the family home so that the girls would have easy access to her home. She planned to attend school during the next year so that she would be employable and financially independent from Rod as soon as possible.

In their final mediation agreement, it was written that they would share joint legal custody of both girls and that the girls would spend Monday through Friday at Rod's house and Friday evening through Sunday at Tanya's house, unless they had other plans. Holiday plans were to be arranged between the parents, and they agreed to reevaluate the plan in a year's time. No further details were needed, since they felt quite able to negotiate those between themselves.

A follow-up a year later found things working well with the family. They agreed to keep the same arrangements for the next year, since Tanya was going to be very involved in her school program for another year or two. The only conflict that did arise had to do with where the girls would spend Thanksgiving, and they were able to resolve it with a family meeting.

This case was a very straightforward one, with clear-cut parental intentions, an absence of spousal strategies, cooperation and flexibility between the parents, and few discordant needs expressed by the children. Hence, the mediator had no need to utilize any counter-strategies and was able to facilitate an agreement in one session, simply through the structure of the mediation process.

11

Why Mediation Efforts Fail: Unsuccessful Cases

Theoretically and ideally, mediation should be effective for solving any conflict between two people. But such is not the case. There are a variety of disputes that will not be resolved by mediation even when the most sophisticated techniques are used by an experienced mediator. The elements contributing to failure in mediation include chronic hostility and mistrust between spouses which does not cease or ease up with structured intervention; strong religious, moral, or culturally based convictions on the part of at least one spouse, which lead to uncompromising beliefs about the needs of children even despite research and clinical evidence to the contrary; consistent allegations by one spouse of severe misconduct on the part of the other, including violence, substance abuse, and sexual abuse; consistent allegations by one spouse of the other's unfitness to parent for reasons of immaturity, neglectful or erratic behavior, or ambivalent intent to follow through on any mediated agreement; and refusal to abandon incompatible spousal strategies that lead to impasses.

Just as success of mediation has two possible definitions,

failure of mediation can also have two definitions. One definition indicates that failure is not developing a written and signed mediation agreement. A second definition indicates that failure is *not developing a written and signed mediation agreement, or developing a written and signed mediation agreement that breaks down over a relatively short period of time.* As indicated by the research cited in Chapter Ten, it appears that we need to apply this second, more rigorous definition.

Interestingly, in comparing couples who were unable to reach agreements in mediation with couples who were never exposed to mediation, Pearson and Thoennes (1982b) found that more couples in the first group resolved their disputes to some degree prior to their court hearings than in the second group. Hence it appears that in some cases, even when the mediation process per se has failed, something of the cooperative, compromising attitude implicit in mediation is retained by the spouses and benefits their future negotiations.

We will now explore five cases in which each of the elements of failure contributed in a primary way to preventing an agreement from being reached or to weakening the durability of an agreement that was reached.

Keith and Jessica

Keith and Jessica had been married for fourteen years and had been divorced for three years at the time of mediation. They had married each other when they were both teenagers and basically had grown up together. They raised three children, Richard, Robin, and Michael, who were fifteen, eleven, and eight years old, respectively, at the time of mediation. When the couple divorced, Keith retained sole legal and physical custody of Richard and Michael, and Jessica retained sole legal and physical custody of Robin. Very shortly, Jessica married a man with two young children of his own, and they had one more child together. Soon after that, Keith married a woman with one infant of her own, and they also had one more child together.

One year prior to mediation, Keith and Jessica had gone

to court in a custody battle over their oldest son, Richard, who had expressed a desire to live at his mother's house. Jessica won the court decision, obtained sole legal and physical custody, and Richard went to live with her. Over the next year's time, their younger son, Michael, became increasingly depressed and withdrawn and began telling his mother that he wanted to live with her and his brothers and sisters. Jessica took him to a therapist who then referred the couple to mediation.

In the first mediation session, after attempting to *preempt* resistance to sharing all the children, the mediator asked Keith and Jessica about their marital relationship. The story revealed a long history of intense struggles. After having raised each other since early adolescence, when they had run off together and had a baby, they had become very attached to each other. At the same time, they regularly had major conflicts over finances and over sharing. Through the years together their dependency on each other became stifling for Jessica, and she grew apart from Keith. This threatened Keith, and he responded by becoming more controlling and, as Jessica phrased it, "oppressive."

As soon as Jessica left, Keith became extremely resistant and mistrustful. Jessica reciprocated, and their communication over the next three years consisted of accusations, condemnations, and legal briefs. There was very little sharing of the children except for the limited and conditional visitation times set by the court.

When Richard, at age fourteen, made his bid to live at his mother's house, Keith accused Jessica of bribing Richard with leniency. After Richard moved, his father cut off all contact with him. Jessica felt that Keith was trying to hang on to the marriage by hanging on to the children. Keith felt that Jessica was too lenient and self-centered. He accepted the court's decision about Richard changing residences only because he felt Richard was probably old enough to make up his own mind. However, he felt very differently about Michael and said he was "not about to give up custody just because Jessica wanted it." Jessica then said that she would be willing to let Michael stay with Keith if that was what Michael wanted, but she explained, "Michael has been very unhappy at your house, and he wants to be at my house, because he misses his brothers and sisters." Keith then said, "He was perfectly happy at my house until you offered him a house with no discipline or rules, where he can do whatever he wants, whenever he wants." The mediator ended the first session at this point, and requested that the couple bring all three children to the next session.

Hoping to get some other perspectives on the history and current status of this dispute, the mediator began the second session by meeting with the children separately and together. Robin appeared to be happy with her living arrangement. She enjoyed staying at her mother's house "with all the other kids to play with," and she liked her alternate weekend visits with her father. Richard was less satisfied and bitterly angry at his father. He felt guilty for leaving his father but said he could not stand to live under his "controlling rule." He also felt very angry at his father for cutting off their relationship; he said, "I don't know why he has to act like such a shithead to me, just 'cause I wanted to live at my mom's house! I don't hate him, but I don't need him anymore. Michael does need him, but my father is holding Michael hostage—he won't let go of him."

Michael appeared very unhappy and forlorn. He said that he had wanted to live with his mother since he was in kindergarten. He did not talk much with his father about it because his father never listened to his feelings. When asked why he was now willing to talk about his desire more openly, Michael tearfully replied, "I love my dad, but he won't let me see my mom often enough, and I really miss my brothers and sisters. I guess I'll have to wait until I'm twelve, when a judge will listen to me."

From these interviews and other data, the mediator concluded that Michael's express desire to live with his mother was not strategically motivated but was genuine and of long duration. The mediator decided that Keith should hear Michael's needs from both the mediator and Michael. Moreover, he decided that if Richard were to express to Keith his own disappointment with the rigidity of Keith's parenting, then Keith might be able to hear Michael's needs more easily. So the mediator then met with Keith and the children alone. The children, reluctantly, told Keith their feelings and preferences for living arrangements, and Keith listened quietly. When the mediator asked Keith whether he had heard them, he said calmly, "Yes, I heard what they said."

Believing that negotiations could then begin, the mediator requested Jessica to join all of them in the room. The mediator first offered (for Keith's benefit) some prefatory remarks about the children's love for both parents and then summarized for Jessica what had been said earlier. He then requested proposals that would allow both parents to share more time with all the children. A number of proposals were offered by Jessica and none by Keith. When asked what *he* wanted, he said, "Just what I have now." When asked about Michael's desire to live at Jessica's house, Keith tried to *invalidate* the child's preference. He said to Jessica, "Michael has been perfectly happy at my house, and if you just stop bribing him and telling him he can stay at your house, he'll stop being in conflict about it and will accept it." He added, "You're not going to get *another* child away from me." On hearing this, Richard retorted, "But, dad, you're holding him hostage. He wants to be with us." Keith then said, "Look, Michael can be with his mother and you guys during visitation times, but the rest of the time he's going to be raised right."

The mediator then dismissed the children from the room and met with the parents alone. After the mediator suggested some mildly compromising options, Keith said, "I'm moving out of the area in about half a year. I'm willing to do some more sharing of the kids until then, but Michael's coming with me when I go." Hearing some room for compromise, the mediator ended the second session and requested a third session with the parents and their new spouses. This decision was based on earlier information that the new spouses were on better terms with each other than Keith and Jessica were with each other. Moreover, the mediator felt that adding a new perspective was the only hope for breaking the impasse.

To open the third session, the mediator asked the two stepparents what they understood to be going on. They each presented rational, objective views and both urged Keith to compromise on his position. A proposal was then offered whereby Jessica would retain sole physical custody of Richard, and both parents would share joint legal custody of all three children, and joint physical custody of Robin and Michael, with the two children alternating between their mother's and father's houses on a weekly basis for one year. At the end of that time, they would all return to mediation to renegotiate the agreement. Keith agreed to this proposal all too easily, which, interestingly, provoked resistance from Jessica. She hesitated and then said that she would have to think about it and would not sign it at that time. The session ended with a request for Jessica to inform the mediator of her decision within two weeks.

One week later, Jessica phoned the mediator and said that she could not trust Keith not to run off with the children or hold them both hostage once he got them and that she did not really want to give up sole custody of Robin because Keith might not really let go of Michael. However, she was willing to agree to joint legal custody for just six months, if it could automatically revert back to sole legal custody at the end of that time.

The mediator then phoned Keith, who indicated that he had had second thoughts about the proposal and would only agree if it was not legally binding, if Jessica paid all medical, dental, and tutoring bills for the children, and if sole legal custody of Michael were to remain with him. When the mediator shared Jessica's proposal, Keith said, "That's outrageous–if she can't trust me more than that, forget it." With this comment, further mediation efforts were suspended, as there was clearly no further room for any constructive negotiation.

For six months after mediation ended, Keith and Jessica continued to maintain the status quo on the time-sharing plan as their lawyers negotiated back and forth unsuccessfully. A court hearing was then held, and the judge ordered them to another round of mediation with a different mediator. After several unproductive sessions, the mediator gave up and referred the case back to court. Three months later, there was another court hearing to decide the custody matter. The judge talked with Michael, reviewed the case, and issued an order giving joint legal custody of all three children to Keith and Jessica and physical custody of all three children to Jessica, with visitations of every other weekend, one day during the week, and half the summer to Keith. However, Michael and Robin had been the only children visiting with their father, since Richard had consistently refused. Moreover, over the previous two months, Robin had been begging Jessica to help her cease her own visitations, as she too no longer wanted to see her father.

The chronic mistrust between Keith and Jessica apparently stemmed from their divorce. After being extremely dependent on Jessica, Keith experienced a deeply rooted hurt that left him feeling vulnerable and defensive. He was unable to appreciate the needs of the children, and he could only view Jessica's requests as evidence of her intention to hurt him further. Moreover, when he did venture out a bit toward compromise, Jessica instantly mistrusted his intent and blocked his proposal. This stalemate, cemented firmly in chronic mistrust, made mediation unworkable.

Ricardo, Angelina, and Grandma

Ricardo and Angelina, a Mexican-American couple, were married for three years and had one child, Maria, who was seven years old at the time of mediation. Never very close in their marriage, they just drifted apart, ending their relationship one day with Ricardo leaving Angelina and the infant Maria. Ricardo was gone for over two years and had no contact with Angelina or Maria. On his return, he found out that Angelina had given up legal and physical custody of Maria to her mother.

Ricardo set out to reestablish himself in Maria's life with visits every other weekend. Angelina continued visiting Maria one day every few months. Soon thereafter, Ricardo and Angelina each remarried and each had several more children. Maria continued to live with Grandma over the years and to get involved with many friends and many social activities.

One weekend, while preparing for his visit with Maria, Ricardo was told by Grandma that Maria refused to visit and that she was frightened to stay overnight at his house. Ricardo insisted on her coming with him. Grandma refused, and Ricardo then filed a petition for modification of custody. The court referred Ricardo and Grandma to mediation; Angelina was not interested in being involved and so was not included in the mediation.

In the first session, the mediator asked about the circumstances leading up to the present dispute. Ricardo told how Maria had come to live with Grandma. He added, "I have always wanted custody, but because I wasn't in a financial position to care for her, and because she really loved her grandma, I let her stay there." He then related how for the previous year Maria had been pulling away from him and withholding herself during visits. He said that at one point she did not want to stay two nights at his house as she had been doing for years and that she insisted on having a night-light on all night. Furthermore, he felt that Grandma had spoiled Maria, letting her be rude and childish, and had sabotaged visits with him. Finally, when Maria refused to visit, he decided to take legal action.

Grandma then explained that Maria felt pushed to act too grown up when at Ricardo's house and complained that he was not sensitive enough to her needs. Moreover she said that since she had raised Maria for almost all her life, a sudden move to her father's house would be traumatic for Maria, especially as Ricardo was planning to move several hundred miles away within a few weeks. The mediator ended the session at this point and requested that they bring Maria to the second session.

In planning the second session, the mediator wanted to find out how Maria really felt about each home and to what degree she seemed to be controlled by her grandmother and pushed by her father.

The mediator first interviewed Maria alone. She appeared easygoing and talked freely and comfortably, but her tone of voice and overall demeanor appeared somewhat babyish. She talked about the fear of the dark she had acquired in the previous few months and said that she greatly missed her grandma whenever she was at her father's house. When asked how it would be different for her if she lived at her father's house and visited her grandma, she said, "I wouldn't like it, but I guess it could be O.K. for a while."

Following this interview, the mediator concluded that Maria's behavior was probably expressing a normal regressive phase of development and a *separation-distress-reducing* strategy, aggravated by Grandma's reinforcement of her regressive behavior and resistance, on the one hand, and by Ricardo's pressure for more mature behavior, on the other. The mediator also concluded that Maria's grandmother had centered her life around Maria and was feeling threatened by the pending loss of the child from her life. Finally, it appeared that in addition to having a genuine concern for Maria's well-being, Ricardo may have sought sole custody partly to *assert power* and *appease his new spouse*. This latter strategy was suggested by Grandma in the first phone call, when she alleged that Ricardo wanted to take Maria so he would have "a built-in babysitter for his new wife's child."

The mediator then met with Ricardo and Grandma and attempted to *pre-empt* their possible strategies and to refocus them on Maria and her needs. After setting the context, the mediator indicated that Maria probably would prefer to stay primarily at her grandma's house but that she could handle sharing more extended time with each of them. Ricardo responded by saying that he had checked with the school that Maria would be attending if she lived at his house and found that she would attend school three months on and one month off throughout the year. He then offered to have Maria spend the off months with Grandma, but live primarily at his house.

Grandma refused this offer and pleaded with Ricardo to consider that such a major move might well make Maria more unhappy. She further pleaded with him to wait until Maria was older. Ricardo responded, "In the short run it probably will hurt her, but I'm thinking about the long run. If she's going to settle into a home with me and my wife, it seems to me the sooner the better."

The mediator then offered perspectives on the pros and cons of her moving and not moving. There was silence in the room for a minute. Then Grandma said, "I cannot let you take her. I'm willing to help her get more comfortable with your visits, but I'm not giving her up." Before the mediator could say anything further, Ricardo suddenly and definitely declared, "It is my *duty* as a father to take charge and raise my child. I will do what I have to do to make it happen." At this point, Ricardo got up, shook the mediator's hand, and said, "I believe we are finished talking." Further efforts to persuade him to stay and talk were futile. He had made up his mind.

A follow-up one year later revealed that shortly after mediation ended, Ricardo and his new wife had moved away and Maria had stayed with Grandma. The two lawyers negotiated a temporary visitation schedule for Ricardo of alternate weekends and additional days during the week. However, because of the distance, Ricardo had been seeing Maria only about one weekend per month. Because Ricardo and his wife had another baby, he had not pursued the court action regarding Maria, but he planned to follow through as soon as the court calendar and his schedule permitted it. He still maintained that he wanted primary custody of Maria.

Although Ricardo was willing to allow Maria to live with her grandma, he had gradually built up concern that his daughter was becoming estranged from him. At the point of her refusal to visit, he was faced with a difficult choice—whether to let her continue being raised by her grandma and risk the loss of his continuing influence on her development or to uproot her and resettle her into his own family, which would enable him to influence her as he so desired. After considering the options, Ricardo acted out of a sense of moral duty and did what he believed was right. This conviction, which was based partly in his Mexican-American cultural heritage, resulted in an uncompromising position, which, when confronted by Grandma's equally uncompromising stance, led to a situation in which mediation was almost destined to fail.

Such uncompromising positions are even more tenacious when a spouse has a deep *religious* conviction about how children "should" be raised. Attempting mediation with a spouse who has such fixed beliefs about parenting is frustrating for the mediator and usually futile for reaching a compromise resolution.

Floyd and Connie

Floyd and Connie had lived together for three years and had been separated for six months at the time of mediation. Though never married to each other, they did have one child together, Joey, who was eighteen months old at the time of mediation.

Both Floyd and Connie had previously been married. Floyd had been married for four years; during that marriage a child was born to his wife, who later claimed the child was fathered by another man. Floyd had a custody suit still in progress from that relationship since he wanted to have paternity rights and custody of the child. Within two months of breaking up with Connie, Floyd married another woman, Dorie, who had been and continued to be best friends with Connie.

Connie's previous marriage had also produced a child, whom she brought to the relationship with Floyd. This child's father had cut off all contact with Connie and the child after the divorce and had not been heard from since. The child considered Floyd to be her father, but Floyd had no legal claim to custody or visitation with her. Within a week of separating from Floyd, Connie moved in with her new boyfriend, Roy, taking Joey and her own child with her.

In the first phone call, Floyd told the mediator that he had filed a petition to get sole custody of Joey after he had heard reports from mutual friends that Roy was a drug dealer and was often under the influence of both drugs and alcohol when with Joey. Floyd said that when he heard these reports he became furious. He told the mediator, "If I ever get more reports on Roy doing drugs around my boy, I'll kill him." He added, "Connie got a restraining order on me for fear that I would beat him up. . . . [chuckle] She has no idea how far I would actually go to protect my son."

Floyd then launched a ten-minute monologue on the investigatory resources that he had developed—a veritable network of espionage tactics, from electronic bugging devices to private investigators and high-powered lawyers working for him. He also claimed that Connie had been involved in grand larceny, breaking and entering, and welfare fraud and had had the nerve to accuse *him* of welfare fraud. He added, "I've only seen my son three times in the last six months because she always had Roy give me some excuse as to why he couldn't come with me. She's not going to get away with that anymore. I've got folders on her activities now from my investigator's surveillance of her."

At this point, the mediator used *reflective listening* and said, "Sounds like you are quite suspicious of Connie," to which Floyd replied, "Not really, I'm just mad at her boyfriend. I think that Connie is a very good mother, but her boyfriend isn't going to get away with this crap!" The mediator then ended the phone conversation, concluding that although Floyd sounded angry and paranoid, he still had some respect for Connie's parenting skills and that it might be possible to neutralize his *power assertion* strategy.

The mediator then phoned Connie. She told the mediator that Floyd always overreacted to everything and that she was very frightened of him because he had a history of violent behavior, adding that he had been in prison for six years for dealing and using heroin. She said she could not understand why he wanted custody of Joey, since he had never shown much interest in Joey before. Connie ended the conversation by asking to be allowed to come to the session fifteen minutes early so that she would not have to be in the parking lot at the same time that Floyd was there.

On the day of the first session, the mediator checked the parking area fifteen minutes before the scheduled appointment time to make sure Connie arrived safely. However, she had not yet arrived. Feeling quite concerned, the mediator experienced a psychological jolt when Floyd and Connie arrived at the scheduled time in the same car. The mediator then hypothesized that Connie's expressed fear was primarily a tactic to prejudice the mediator in her favor.

Proceeding as usual in the first session, the mediator emphasized a bit more than usual the impact of mistrust between parents on children's well-being and lightly explored their pre-separation relationship and previous marriages.

Floyd and Connie both gave details of their previous relationships and of the quiet nature of their own breakup. Floyd was well-mannered and appeared in good control as he expressed his concerns about Joey's safety when with Connie and Roy and his anger about the frustrated visitation attempts. Connie matter-of-factly explained that both she and Dorie, his new wife, were concerned about his violence. Floyd said, "Well, I admit, I *have* lost my temper a bit at times, but I would never hurt Joey." Connie then said, "It's true that he doesn't get violent with children, only with adults, and mostly with close family members. But he also tries to get power over people through legal channels whenever he gets mad about something." Floyd admitted this, proudly. He boasted of all the lawsuits in which he had been involved and of his legal resources, knowledge, and friends. Then he said, with a big, confident smile, "Sometimes the law is real good for getting done what you want, but sometimes I just have to take the law into my own hands."

After some more discussion, the mediator felt it was an appropriate time to request proposals for time-sharing. Floyd responded with a well-thought-out plan, which included having Joey every other weekend and alternate holidays. He once again declared that he respected Connie as a mother and wanted her to continue as Joey's primary caretaker. He added several other clauses that gave him access to medical and school information. He also wanted to be able to talk directly with Connie and not have to deal through Roy, and he wanted a doctor's note if Joey was not able to participate in a visitation. Finally he reprimanded Connie for exposing Joey to drugs and reminded her that even though he himself was "clean" of drugs now, he knew well how the drug world operated, adding "so don't try to bullshit me about it!" Connie said that she needed time to think about Floyd's proposal, so the mediator ended the session and scheduled another for two weeks later.

Five minutes before the second session was scheduled to begin, Connie suddenly entered the mediator's office as he was saying good-bye to his earlier client. She told the mediator that she needed to talk to him right away. He invited her to sit down, but she could not, as she was shaking convulsively and sobbing. Hardly able to speak, she explained that Floyd was with her in the waiting room and was threatening to kill her. She said he had sat down next to her and said, "I'm gonna put you six feet under unless you give up Joey to me. I'm gonna get him from you." She added, "I think he'll really do it." After ten minutes, she was still shaking like a leaf and said, sobbing, "I am too afraid to be in the same room with him—may I please go out the back door and leave before he does? There's no point in my staying, anyway, because my lawyer told me not to agree to *any* visitations at all."

The mediator allowed her to leave, then asked Floyd to enter his office. He talked with Floyd about Connie's fear and about her choice to leave, and Floyd said, smiling, "Well, I'm gonna get her in court, then." He rattled on for another fifteen minutes, boasting again of his control of a vast network of legal resources. The mediator, feeling physically intimidated by this aggressive, threatening, six-foot five-inch man, verbally supported Floyd's efforts to use the legal system and all his obvious skill at it to get what he felt he deserved. He then tactfully ushered Floyd out of the office as soon as it was possible. The mediator then alerted the judge in the case about the present danger of violence from Floyd and officially referred the case back to court.

A follow-up six months later found that there had been five court hearings since the end of mediation. Less than five days after mediation ended, there had been a court hearing in which Floyd was ordered to refrain from harassing Connie. One month later, at the custody hearing, Connie was awarded sole legal and physical custody of Joey, and Floyd was given one weekend daytime visit per week, to be supervised by a third party. A third court hearing a month later was held for Connie's petition alleging sexual molestation by Floyd; after an investigation, the court found Floyd not guilty. A fourth court hearing was held two months later on Floyd's petition alleging that Connie was involved with drug use. This resulted in a court order for a restraint from use of drugs (by Connie). This was followed one month later by a fifth court hearing, on Connie's petition alleging that Floyd was making more threats of violence. The court issued another order for restraint from harassment, with more detailed conditions. It certainly appeared that Floyd and Connie would be spending considerable amounts of time and money in the future carrying out their ongoing battle in the courts.

What appeared early in the mediation process as usual strategic maneuvers on the part of Connie and Floyd for leveraging their respective positions turned out to be very serious threats of harm, which were not possible to mediate. Floyd's alleged history of violence was corroborated by his delusional-sounding monologues about his power. Such intimidation on the part of one spouse does not leave any room for reasonable compromise on the part of the other. Moreover, when there is a real risk to the physical safety of either a parent or the children, as in cases of alleged violence, sexual abuse, and sometimes substance abuse, the mediator cannot conscionably ignore the problem. Moreover, mediation efforts in such circumstances are an empty exercise because the level of mistrust typically is far too great for the couple to agree to any sort of unsupervised co-parenting arrangement. Finally, the mediator is faced with the added moral difficulty of trying to be an advocate for the child while also facilitating a compromised mediation agreement. A further discussion of these dilemmas is presented in Chapter Twelve.

Brad and Jocelyn

Brad and Jocelyn were twenty-two and twenty years old, respectively, at the time of mediation. They had lived together for one and one-half years and had married just four months before mediation. Their stated reason for getting married was to establish paternity for their child, Monique, who was one year old at the time of mediation. Three months after getting legally married, Brad backed out and they agreed to get a divorce, with Jocelyn retaining custody of Monique. Jocelyn began to carry out a self-divorce procedure from a book and then decided instead to hire a lawyer and take care of her divorce through the courts. On being notified of the formal divorce hearing, Brad initiated a *point-counterpoint* retaliation strategy and filed a petition for sole custody. At the hearing, the judge ordered the couple to mediation.

In the first phone call Jocelyn told the mediator that she was against Monique's staying overnight at Brad's house because it was dirty, crowded, and unsuitable for a child. She added, "Brad is just getting revenge. He would accept reasonable visitation if I had gone through with the self-divorce, but because I changed my mind and went through the court, he wants to hassle me." She then said, "We've been getting along fine in the past two months. I've been bringing Monique over to see him on all my days off."

On calling Brad, the mediator was informed, "We get along very well—there's no problem—we'll probably get back together, but until we do I just want to make sure that I see my daughter."

Brad and Jocelyn arrived in the same car for the first (and only) mediation session. They were very friendly with each other, giggling, joking, and sitting very close to one another. They told how they met at a party, dated for a year, then decided to get Jocelyn pregnant. However, after the baby was born, Brad initiated several separations.

Jocelyn pointed out that Brad had had three other children by two other women, none of whom he had ever visited. During their own relationship, Brad lived with two other women off and on during separations and may have fathered another child. She said her own parents did not like Brad "because he was irresponsible and could never hold a job and because he was cheatin' on me." She added that she had not trusted Brad for some time, but then said, "It might change though, 'cause he's been faithful for five months now."

While Jocelyn was speaking, Brad sat smiling in his chair. He seemed to be proud of his exploits and smug about Jocelyn's "hanging in there" with him. He teased Jocelyn flirtatiously, as if he were a courting teenager, and said, "We're going together now." When the mediator asked what he meant, Jocelyn smiled and said "We're dating each other again and seeing a lot of each other. I come over with the baby nearly every night, but I won't let the baby stay there overnight alone."

At this point, it appeared to the mediator that there was little he could do for this couple except help them discuss their future plans a bit more, which they did, and then request proposals for sharing Monique until they decided on the direction of their relationship.

Brad agreed to Jocelyn's request that Monique not stay alone with him overnight. He did insist, though, that he see Monique at least three days every week. Jocelyn smiled at Brad, affectionately slapped his arm, and said flirtatiously, "Come on, you *know* I come over more than *that*!" Brad and Jocelyn then proceeded to work out a fairly detailed plan of holiday sharing, splitting each holiday in such a way that Monique spent a sizable period of time with each parent. Moreover, they decided that Jocelyn and Monique would come over to Brad's house at least three days a week and that Brad, Jocelyn, and Monique would spend Saturdays together. Brad, Jocelyn, and the mediator all signed the agreement, and the couple walked out smiling and joking with each other. The mediator assumed that the young couple would probably reconcile and the agreement seemed a satisfactory interim plan until that time.

Two and a half weeks later, Jocelyn called the mediator and asked, "Can I break the agreement that Brad and I made? Brad said he's not going to pay me child support." The mediator urged her to stick with the agreement and to contact her attorney regarding the child support payments. She also was encouraged to return to mediation if the difficulties continued. However, Jocelyn replied, "We can't—Brad laughed at me when I suggested that, and said that he's not going back to no mediator—that he doesn't need to."

A follow-up a year later found that within a month after mediation ended, Brad had stopped seeing Monique and Jocelyn and had had two other girlfriends since. Jocelyn said that that was fine with her and that Monique was doing well, "as long as he doesn't come around and we don't have to argue." She added, "Brad is very irresponsible—I knew he couldn't follow through on the agreement. I don't believe he even cares about his child."

The immaturity of this young couple prevented them from consistently following through on a time-sharing plan. The mediator at first believed that because they seemed to have some degree of positive feeling for one another, there was a chance they could carry out a basic time-sharing plan. However, the inconsistency of their feelings for each other prevented this plan from working.

Immature parents intent on retaliation can sabotage mediation efforts by blocking any compromises. Alternatively, their ambivalence in following through on any commitment can prevent an agreement from being honored. Such parents appear not to have the experience or the emotional flexibility necessary to consistently set the needs of their children higher than their own needs.

Frederick and Michelle

Frederick and Michelle had been married for seven years and separated for six months at the time of mediation. During their marriage they had one child, Erica, who was three years old at the time of mediation.

Frederick was a man of wealth and power who came from a long-established New England family. He had, for the most part, got all that he wanted of worldly things—travel, possessions, comfort. During five of the seven years of his marriage, he had had extramarital affairs. Always feeling emotionally distant from Michelle, he had hoped to fill the void by being involved with other women, but he never quite felt fulfilled. He then attempted to get closer to Michelle by "giving her a baby." As he put it, "The baby was my last hope to get closer to Michelle." However, the baby just consumed more of Michelle's time and emotional attention, so Frederick continued his affairs.

At the time that Erica turned two and a half, Michelle found out about Frederick's longest and latest affair and announced that she and Erica were leaving. Six months later she filed for divorce. During those six months, Frederick made numerous pleas to Michelle to reconsider her decision. She became increasingly angry and resentful of him, and she pulled away even more. Transferring Erica was always accompanied by the same scene—Frederick pleading with Michelle to come back home, and Michelle screaming at Frederick to leave her alone. During these scenes, Erica would wind up crying hysterically and clinging to whichever parent she had just left.

After a two-month period of relative calm, Frederick decided to seek sole custody of Erica. This decision was made right after Erica initiated what appeared to the mediator to be a *parent-esteem-protecting* and *reuniting* strategy. She told Frederick in one of his most vulnerable moments that she did not want to live with her mother. Frederick then told Michelle of his decision and suggested that he might consider changing his mind if she agreed to have Erica evaluated by a child psychologist to find out whether she was being damaged by her mother. Michelle agreed to this and contacted a psychologist, who referred her to mediation. Both Frederick and Michelle consented to explore their situation with a mediator. Frederick added that he believed it would take "about a dozen sessions."

After gathering some initial information, the mediator concluded that Frederick was following a reuniting strategy in *pursuing sole custody* and *requesting extended mediation.*

During the first session, Frederick continually talked about the good times in the marriage, appealing to Michelle to change her mind about going through with the divorce and retaining sole custody of Erica. However, for each pleasant memory that Frederick brought up, Michelle would bring up two unpleasant ones. As the discussion progressed, Michelle became increasingly agitated and soon began an emotionally disengaging strategy of *invalidating* her ex-spouse by telling the mediator that Frederick knew nothing about parenting, that he had no empathy for children, and that he basically had little to offer Erica himself, save what his servants would do for her. At this point the mediator diverted the conflict and ended the session. The second session was scheduled for three weeks later, and the couple were given the task of considering a time-sharing plan that would work until they could decide on a long-term plan.

In the second session, Frederick announced that he had thought about the situation further and decided that since Erica really loved and needed her mother, she should have the chance to be with her on a frequent basis. He said he was willing to share joint custody with Michelle and pointed out that they would thus be able regularly to share information about her with each other. On hearing this, Michelle bristled with fury. Apparently, Frederick was now initiating a new reuniting strategy of *pursuing joint custody,* so as to guarantee frequent contacts between him and Michelle. Michelle immediately said firmly, "I too have thought this over and have decided that you can have physical custody of Erica if you insist, but there will be some definite conditions that you will have to follow. I will not share custody with you—either you accept *me* taking custody or *you* take custody."

Michelle's strategy of *taking or giving sole custody* was her desperate attempt to disengage from Frederick. In response, Frederick pleaded with Michelle not to be so harsh, that Erica needed both of them working together: "If you won't come back home, then let's make it easier on our daughter by sharing her." Attempting to call his bluff, Michelle again said, "I will share Erica, but I will not share you. Tell me your decision—either you take her or I'll take her." Frederick hesitated and then said, "I cannot decide that now; we need more mediation sessions to talk about it further. I'm sure that we can reach a compromise." Michelle responded, "There will be no further compromises, and I will not participate in any further sessions here because they are a waste of time—you make up your mind what you want and let me know."

Michelle then said that she was leaving and that she needed to hear Frederick's decision within the next week. The mediation efforts thus ended. Two weeks later the mediator received a call from Frederick informing him that Michelle had tried to force him to decide too quickly and that he could not decide, so they were going to have the matter settled in court.

A follow-up one year later found that several months after mediation efforts ended, the couple had had a full probation evaluation completed. Then, in their court hearing, they were awarded joint legal custody, with physical custody to Michelle (because she had been Erica's primary caretaker) and reasonable visitation to Frederick, consisting of alternate weekends, alternate holidays, and two weeks in the summer. Frederick's attorney also managed to include a stipulation that Erica would be administered a psychological evaluation yearly to assure that Erica was not being psychologically harmed by living with her mother.

During the year after the court hearing, Frederick had made several more pleas to Michelle to reunite but had become somewhat less persistent over time. Moreover, Michelle was more able to refrain from overreacting to these pleas, and she managed to minimize communication with Frederick about anything except the barest necessities of Erica's life.

Because Frederick wanted to reconcile with Michelle, he could not accept her decision to divorce. Instead, he attempted a variety of reuniting strategies aimed at coercing Michelle to interact with him and at taking control over what she wanted (namely, Erica) unless she agreed to reunite.

Because of Michelle's desperate need to disengage, she was willing to sacrifice control over Erica just to keep apart from Frederick. Although she knew that she probably would be able to call his bluff in initiating her strategy of *taking or giving sole custody,* there was a decided risk involved. She did make it clear, though, that her intention was to disengage permanently.

If Frederick had accepted Michelle's decision to be apart from him and had not pushed so hard for reunion, or if Michelle had been more able to tolerate and resist his efforts, a workable compromise might have been achieved. However, because the complementary strategies of reuniting and disengaging were so strongly polarized, there was no room for compromise and therefore no mediated settlement.

12

Special Circumstances Affecting Mediation

In the normal course of mediation work, the mediator encounters a number of issues that present a special challenge to both the mediator and the local courts of jurisdiction. In this chapter, we will discuss some of the more important of these issues.

Visitation Disputes

Not infrequently a couple is referred to mediation for a dispute over visitation but not over custody. In these situations, the mediator must alter his or her approach to some extent. A number of factors must be considered before mediation begins, including the context of the dispute, the local jurisdictional options available to the couple, and the limits placed on those options by the couple's knowledge, needs, and desires.

Occasionally, as the mediation process unfolds and the spouses come to understand why their time-sharing arrangements have become difficult, they appear much more receptive to a joint custody arrangement. Where joint legal and/or physical custody is a legal possibility within the court's jurisdiction of the couple's dispute, the mediator may be facing a real dilemma. If the mediator restricts his scope to visitation issues and does not present the joint custody option, then the children will lose the potential benefit of a joint custody arrangement. Of course, if the parents are not dissatisfied with a sole custody arrangement, then the dilemma is minimal.

However, if the mediator does expand the custody options available and discusses their benefits, then he or she may unwittingly threaten the custodial parent, who may have appeared receptive but was actually not expecting anything but visitation matters to be discussed. That parent may then become very resistant, forcing the other parent into an antagonistic position and setting off a true custody battle.

The situation is further complicated when the visiting parent has never even known that he might be able to obtain joint legal custody and/or joint physical custody if he simply requested it. Fathers, particularly, are often in this position because, never hearing anything to the contrary, they assume that the tradition of the visiting father is still the only available option. If the mediator educates the father within the mediation context about the other options, he or she is guaranteed to upset the delicate equilibrium between the parents and risks generating more conflict between them as a result. This dilemma must be confronted anew with each case of a visitation dispute.

In expanding the custody options, even when it results in a workable joint custody arrangement, the mediator also might unwittingly antagonize the judge and either or both attorneys. Some judges may feel that the mediator oversteps his or her boundaries in altering custody arrangements when not specifically requested to do so. And some attorneys may resent a mediator for persuading their clients to compromise without the attorneys either controlling or at least directly stipulating to such a modification. Moreover, an attorney might also experience a backlash effect when his or her client on second thought complains of feeling coerced into a shared custody arrangement.

Disputes over visitation are frequently much more difficult for the mediator than are custody disputes. Whereas the majority of custody disputes arise within the divorce proceedings relatively soon after the marital separation, visitation disputes typically reach mediation years after the divorce. A fundamental difference between these situations is that in custody disputes the parties are relatively equal in their initial bargaining positions (notwithstanding severe imbalances in their respective parenting skills, involvement, or circumstances), whereas in visitation disputes, the balance in bargaining power is typically rather skewed. The custodial parent has already unilaterally captured the affections of the child and may well be sabotaging visitations of the other parent. Wallerstein and Kelly's research confirmed that nearly half the children in their research sample "witnessed intensely antagonistic exchanges between parents at the time of visiting [so that] it seemed to some youngsters that crossing a mined field was the prerequisite for reaching the absent fathers" (1980, p. 141). Such hostility frequently reached such a point that the children would refuse to visit. As Wallerstein and Kelly further noted, "The mothers of each of the girls refusing to visit had powerful holds over their daughters, and the girls' own sadness and anger at being abandoned by the father resonated and meshed with the mothers' outrage at being similarly abandoned, creating insurmountable barriers for their fathers" (p. 137).

Hence, by the time these couples reach mediation for visitation disputes, the visiting parent typically feels powerless and at the mercy of the custodial parent. As a result, the pre-empting monologue for setting the context in custody disputes is inappropriate for visitation disputes unless it is desirable to discuss the custody arrangement as well. The context must be set according to the range of options that it is feasible to consider.

In addition to feeling powerless, the visiting parent also is frequently placed in the position of having to *prove* that he or she is worthy of increased visitation. As a result of a combination of factors, the previously designated schedule of visitation may not have been followed. The visiting parent usually sees this as evidence of sabotage by the other parent. But the custodial parent may see it as evidence of the visiting parent's irresponsibility, lack of consistency, and lack of genuine interest in the children. There may be evidence to support one or both positions, but because the visiting parent is already in a weaker position, the burden of proof usually lies with him or her.

The mediator, then, is faced with the onerous task of dealing with the needs of the children for regular, continuing, and (if possible) frequent contact with both parents within the context of an obvious imbalance in bargaining power. Awareness of this dilemma can prevent the mediator from causing a major crisis as he or she tries to equalize the imbalance between the parents.

When a Parent Moves Away

Mediating custody disputes when one parent is moving a long distance away from the other brings up a number of special considerations. The idea of large geographic separations typically represents a major threat to all the family members. As Ricci (1980, p. 206) noted, "There are two bottom lines to big geographic separations. First, distance feels final, and gives tangible proof that the parents are separated. If one member of the family has harbored, however unconsciously, a sense that the old family feeling or the old marriage was not finished, long distance will bring that hope painfully to the surface. Second, the physical separation hurts. Many miles means no way to hug, to brush back a forelock of hair, to drop in on football practice, or to watch a first book report being written. The parent separated from the child feels this pain and so does the child."

The threat represented by a major move increases the probability of an escalation of the parents' and children's strategies. The mediator must assess the motives and reactions of the family members extra carefully, since the stakes are higher for all concerned.

As part of this assessment, the mediator needs to know the intentions and circumstances of the parent's decision to move. If the move is being made for a legitimate reason such as employment, the mediator can proceed with facilitating an agreement. MacGowan (1981) points out that such unimpeachable reasons for moving probably would not sway a court to impose sanctions. If, however, the parent cannot give a valid reason for moving, or the reason is to get far away from the other parent, then the mediator should alert the parent to the legal and psychological consequences of such a move. The legal consequences, of course, will vary, depending on the particular jurisdiction. In California, for example, under the joint custody law the parent more willing to share the child is preferred: "In making an order for custody to either parent, the court shall consider, among other factors, which parent is more likely to allow the child or children frequent and continuing contact with the non custodial parent" (see Appendix A).

The psychological consequences of a prolonged separation from a parent (as discussed in Chapters One and Three) should be discussed with both parents. Particularly if the move is motivated by bitter feelings, the child could suffer greatly. Without the opportunity to communicate and maintain regular contact with the absent parent, the child can easily misinterpret a distant move as sure evidence of rejection and abandonment. The parent who is moving needs to be fully informed of these consequences. Not uncommonly, after hearing about these factors the parent is persuaded to delay or even terminate the plans for moving. Moreover, by presenting these consequences in the presence of both parents, the mediator can effectively dissuade geographic moves that are based upon poor reasons, by indirectly providing the remaining spouse with leverage for retaining a continuing relationship with his or her children.

If the move is being made for valid reasons, the mediator must then consider the ages, preferences, and needs of the children involved, the nature of the parent-to-parent and parent-to-child communication that will be possible over a distance, and the financial circumstances for supporting such communication, whether by phone calls, letters, or travel.

With school-age and older children, time-sharing must depend first of all on a plan for spending the school year at one home. Periods of more extended contact with the other parent can be found primarily in summer, Christmas, and Easter vacations. Individual differences among children should be assessed so as to maximize good matches of temperament, interests, available resources, and other factors (as discussed in Chapter Three). With these factors in mind, the parents can proceed to make a plan to last a year or two, with periodic reevaluations built in to protect the needs of the children.

With infants and preschool children, the decisions become much more difficult. Questions arise such as: At what age is it advisable for a very young child to stay with a noncustodial parent for the whole summer? What are the consequences for a ten-month-old infant of being away from its primary caretaking parent for four weeks? How often should a custodial parent call a three-year-old child when the child is with the visiting parent for six weeks, given that this is the only contact during the year with the visiting parent? Many of these questions are the very ones asked of mental health professionals when called to testify in court. The answers are quite complex since they involve a wide range of variables, beginning and ending with the support and explanations offered the child by the parents.

A central task for the mediator in dealing with issues regarding very young children is to emphasize the importance of supportive communications between the parents and to try to optimize such communication. Moreover, it could be argued that if two parents are genuinely respectful and supportive of each other's importance to their child, they can make *any* sharing arrangement work well for their child. And to the degree that this ideal is less attainable, the mediator must help to build structures that will safeguard the child's emotional and psychological well-being.

For an excellent set of guidelines for facilitating coparenting when one parent moves far away, the reader is referred to Isolina Ricci's very practical book, *Mom's House, Dad's House* (1980, chap. 15).

Stepparents and Grandparents

Inclusion of stepparents and grandparents in the mediation process offers additional possibilities for resolving deadlocks and for maintaining agreements that are reached. However, the inclusion of extended family members entails certain risks, and both risks and benefits must be duly considered before deciding whether and how to include them in the mediation process.

Stepparents frequently play a significant role in the lives of children and parents of divorce. If the circumstances of the remarriage are positive—as is more often the case when the remarriage is not a contributing factor to the divorce and occurs a substantial length of time after the divorce—then the stepparent can become a helpful ally to the new mate. By offering a more neutral perspective and a leveling of the spouse's emotions, the stepparent can facilitate the negotiation process. The stepparent can also help the children by listening dispassionately to them and supporting them through the stresses of divorce. The stepparent can also provide alternative, and sometimes more constructive, parenting practices to supplement those of the children's parents. And finally, the stepparent may become an ally of the ex-spouse. Not infrequently, for example, a stepmother can offer the children's mother help in dealing more effectively with the father.

Generally, stepparents who play a positive role in the lives of the disputants are best utilized in the mediation process at the point of an impasse where other mediator strategies are unsuccessful. Bringing them in as consultants to the mediator can provide the fresh perspectives needed to reach an agreement. Moreover, it is tempting to speculate that including stepparents in the mediation process may facilitate the maintenance of the agreement over time.

Several factors, however, suggest that a mediator should be cautious about including stepparents in the mediation process. First of all, it is not uncommon for a spouse to divorce his or her mate specifically in order to remarry. In such circumstances, the stepparent may be scapegoated by the other spouse and the children. If, for example, the stepparent is viewed as "the other woman," including her in the mediation process may escalate the antagonism between the parents.

Second, a stepparent may be the force behind a petition for modification of custody. If, for example, a father petitions for sole custody as a strategy for appeasing his new spouse, the other parent usually suspects so and becomes suspicious of and openly hostile to the stepparent. Bringing them together in the mediation room would then be counterproductive.

Third, if only one parent is remarried, including that parent's new mate in a session with both parents may imbalance the negotiation process so that the single parent feels outnumbered and intimidated. This also will increase resistance and decrease the probability for reaching a mediated settlement.

Similarly, grandparents who have been significantly involved in the lives of the children can offer a mature perspective to the couple and serve as family consultants to the mediator. In this role, they express an historic tradition in families, offering experienced advice on how to conduct one's life, how to raise children, and how to relate as marital partners. Unfortunately, grandparents can also be less than ideal in their contributions to custody disputes. If they have taken sides with their respective children, they simply add to the adversarial atmosphere. They each are then viewed by the opposing parent as a judgmental enemy. If grandparents become overinvolved with the custody battle, the mediator needs to think twice before inviting them into the mediation process.

Parental Sexual Conduct

Historically, the sexual conduct of parents has heavily influenced awards of child custody. Trial courts generally have frowned on forms of sexual behavior or sexual relationships that did not conform strictly to societal norms. However, with the recent trend among trial courts to liberalize their attitudes, parental behavior that used to be considered immoral and clear grounds for denial of custody to a particular parent is weighted less heavily in court decisions (Fainer and Wasser, 1978).

Nevertheless, the mediator not infrequently encounters the issue of sexual conduct in the form of allegations by one parent against the other. Several specific concerns are regularly expressed.

It is not uncommon for one spouse to deny or resist overnight visitation of a child with the other spouse because that spouse is cohabiting with a lover while unmarried (see the case of Warren and Lorraine in Chapter Ten). Such concern can spring from a religious conviction that this kind of relationship is sinful, or a fear that such a relationship is psychologically harmful to children, or any of a number of strategic motives such as reuniting, emotionally disengaging, power asserting, and retaliation.

If the concern stems from a religious conviction, then the other spouse will usually respect it. The mediator must respect such convictions in *all* cases or forfeit neutrality. One cannot persuade a person, with logic, to give up or suspend a deep religious belief.

If the concern is about psychological harm to the children, the mediator can probe the specific worries and present pertinent information about how children experience a parent who has a new mate. This information should include the fact that children at different ages will experience the very same objective event in radically different ways and that because of the wide range of individual differences among children, different children of the same age also will have very different experiences of the same event. Moreover, the significance to a child of a circumstance such as parental cohabitation is largely a function of what it does and does not mean for the child. For example, a young child may interpret his father's sleeping with a woman to mean that his mother is no longer his mother and therefore does not love him any longer. Or a child may interpret her mother's sleeping with a man to mean that the mother will not care for her any longer. If both of the child's parents were to explain clearly and periodically that cohabitation does *not* mean that the child is unloved, will no longer be provided for, or will lose one of his parents, then the child could well accept cohabitation as a reality of life.

If the other parent's allegations about cohabitation are strategically motivated, they will tend to diminish in importance as other issues are dealt with. By not drawing too much attention to such concerns during the mediation process, the mediator can discern the sincerity of the parent's concern. If the concern holds up consistently through the first phases of the mediation process, then it should be faced squarely and dealt with in terms of its motivation.

As one immediate result of a marital separation, a spouse may begin to express his or her sexuality flagrantly more openly than he or she did in the marriage. Partly out of a need to "bust free" of the restraints of the marital bond, and partly out of a need to prove that one is still sexually attractive, a parent may engage in openly affectionate and overtly sexual behavior with a date or new mates in the presence of the children.

Typically, the other spouse finds out about such sexual conduct from the children after they return home from spending time with the other parent. Children may report such behavior out of several motives, depending on their developmental stages. A preschool child may feel jealous of the intimate attention being given to the other person and worry about not getting enough attention and love for himself. An older child may simply feel embarrassed or confused about the nature of such intimacy. A young teenager may feel overly excited and stimulated at seeing overt displays of sexuality and may report the incident as "disgusting" or "gross" in an attempt to defend psychologically against his or her own sexual impulses. An older teenager may view such behavior with contempt because it represents a blatant betrayal by one parent of the other parent. Lastly, children may express concern about such behavior out of such strategic motives as reuniting the parents, detonating tension, and proving loyalty.

In planning the best way to handle such concerns, the mediator must carefully assess the children's concerns developmentally, as well as the accusing parent's motives. As with the cohabitation issue, a parent may make allegations of sexual indiscretion out of a variety of strategic motives as well as out of genuine concern for the welfare of the children. Solid developmental information given to both parents about children's interpretations of adult sexuality should alleviate or put into perspective unwarranted worries and should inform the sexually expressive parent about the benefits to children of showing discretion. Agreements to refrain from overt sexual expression in the presence of children can be helpful in minimizing such concerns in the future. Unfortunately, however, the accused parent will frequently deny such allegations, which forces the other parent to choose between trusting the parent and trusting the children. The mediator can also sometimes help to clarify incidents and interpretations that have been distorted, so that the negotiations can move on to other, less volatile areas.

Among the sexual issues that may arise in custody disputes, homosexuality has historically been the most unacceptable of parental sexual conduct. However, society's tolerance for homosexuality has recently increased significantly. This change was formalized by the American Psychiatric Association's 1974 deletion of homosexuality from the category of mental disorders and its acceptance of homosexuality as a valid preference of sexual orientation. Moreover, recent court decisions have begun to award custody to homosexual parents. According to the Lesbian Mothers National Defense Fund in Seattle, Washington, the number of contested custody cases won by lesbian mothers has increased from 1 percent to 15 percent in just ten years. Trial courts cannot now impose their own standard of proper behavior on parents and cannot legally conclude that parental homosexuality per se is a reason to deny a parent custody of, or continuing visitation with, a child. However, homosexuality can, by law, be considered as a significant factor in evaluating the overall home environment and the psychological well-being of the parent. If evidence is presented that the parent's sexual conduct is, or could be, detrimental to the best interests of the children, then a trial court could deny residence of the children in a homosexual household (Fainer and Wasser, 1978; MacGowan, 1981).

In dealing with the issue of homosexuality, the mediator must be able to inform both parents of the factors that are truly relevant to childrearing. The myths and generalizations have to be dismantled, and the particular circumstances must be fully explored, so that the parents can make informed and intelligent decisions about child sharing. Moreover, the mediator should be informed about the current attitudes of the local courts toward parenting by homosexuals in case he or she needs to leverage the negotiations so that they stay within the parameters of likely court decisions.

In general, the homosexuality of a parent can be a relatively insignificant factor if he or she is a loving, responsible person who shows consistency, stability, and other qualities of good parenting on which all children thrive. However, if the homosexual parent shows poor parenting characteristics, then parenting effectiveness is bound to decrease and the best interests of the children may be compromised, not because of the homosexuality, but because of other factors in the overall conduct of that parent. Moreover, if the parent is indiscreetly acting out his or her sexual life, or expressing generalized hostility to the opposite sex, in a way that is insensitive to the needs and feelings of the children, then this could adversely affect their well-being. The mediator should deal with such difficulties in much the same way that he or she deals with general parental sexual indiscretions. The parent should be alerted to the effects on children's self-esteem development of exposure to categorical hostility toward a gender.

Often, a more central concern for the heterosexual parent is the way in which the children's sexual development will be influenced by the homosexual parent. Currently, there is no agreement among the experts about the causes of homosexuality. Whereas traditional psychodynamic theories based homosexuality exclusively in aberrant family relationships, more recent evidence suggests that genetic, biological, and hormonal factors may play significant roles in its etiology (Maccoby and Jacklin, 1974). It may well be, as with so many other human conditions, that homosexuality does not have a single origin but results from a variety of contributing factors.

Several experts in the fields of sex research and child development interviewed by Ramos (1979) concluded that children of homosexual parents are no more likely to become homosexual than are children of heterosexual parents. Moreover, as the renowned child expert Benjamin Spock noted, almost all homosexuals are the children of conventionally heterosexual parents. It is also the case that children learn sex-role behavior from people of the opposite sex as well as from people of the same sex and that people other than parents can contribute significantly to a child's sex-role development.

Another typical concern of the heterosexual parent is

that the child living with the homosexual parent is likely to have to face peer ridicule. However, as psychiatrist Judd Marmor pointed out, "Difference is not easily accepted in our culture, but it is a fact of life. Just as intelligent black or Jewish parents can help their children to cope with bigotry, so can homosexual parents" (Ramos, 1979, p. 166).

Although there are not yet enough data on the effects on a child of living with a homosexual parent, it is likely that if the parent is effective and sensitive and remains supportive and respectful of the other parent's importance to the child, then homosexuality per se need not be an issue. However, the mediator must be very careful to remain objective in assessing the implications for the children of these circumstances. Because of the typically loaded nature of these situations, it is all too easy for the mediator to succumb to personal prejudice rather than stick with real child-related concerns. Keeping abreast of developmental research in this area can facilitate the mediator's effectiveness.

Substance Abuse

Among the most frequent allegations made by one spouse about the other are those that refer to substance abuse. These may include, in more serious forms, alcoholism, heroin addiction, and amphetamine and barbiturate addictions, and in less serious forms, chronic or recreational use of cocaine and marijuana. Because of the personal and seemingly victimless nature of these abuses, the accused spouse frequently denies such allegations. Moreover, even when the spouse does not deny use of these substances, he or she may deny that it presents any danger to the children. This is best characterized by the frequently heard assertion, "I'm in control and I know exactly what I'm doing when I drink, so there's no need to be concerned."

When substance abuse is presented as an allegation in court custody disputes, it is a difficult issue to deal with. For one thing, it is often difficult to produce admissible evidence, other than hearsay, of alcohol or drug abuse. Second, contrary to the tradition of trial courts, recent appellate court decisions have emphasized that the award of custody should not involve punishment of a parent for past behavior such as drug or alcohol abuse (Fainer and Wasser, 1978). In each case, proof must be submitted showing how drug or alcohol abuse renders the particular parent unable to care adequately for the child and results in detriment to the child's best interests. Because the only available evidence is typically the report by the child to the other parent, such allegations are often dropped as unsubstantiated. Moreover, even when there is enough evidence to suggest judicial concern, the most that a judge can usually do is to order a restraint from the use of drugs or alcohol while the parent is in the presence of the child. This frequently results simply in the parent becoming more discreet in his or her continuing substance abuse.

For the mediator, the same kind of dilemma exists. Without any way to investigate the truth of such allegations, the mediator is left to treat them as he or she does any other allegation, by remaining as balanced as possible. However, in a case involving substance abuse where the alleging parent persists with his or her concerns and the children confirm such allegations, the mediator has a duty to confront the issue. Discussing the effects of parental substance abuse on children in general can be an informative and relatively nonthreatening way to make the point. The mediator can talk about the direct risks to children of being unwittingly exposed to dangerous circumstances at home (for example, fires, poisons, falls, other medical emergencies) while the parent is in an altered state of consciousness. Or he could talk about the serious risks that children face while in a car with a driver who is drunk or drugged. He can add to the impact of this perspective by telling a few graphic horror stories emphasizing the severe legal and personal consequences to parents who injure or kill their children while under the influence of drugs or alcohol.

The mediator can then talk about the indirect effects on children of parental substance abuse. These include children's feeling scared, insecure, and confused when around the parent. Over time, the children may well refuse to be with the parent at all. Moreover, their own self-esteem can be weakened by the lack of security they feel around a neglectful or unpredictable parent. Finally, there is the indirect effect of modeling negative behaviors for the children. When children repeatedly observe their parent engaging in some self-gratifying behavior, whether it be smoking, drinking, or pill taking, they may well be learning to use the same behaviors as they get older and are under their own life stresses.

Because parents going through a divorce are so stressed, and because our society is so drug-oriented, it is difficult to be assured that a parent will refrain from substance abuse when with the children. However, if the mediator informatively, tactfully, vividly, and sincerely presents the real risks to children of exposure to this behavior, and includes clauses of self-imposed restraints in the agreement, he or she has done all that is possible to protect the children. Enforcement of such restraint agreements is clearly out of the mediator's domain.

Domestic Violence

Wallerstein and Kelly (1980) reported that of their upper-middle-class, Marin County, California, research sample of 60 families and 131 children of divorce, a full one quarter of the couples regularly exhibited violence during the last part of the marriage and in the course of their divorce. Moreover, 57 percent of the children personally witnessed one parent hit the other. Forty percent of the children had exceedingly poor relationships with their fathers, including gross neglect and verbal, physical, and sexual abuse of one or more children in the family. One fourth of the mother-child relationships were also quite poor, characterized by serious neglect and threatened abuse. This behavior among well-educated, well-to-do families suggests a much more widespread occurrence of domestic violence among the larger population of divorcing couples.

Because of the immediately serious nature of overt spousal violence, or violence to children, courts will readily act to deny custody to, or restrict visitations of, the allegedly violent parent. Unlike allegations of substance abuse, acts of violence are more easily documented, and therefore detriment to a child is easier to prove. Sometimes, however, a parent is denied visitation with the children by the court on the basis of allegations of wife battery alone. The court's conclusion may contain the assumption that if a man hits his wife, then he is also likely to hit his children. However, Wallerstein and Kelly pointed out that "parenting can be maintained as a relatively conflict-free sphere of behavior within a very deprived and unhappy marriage—though, of course, not always. We were interested, in this connection, to discover that men who readily resorted to violence in response to their wives did not necessarily beat, or even spank, their children. Parenting, in fact, could become a means of offsetting marital unhappiness by cultivating a special relationship with one or more of the children" (1980, p. 15). In short, there is no necessary connection between wife battery and child abuse. In such situations, a father and his children may all be punished by restricted contacts as a result of a questionable court decision. However, to the degree that children experience the results of, or worse yet, directly witness spousal violence, any restrictions that will eliminate it are certainly called for.

As with allegations of sexual misconduct and substance abuse, allegations of violence by one spouse about the other can be strategically motivated. If such allegations do not persist, the mediator can usually assume that they were not significant or, perhaps, even valid. However, such assumptions must *always* be made with a certain degree of cautiousness, as it is not uncommon for spouses and children who have been threatened to minimize the dangers of potential future violence. If the mediator remains cautious and sensitive to the discussion of such issues, he or she usually will be able to sense when real intimidation is being experienced. In such situations, individual sessions with the parties involved usually provide enough of a sense of safety to uncover any real dangers.

Occasionally a wife is suspicious of possible future incestuous behavior of the husband based on past incidents but has no current evidence to back it up. In such cases, the husband will sometimes voluntarily agree to restrict his visitations to daytime visits and/or visits with a third party present, in order to allow time to build up trust. The mediator can suggest periodic reevaluations to build in further security for the children and to offer comfort to the wife.

In the case of persistent and serious allegations of spousal violence or violence to the children, the mediator has few options. It is not possible to facilitate constructive mediation in the face of real evidence or threats of physical, emotional, or sexual violence. And when the allegations of violence specifically regard the children, it is the moral and ethical duty of the mediator to facilitate bringing the matter to the attention of the appropriate authorities. In some states, there are even child abuse reporting laws; in California, for example, the law mandates any person who has even a reasonable suspicion of the occurrence of physical or sexual abuse or neglect of a child to report the matter (anonymously) to the children's protective services and/or to the sheriff's or police department for investigation. Penalties can be incurred for not reporting the matter.

The mediator can confront the issue with both parents or with each spouse separately if there is a chance of violence erupting as a direct result of the confrontation. He can simply tell the alleging parent that an accusation of violence is a matter for the courts to deal with and is not appropriate for mediation. He should refer the parent to the appropriate authorities and then refer the case back to the court and/or to the attorneys involved. If, after the investigation, the allegations prove to be unsubstantiated, the case may be returned for mediation, assuming enough interspousal trust remains for mediation efforts to be feasible.

Converting Court-Ordered Evaluation into Mediation

On occasion, family therapists and mediators are requested by courts to conduct evaluations of family situations in which divorced or divorcing spouses are having disputes over custody or visitation. Such requests regularly come from courts in states where there are neither mandatory mediation laws nor informal mediation services. Even in California, a judge may override the mandatory mediation law and make such a request if, in his or her discretion, a particular case seems inappropriate for mediation. The judge may order a written report of the evaluation with recommendations for a workable custody and/or visitation plan.

The therapist or mediator receiving such a request has several choices. She may choose to follow through strictly as requested. Or she may attempt mediation and, if it is unsuccessful, then make recommendations to the court as requested. Or, with the judge's permission, she may decide to function exclusively as a mediator, with full confidentiality, and, if unsuccessful, refer the case to an evaluator who will then make recommendations as originally requested.

The particular approach chosen depends on several factors, the most important of which may be the mediator's opinion of whether the case can be successfully mediated. Judges will sometimes conclude that a particular case is not suitable for mediation on the basis of superficial or erroneous factors. These may include strategically motivated spousal assertions or allegations, spousal concerns that have little to do with the best interests of the children, or a high degree of hostility expressed between the spouses within the adversarial context, which, as Wallerstein and Kelly (1980) found, may have little to do with workable co-parenting decision making. Other factors include the mediator's relationship with the judge and the attorneys, their receptivity to mediation, and considerations of time and finances.

In assessing which approach to take, the mediator should first consider the details of the case within its adversarial context. If the case seems amenable to mediation, he should then consult with the attorneys. If both attorneys are supportive (or can be persuaded to be supportive) of mediation, then the mediator has a solid base from which to approach the judge. If one attorney is supportive and the other is resistant, then the mediator may need to be more convincing with the judge. If both attorneys resist mediation, then the mediator may not be able to use mediation unless he or she can persuade the judge to override the attorneys. The mediator, though, needs to be fully aware of the effects of resistant attorneys on their client's cooperation in these circumstances. Any efforts that he or she can make to include the attorneys, to inform them about mediation, and to elicit their support will aid the mediation efforts.

If mediation is acceptable to the judge, then the mediator needs to understand clearly what the conditions will be. The judge may only agree to mediation if the mediator submits a written report with recommendations in the event that mediation is unsuccessful. Or, the judge may agree to allow mediation to proceed with complete and exclusive confidentiality, such that no recommendations would be made if it were unsuccessful. Being clear with the judge ahead of time about mutual expectations can prevent later misunderstandings.

Although it is easiest at the outset, the mediator can attempt to convert an evaluation into mediation at any point along the way. If confidentiality is to be maintained, then, of course, this should be clarified and formalized at the outset. However, if recommendations are intended as part of the process, the mediator can at any point urge the couple to reconsider their options for resolving the dispute. Assuming that mediation is feasible for the case, as discussed earlier, the mediator can educate the couple about the benefits of mediation (see Chapter Three) and can utilize the strategies for eliciting cooperation (see Chapter Eight). Once there is consent—implicit or explicit—the mediator can proceed as usual to mediate the issues. In most cases, convincing the couple that mediation is in their best interests is a difficult task, but it is eased when they are already familiar or comfortable with the concept of mediation, when the judge and attorneys are supportive of this approach, and when the mediator feels hopeful about resolving the particular case with mediation. When successful, the mediator feels a tremendous sense of accomplishment, and the success certainly adds to the growing credibility of the mediation approach in the eyes of the court.

13

Ethics, Values, and Morals in Mediation

Throughout this book, it has been stressed that the mediator must remain neutral and balanced at all times to be effective in facilitating an agreement between disputing spouses. It has also been stressed that the mediator must function primarily as an *advocate for the child,* not as a representative of either spouse, and that, according to the most current research, what is best for children after a divorce is a continuing and regular relationship with both parents. Although such advocacy for the regularity and continuity of children's relationships with both parents might seem to be a relatively objective, nonjudgmental, and value-free position for the mediator to assume, it is not. Mediation work involves the mediator in numerous moral dilemmas that present even higher challenges than the process of the work itself.

For example, while attempting to remain neutral, a mediator occasionally experiences bias against one spouse. This bias may be due to the personal style of the spouse, to his or her beliefs, attitudes, and values, or to the uncooperative stance the spouse assumes in mediation. The spouse may enter mediation with a chip on the shoulder and verbally attack the mediator. He or she may be late for sessions and may challenge every procedure of the mediator. Moreover, he or she may elaborate on beliefs, attitudes, and practices regarding childrearing that may be personally offensive to the mediator. While falling short of child abuse, these practices might include the regular use of corporal punishment and excessive strictness or, alternatively, the absence of limit setting and a totally laissez faire approach to raising young children. In contrast, the other spouse may be a relatively open, loving, generous, compromising, cooperative person, whose beliefs and practices of childrearing are highly congruent with those of the mediator.

Several factors make this a difficult situation. For one thing, the mediator generally does not have time to work through these feelings of bias by getting to know other, more positive facets of the spouse who seems offensive. Again, it is usually not possible to spend the extra time that would be needed to become better acquainted with this spouse, not least because the mediator would have to do the same for the other spouse. Morever, even when individual sessions *are* offered to spouses, complications can arise. In a follow-up study of mandatory mediation cases, Saposnek and others (1983) found that spouses would sometimes interpret the empathy shown by the mediator during individual sessions as implicit support for their respective sides and would later feel betrayed when the same degree of one-sided empathy was not shown during conjoint sessions with both spouses.

A second contributory factor is that in order to carry out the mediational goal of maximizing the children's access to both parents, the mediator must be supportive of both parents' importance to and involvement with the children. This means, however, that the mediator not only must ignore the offensive behavior of one spouse but also must be positively supportive of that spouse. Of course, to the degree that the mediator does support this spouse, he or she may alienate the more cooperative spouse. A cooperative spouse may well interpret the mediator's equal support of the less cooperative spouse as evidence of the mediator's professional blindness and obvious bias. That spouse may feel that the mediator is condoning uncooperative behavior and minimal or poor-quality parenting and is ignoring behavior that may appear to that spouse to be detrimental to the children. However, if the mediator questions, lectures to, or expresses a judgmental attitude toward the uncooperative spouse, then the bias becomes overt and the mediator may well forfeit neutrality and further exacerbate the uncooperative spouse's resistant behavior.

In attempting to protect the best interests of the child, the mediator tries to implement a plan that allows the child a regular and continuous relationship with both parents. Generally, the mediator must assume that short of blatant child abuse or parental behavior that is clearly antithetical to the child's welfare, both parents are adequate to be caregivers to their child and both have important individual contributions to make to the rearing of their child. Not only do these assumptions generally follow from the research on the needs of children of divorce, but they are congruent with the mediator's need to maintain balance and neutrality, to cut through the various strategies of spouses and children, and to equalize parental negotiating power.

Unfortunately, these assumptions lead the mediator to deemphasize or perhaps even completely ignore *quality of parenting.* They suggest that minimal parental competence is perfectly adequate to support the child's best interests. Hence, a parent who manifests very minimal parental competence may be given the same consideration in the development of a mediated co-parenting plan as is given to a highly competent parent. Although there is, no doubt, a continuum between a mediator's personal bias and a mediator's professional conviction about parental incompetence, a spouse who falls at the latter end of this continuum clearly poses certain dilemmas for the mediator.

As an example, consider the following case: Walter and Yolanda have been divorced for two years and have three children, Nathan, aged nine, Katie, aged eleven, and Jordan, aged twelve. Nathan and Katie have been living with their mother, and Jordan with his father. Walter files a petition to modify Yolanda's sole custody of Nathan and Katie to joint legal and joint physical custody. In mediation, Yolanda reports that Walter has never known how to be a father, that he is completely self-centered, and that he has no conception of the needs of his children. Furthermore, he has deprived Jordan continually, and Nathan and Katie during visitations, of food, clothing, and, on several occasions, even shelter ("accidentally" locking the children out of the house). His refrigerator is frequently empty or sparsely stocked with food, and he has not bought shoes or pants for Jordan in over a year. Moreover, he is seriously in arrears on child support payments and reports to Yolanda that he does not have enough money to catch up but is working on it—although he recently purchased for himself a new sports car, a small boat, and new wardrobe. He is home infrequently and very often leaves the children home alone or with a young teenage babysitter. When angry at the children, he spanks them harshly and sends them to their room without dinner. About twice a year, he takes all the children to a movie, but otherwise he has instructed them to entertain themselves, since he does not have enough money "to squander on frivolous things." Walter rationalizes his overall parental incompetence by saying, "Children will learn to survive best if they go without."

Yolanda, in contrast, has consistently sacrificed for the children, and has held the family together through the twelve years of the marriage and the two years postdivorce. She has lived on a meager budget, yet has managed to take the children to special events, spend lots of time with them, and nurture them emotionally and materially as best she could.

In separate interviews with the mediator, the children basically confirmed this imbalance in parental competence. However, all of them said that they would agree to whatever their parents worked out because they just wanted to stop the arguing. Moreover, they all said that their father would make them feel guilty if they did not spend enough time with him, and because they felt sorry for him being all alone, they wanted to keep him company.

Throughout the negotiations, Walter insists on an equal sharing arrangement, Yolanda agrees to respect the wishes of the children, and the children want their parents to decide. Given this setup, it is likely that Walter's proposal will prevail.

At this point, the mediator confronts a large dilemma. Should she suspend her professional concern about the imbalance of parental competence and act as if there were a genuine equality of competence—that is, assume that a questionably minimal level of parental competence is sufficient to protect the children's best interests? Can she rest assured that having any two parents who agree on a co-parenting plan is really better for children than having one competent and involved parent, and one incompetent and peripheral parent who do not agree to a co-parenting plan? Or should the mediator strategically try to influence the decisions about the co-parenting arrangements so that a disproportionate amount of the children's time would be spent in their mother's care? This tactic might seriously risk the mediation efforts if Walter were to continue insisting on a strictly equal arrangement. Or should the mediator simply abandon neutrality altogether and directly confront Walter with the fact that his parenting skills are inadequate and his proposal clearly is not in the best interests of the children? Or should the mediator refuse to participate in the decision-making process and inform the couple that because she does not believe that it is best for the children to spend more time with Walter, she is referring their case back to court for a probation investigation?

While it is possible that having more time with the children could increase Walter's sense of responsibility, the risks to the children of such minimal caregiving make the mediator's choice of action quite difficult.

Even more difficult is the case in which *both* parents are only marginally competent, or clearly incompetent, to offer constructive caregiving to the children. Consider the following case: Johnnie and Bertha had been separated for six months, and their six-year-old daughter, Babs, had been living with her father and seeing her mother every other weekend. Bertha, who also had a three-year-old daughter from another relationship while she was married to Johnnie, petitioned for custody of Babs. In mediation, Bertha, a sarcastic and hostile woman who carried the intense anger at her own parents into her spousal and parental relationships, told how Johnnie always worked and was never home. "He never learned to be no father—just like *my* ol' man. May the Lord burn his ass in hell, and my ol' lady too, while he's at it!" Bertha explained that she sought custody of Babs after finding out that Johnnie was never with Babs but was leaving her with his fiancee, Ginger. She added that Ginger "spanks, whips, and is severely strict with Babs. She refuses to let Babs talk or even make a sound at the dinner table, because, she says, 'Babs spits food when she talks, and I don't want to clean it up.' Babs also told me that she has to eat at the kitchen table while Johnnie and Ginger eat in the living room, so they can watch TV. And Babs is not allowed to watch TV, 'cause it's bad for kids." When the mediator asked Johnnie if all this was accurate, he said, "Yeah. Ginger is real religious and knows what's right, and besides, as Ginger says, it's been ten generations that kids should be seen and not heard."

On hearing this, Bertha launched a tirade about Ginger for not caring about Babs. With a gush of anger and accusations, she accused Johnnie of neglecting Babs, and then, in an angry and rambling fashion, expounded on her own deep need for Babs. At one point she bragged about how well she could control her own anger: "Like last night at 10:30, the baby [her three-year-old child] was watching TV and spilt some milk on the carpet. I got furious, but I just got up and started running as fast as I could down the block. I ran three and a half blocks to get away, otherwise I would have smashed her head in. I had the good judgment to leave. She was asleep when I got home—instead of dead. But Johnnie, he don't even care about Babs."

Bertha then continued, "I need Babs so badly to live with me because she is the only person who kept me out of an institution when I was about to crack. She's been my source of reality. She needs me and loves me—no one else does like her! I can't make it without her. I swear I'll get her—I'll take her and leave the country if I have to."

The mediator's choice of action in this case is even more limited than in the previous case of *one* inadequate parent. If the mediator does have the power to slant the negotiations, and chooses to do so, which way should she slant them—toward Babs' moving in with her angry, explosive, unpredictable mother or toward Babs' remaining under Ginger's strict, questionably adequate care and living with an essentially absent father?

However, if the mediator chooses to act as if both parents

were adequate, she has to be able to tell herself that whatever plan the spouses agree to is probably in the best interests of the child. To justify this position, the mediator probably has to accept the fact that most children in the world grow up with far less than optimal parenting.

Or are there some legitimate and consensually agreed-on standards of minimally adequate parenting? Certainly our vast research in child development offers numerous guidelines for effective parenting, but how many parents actually follow such guidelines? Moreover, the history of the childrearing literature is a history of pendulumlike alternations in styles, practices, and even "truths" about what is important for children. Clearly, our values about children and childrearing across the generations have been grounded in relativity, rather than in absolute truths.

A last and most serious option for the mediator to consider is the possibility of referring the case back to court with a recommendation for temporary foster placement of the child or perhaps even for the permanent relinquishment of parental rights, which would free the child for adoption. However, this would indeed be a drastic move. For one thing, if she is bound by a confidentiality agreement, she might have to breach it, which would put her in a difficult position. Second, such an action would certainly stretch the role of the mediator into questionable areas. And, third, while the possibilities are perhaps somewhat better for temporary foster placement, the possibilities are very slim for permanently relinquishing the rights of biological parents who express interest in and involvement with their child. The right to parent one's child is held to be a basic right that lies at the heart of most court decisions and legislative enactments, and it is not relinquished easily in any court of law. In fact, MacGowan (1981) cites several cases in which it was held that the killing of one parent by the other disqualifies the surviving parent from obtaining custody only if the homicide constitutes neglect of the child.

The ethical questions faced by the mediator are numerous and challenging when confronted with a case like that of Johnnie and Bertha. It is difficult to leave such a case feeling comfortable, no matter what action one chooses to take.

After a divorce, it is not uncommon for a parent to cope

with the crisis by making a sudden and radical change in life-style and/or personality. This could involve a change from a stable middle-class life-style to that of a swinger, or it could involve a change from an emotionally distant personality to one that is open and emotionally labile. Moreover, the spouses may begin to proselytize about the teachings of any one of a variety of systems for personal growth, such as *est,* primal therapy, meditation, massage, or Scientology. A sudden personality change can also occur as a result of a profound drug experience, religious conversion, or initiation into a cult.

In attempts to explain the phenomenon of sudden, radical changes of personality and life-style, Conway and Siegelman (1978) coined the term *snapping,* which connotes a sudden qualitative and unpredictable alteration in one's functioning. Although these authors were concerned mainly with accounting for what they called "America's epidemic of sudden personality change," the concept of snapping has much relevance in explaining the sudden changes of certain divorced persons as well. Sudden, radical changes in personality and life-style generally are quite unstable, and this instability is compounded for a newly divorced spouse. The deterioration of parental behavior for at least the year following the divorce has been well documented (Hetherington, Cox, and Cox, 1978; Wallerstein and Kelly, 1980) and, as previously noted, has been characterized as a state of diminished capacity to parent.

When a mediator deals with a parent who is experiencing the chaos of a new divorce and has also undergone a snapping experience, various dilemmas arise. Let us consider an example: Mark and Marion had been married for fifteen years and had four children, aged nine, ten, thirteen, and fourteen. When Marion left Mark, he was extremely distraught and depressed for several months. After making several bids to reunite with Marion, Mark finally seemed to accept the pending divorce and wanted Marion to have primary custody of the children.

Several weeks before the divorce hearing, however, Mark got deeply involved with an Indian cult and had a profound conversion experience similar to several he had had during the marriage. During his visitation times, he talked at length with the children about living in the community of this cult. When they expressed interest in his idea, he took them for a visit to the state where the community was established. The children became entranced with the apparently loving and free atmosphere there, and they made some friends.

In the mediation negotiations, Mark appeared very rational, reasonable, and "hypnotic" as he described the structure of the religious community. He also seemed very cooperative, until he said calmly that although he would like to share parenting with Marion, he was moving to the religious community out of state and would like the children to join him there. Marion agreed that it would be fine for the children to spend the summers there but that they would need to spend the school year with her. Mark added calmly, "I've talked with the children and they said that they wanted to live in the community with me." Marion was startled and said she would need to talk with the children about this decision.

At the next mediation session, the day before Mark was to move out of state, Marion came in looking dejected. She explained that she had talked with the children and wound up in a nasty argument with one of the older ones. Against her wishes, all four of the children did say that they wanted to live in the commune. However, she felt that Mark must have made some far-reaching promises to them to get them to change their minds so easily. The mediator met with the children and heard them express their wish to go with their father. To the mediator, the children were unsettlingly consistent with one another in their expressed change of heart.

The mediator then met with Mark and Marion again, and tried to support Marion in being cautious about this decision. He explained the various dynamic and strategic reasons why children might state such a preference. Moreover, because of his unsettled feelings about the turn of events, he attempted to steer them toward a time-limited plan with lots of mutual time-sharing and mutual decision-making clauses built in. However, Mark countered these attempts in a calm, rational, and calculated fashion. He finally played his trump card, saying, "I would be willing to let Marion visit with the children anytime she wants, with twenty-four-hour notice, but the leader of the community and his board of legal consultants informed me that if I bring my children even for a short time, I must have sole custody of them, or I cannot live there." When asked why, Mark replied, "They apparently have had some difficult situations come up between ex-spouses over their children, and they don't want to deal with those problems anymore."

Marion looked even more distraught and dejected and said "All right! I'm tired of all this. You can have what you want. Since the children have obviously been brainwashed by you, there's nothing I can do about it. Besides, I don't have any money to go back to court to fight this." The mediator urged Marion to take her time and think it out further, but Mark kept reminding her that he was leaving the next day and needed a decision immediately. Marion was feeling rejected by her children, persuaded by their stated desire to move with their father, and rushed and intimidated by Mark. As a result, she would not heed the mediator's advice to refrain from a hasty decision and insisted on the mediator's writing up the agreement as Mark had proposed it.

Both Marion and the mediator knew that the sudden change in Mark would probably not last, yet Marion felt powerless to counter Mark's well-devised plans. The mediator was placed in the position of either allowing this plan to proceed and implicitly condoning it or else asserting his professional judgment (and, perhaps, personal values) and refusing to condone such a plan being carried out. Efforts toward a compromise were repelled by Marion and blocked by Mark.

In such a circumstance, where the spouses are willing to agree to a proposal that seems very questionable to the mediator, but the mediator has no leverage for significantly modifying the proposal, what options does the mediator have? If the case were to go to court, and the children were to persist in their expressed desires, a judge might well rule in favor of Mark's plan. Although its instability is obvious to the trained eye, it might well look to a judge like an acceptable plan developed by two concerned and involved parents. If, after hearing the mediator's concerns about and attempts to modify the agreement, the two spouses decide to proceed with the agreement, should the mediator simply trust their decision? Or does the mediator's role as an advocate for the child obligate him or her to go one step further and take other action to preclude the development of a questionable parenting agreement? And what could be the nature of such action? What sacrifices would need to be made in order to carry out such action?

Another issue is whether it is always better to protect children from court battles even if it means allowing them to participate in a questionable agreement. Does the acrimony generated in the adversarial court process always have a worse effect than the results of even a questionable mediated agreement? Or are there some issues, such as risks to physical and emotional safety, that should always preclude a mediated settlement on the grounds that the child will do much better in the long run by undergoing a court custody battle? When can a court-rendered decision really offer more protection for a child's well-being than what is offered by a mediated agreement?

Even assuming that most agreements reached between spouses, with or without mediators, are better for the children than are most decisions rendered by the court, there are still a number of ethical issues that arise for the mediator. In order to achieve the compromises that permit agreements to be reached, the mediator often has to orchestrate sacrifices on the part of one spouse and/or the children. These sacrifices are based on certain values that the mediator believes to be important for children. If these values are not valid for the parties involved, then the mediator may cause undue discomfort or harm to the family members.

Consider, for example, a case in which a mother wants to retain sole legal and physical custody of her nine- and twelve-year-old children, while the father makes a strong and insistent plea for joint legal and physical custody. Although the father is partly motivated by a power-assertion strategy, he also sincerely wants to share half-time parenting responsibilities. The children, however, would like to reside with their mother but would agree, reluctantly, to an alternating weekly sharing schedule. The father and mother have remained in constant conflict because the father has felt dominated by the mother. By having sole custody, she has been able to control the father's access to the children. The children have tried many strategies for getting the parents to stop arguing, but the arguments have persisted, largely because the father has been in a "one-down" position since the divorce, a position he has constantly resisted.

With just a few strategies, the mediator could achieve a joint custody agreement, since with the mediator's support, the mother would compromise. Alternatively, the mediator could discourage such an agreement and risk having the case returned to court. He might choose the former solution with the following justification: If the father had a sense of sharing equal power with the mother, then he would be less resistant and more cooperative with her, which in the long run would benefit the children by reducing the interparental tension. The mediator would thus have to sacrifice the short-run comfort of the children in trying to achieve increased harmony between the parents. This plan, then, would be feasible but not quite fair to the children. It requires the mediator to maintain a strong conviction that an equal-custody plan will result in reduced acrimony between the parents and that it is more important that the parents reach any workable agreement between themselves than that the mediator risk escalating the parental battle by yielding to the children's preferences.

In such a case, where the mediator can influence the outcome, what should the mediator choose to do? Should children be expected to make a sacrifice on the chance that it would reduce their parents' conflict? Or should the children be allowed their preference even if it results in further interparental tension?

The issue of feasible versus fair agreements comes up frequently when both spouses have positive parenting skills and good intentions but have an unbalanced spousal dynamic. Typically, the husband is dominating and aggressive and the wife submissive and yielding. When they negotiate their proposals, their spousal relational positions are directly represented in their agreement. The parenting plan to which they agree will be feasible for the children but not very fair to the wife. Feeling, as always, intimidated by her husband, the wife is unassertive and allows him to plow right past her own needs.

In this situation, to what extent should the mediator be protective of the wife's needs? Should he make mild, moderate, or vigorous efforts to encourage her to take a stronger stand on her own behalf, knowing full well that such action may antagonize the husband into a refusal to compromise at all? Or should he make no efforts at all and just assume that the spousal balance which exists at that time has no doubt existed for many years and is not likely to change in mediation? As marital therapists know well, tipping the balance of power in a marital relationship is almost always guaranteed to trigger a conflictual crisis of some proportion. However, would not the mediator's laissez faire attitude be encouraging the continuation of the imbalanced decision-making process? Should the mediator allow an agreement to be made that is feasible but unfair to the wife and encourage the wife to seek counseling later, in order to become stronger so that she could be more assertive in future modifications of the time-sharing plan?

In the above case, the mediator's dilemma is how and whether to halt the development of an agreement that, in the mediator's view, is not desirable. In other cases, however, the dilemma is the extent to which it is legitimate to force a couple to reach an agreement. In many cases, using the strategies described in Chapter Nine, a skillful mediator can maneuver and even coerce a couple into reaching an agreement even when it seems at first to be an impossible task.

There are several motives a mediator might have for choosing to force an agreement. First, the mediator may believe that *any* agreement will be better than a court-rendered decision. Second, the mediator may feel that if she just gets a couple past the impasse of the custody power struggle, they will be able to establish a new way of relating to one another that in the long run will work out better for the children. Third, the mediator may have an excessive case load to get through and thus not have the time for more prolonged negotiations that might yield more mutually acceptable agreements. (It has been suggested that this is frequently the situation in conciliation court settings, where there is often a large backlog of case loads.) Fourthly, the mediator may strive to reach as many agreements as she can, as a personal test of her skill and influence as a mediator.

Regardless of the reasons for it, forcing an agreement can have certain negative consequences. At least one and often both spouses may feel shortchanged, manipulated, or bullied by the mediator. This can cause one or both spouses to sabotage the agreement shortly after mediation ends and to resist returning to mediation for future modifications of the co-parenting plan, because of adverse feelings about the mediator and mediation. Moreover, it can result in a hastily made agreement that is unsatisfactory for the children. In the mediator's vigorous attempts to break an impasse, he or she may overlook risks to the children presented by a particular agreement.

However, forcing an agreement can result in benefits for the children even if one or both of the parents are dissatisfied with the process. The agreement may in fact be better than any court-rendered decision, and it may help the couple establish a new way of relating to each other.

Can the mediator push too hard for compromise? Is compromise always the best solution? May the mediator's stance of "peace at any cost" not sometimes have excessive and unwarranted consequences? Are there not some circumstances in which higher human principles of morals and values should legitimately be ascendant over a forced compromise? Are there not some situations in which there is a *right* side to a dispute, a *right* resolution, a morally *correct* parental position that supersedes a compromised co-parenting arrangement?

Recognizing that the mediator often has a good deal of power to influence the outcome of negotiations between parents, we must consider several broader issues regarding ethics, values, and morals.

To begin with, almost all mediation cases come out of an adversarial context in which each of the spouses is attempting to assert his or her parental rights at the expense of the other parent. Moreover, each parent typically retains a legal advocate to ensure that these rights are protected to the maximum extent possible. In the context of litigation, the court is presumed to be responsible for protecting the rights and needs of the children. In the mediation context, however, it is the mediator who must protect these rights and needs, particularly when a parenting agreement reached in mediation is not likely to be closely scrutinized by a judge. But what values should the mediator advocate? To what extent should the mediator support a parent's *legal* rights if the mediator feels that doing so would compromise the children's needs? Or are his responsibilities limited exclusively to protecting the rights and needs of the children?

If a father's legal rights to regular and frequent access to his young child have clearly been violated by the mother, and the child is supportive of the mother, what position should the mediator take? Suppose, further, that the father expresses very minimal affection for the child but offers much more in the way of material things and educational opportunities than the mother can. And suppose that the mother offers much deeper affection for the child but lives in near-poverty conditions. Finally, add the facts that the child and mother are quite dependent on each other, that the child prefers to maintain the existing time-sharing arrangements, and that the father and his lawyer are pushing for an equal time-sharing arrangement.

This case presents a three-way intersection of conflicting rights and needs. With the strong support of his attorney, the father insists that his parental rights have been violated and he deserves redress in the form of an equal parenting arrangement. The child's rights to have open access to both parents presumably would also be satisfied if the father's proposal were adopted. However, the child's needs, which certainly are open to differing interpretations, might be best satisfied if he maintained his close relationship with his mother—that is, the existing living and time-sharing arrangements were preserved. Yet, could it not be argued that, in the long run, the child's needs would best be met if he were emotionally closer to both parents? But what would be the consequences to the child of decreasing the special closeness with his mother in order to spend more time with his father, only to find that his father continued to be very limited in the affection that he was able to feel for the child? Does some universal justice prevail such that if both parents' rights were fully respected, the resulting balance would optimally meet the child's needs? Should the mediator not act strictly as an advocate for the child, but rather as an advocate for the whole family unit? In this way, he would be concerned with the rights and needs of both parents and child. Is this role too similar to that of the judge, and does it not overlap the roles of the attorneys? Is it an inappropriate role for a mediator? Is it even possible?

Whether the mediator's role is as an advocate for the child alone or for the family unit, how far should this advocacy extend? If a child has deep and close relationships with grandparents or other relatives, in addition to bonds with the parents, what position should the mediator take? Should she limit her concern to the nuclear family unit, or should she take the liberty that comes with being a mental health professional and expand her influence to include extended family members?

If all else is equal, is a parent more important to a child than a very close grandparent? Or a close aunt? Should they be considered on an equal level with the parents if the child's emotional attachment to them seems equal? At what generation and at what degree of kinship should the mediator stop in considering the best interests of the child? Should family pets be considered part of a child's extended family? These questions become especially significant when one parent is moving away from the area where the other parent and all the child's extended family members reside.

The courts have repeatedly made it clear that parents shall be first in line for awards of custody, before grandparents, other extended family members, or any other interested persons. However, for the mediator, this simply means that *legal* custody should be assumed by one or both parents, unless there would be detriment to the child in doing so. Time-sharing arrangements, however, can be worked out in any way that would be in the child's best interests, and that both parents would agree to. So the mediator may actually have considerable latitude in shaping the parenting agreements. Although it increases the complexity of negotiations, the mediator may be able to optimize a child's support network by including extended family members in the time-sharing plan. Maintaining such bonds has been shown to decrease the sense of isolation and loss for children of divorce (Kellam, Ensminger, and Turner, 1977; Hetherington, 1981).

Historically, in legal matters, attorneys have had two roles, that of *advocate* for their client's rights and interests and that of *counselor* for their client. Attorneys vary considerably in the respective emphases they place on these functions. Regarding lawyers who practice child custody law, the Committee on the Family of the Group for the Advancement of Psychiatry (1980) concluded: "At one extreme are those who function primarily as counselors; at the other extreme are the inveterate litigators. In handling divorce and custody matters, some lawyers explore in detail the alternatives for reaching agreement, seeking therapy, or trying arbitration. They view their duty as one to the whole client in terms of long range advantage, with due consideration for intra-family relationships. The aggressive lawyer, on the other hand, battles on behalf of his client to press for immediate advantages. Some clients who are not in a compromising mood seek out this sort of lawyer. Most lawyers, of course, fall somewhere between these extremes" (pp. 44–45).

Even when lawyers are functioning in their least adversarial way, they are bound by professional ethics to represent their client, and only their client, to the best of their abilities (as discussed in Chapter Two). As Haynes (1981) further noted, the American Bar Association's canons of judicial and professional ethics state: "The professional judgement of a lawyer should be exercised, within the bounds of the law, solely for the benefit of his client and free of compromising influences and other loyalties. Neither his personal interests, the interests of other clients, nor the desires of third persons should be permitted to dilute his loyalty to his client" (McKinney, 1975, p. 438).

How, then, can attorneys facilitate achieving the best interests of the child in custody and visitation disputes when they are bound by their ethical codes to take only the perspective of their own client? Is there any room for lawyers to consider the effects of their one-sided advocacy on the larger family unit? Ethically, can they care about the effects of their maneuvers on the children? Is it possible for "family law" to be true to its designation, in a literal sense, and for lawyers in this specialty to be concerned with protecting the rights and interests of a family unit as a viable, dynamic, and emotionally integrated entity, which undergoes rearrangement, not disintegration, after a divorce?

MacGowan (1981) suggested that "an attorney deciding whether to accept a child custody case should consider an ethical obligation not specified in the Rules of Professional Conduct: the obligation to influence the client to act in a manner beneficial to the child" (p. 386). She cited cases in which this ethical responsibility in custody proceedings has been recognized by both trial and appellate courts. Of course, some attorneys would claim that they always do fulfill this obligation, because their clients are always acting on the best interests of the child. Fortunately, not many attorneys would claim more than that they are merely fulfilling their professional obligation to advocate for their own client.

Several factors contribute to lawyers' difficulty in viewing custody contests from the family systems perspective. First, the one-sided data gathered by attorneys typically is emotionally loaded and therefore very seductive. Second, shifting one's conceptual paradigm from an individual to a family systems perspective requires a leap that is difficult even for many trained psychotherapists to make (Watzlawick, Weakland, and Fisch, 1974; Haley, 1976). It is even more difficult for attorneys, who not only practice from an individually oriented perspective but also are bound by their code of ethics to keep it that way. However, if the mediator can get the attorneys in a case to suspend their adversarial role temporarily, they may be more receptive to considering a higher order of perspective in custody disputes—that is, that a child's interests are almost always served best when the parents stop fighting with each other.

Among the most frequent scenarios of contemporary divorces is that in which one spouse leaves the marriage explaining, "I'm leaving in order to find myself—to explore who I am, to be free, to get my act together, to do my own thing." Some of these spouses are leaving very conflictual, tension-laden, and oppressive marriages, but many are leaving marriages that may be structurally sound but are dynamically dampened.

Many factors have been posited to explain the alarming divorce rate of the last decade. Apart from increased mobility, economic stress, and the legal ease of obtaining a divorce, there is what is perhaps the most intriguing factor of all: the sociocultural approval for seeking individual freedom. Spurred on by the generation of the 1970s—dubbed by Lasch (1978) "the culture of narcissism"—divorce has gained popularity as a socially condoned method for attaining personal happiness. Moreover, the escalation of divorce has tended to be self-perpetuating—hence, it is probably accurate to say that a central cause of divorce has been the high rate of divorce. However, to whatever extent popular books reflect and contribute to popular trends, a deescalation in the divorce rate may be imminent. An omen of this may be the recent publication of a charming book entitled *How Not to Split Up* (Appleton and Appleton, 1981).

An unfortunate but major consequence of one spouse's seeking his or her individual freedom is that family integrity is ruptured, and the lives of the children often severely disrupted. This brings up a number of significant issues regarding individual and family values. Is it morally defensible for a spouse to leave a marriage and rupture a family solely to attempt to satisfy his or her individual need for freedom? Should a spouse be willing to compromise individual needs and desires in order to preserve the family unit? Is there not some higher human principle that each individual should make personal sacrifices for the sake of a more significant social unit, that is, the family? That the welfare and security of children are more important than the satisfaction of individual adult needs? Is such a notion just relative to culture and time, or is it a much more basic value?

Certainly there are marriages that are best dissolved for the sake of both the parents and the children. For instance, when there is violence or abuse, chronic conflict, or incompatible and unchanging expectations of the marriage, one could hardly fault a spouse for leaving. However, how shall we view the actions of the spouse who leaves a relatively stable marriage to seek personal enlightenment and is unwilling even to attempt reconciliation? This action might well be condoned from a psychological viewpoint, which tends to place value on the expression and gratification of individual needs. From a moral viewpoint, though, this action might well be viewed as selfish and not in the best interests of the children or of the family as a whole. For example, is it fair for a mother who leaves the family to expect equal time-sharing with the children whose lives she disrupted? Should a father who abandons his wife and children be given the same rights and privileges to the custody and control of the children as the mother, who chose to stay and work things out? Is it fair that the children have to accommodate to the needs of the parent and divide their time between two homes? Or would it be more fair for the parent to have to pay a price for leaving and sacrifice frequent contact with the children? These questions must be pondered with full awareness that societal values swing back and forth from generation to generation, making their answers all the more difficult.

For the mediator, the issue of individual freedom versus family integrity presents imposing dilemmas. Can the mediator afford to function purely on a psychological/legal level and ignore the moral implications of his work? If he chooses to attend to these implications, will his task of being neutral be impeded? Is it possible to be somewhat, but not completely, morally concerned? Or are these perspectives fundamentally incompatible, forcing the mediator to choose to be either wholly concerned or wholly unconcerned?

One of the central changes in society's values brought about by the feminist movement is the increased permission for men to be primary caregivers to children. In general, men have become increasingly comfortable in expressing their gentleness, their playfulness, their nurturing capacities, and their emotional closeness to children. This emotional balance between men and women has developed concomitantly with changes in employment structures. More women now work outside the home, and household and childcare responsibilities are more frequently shared between parents. Moreover, with the increasing numbers of joint custody arrangements, fathers more often are becoming primary, or at least equal, caregivers for their children.

Although society has given fathers both permission and the appropriate legal structures to function as primary caregivers, it has not yet provided them with the *skills* necessary for primary childcare. In spite of how liberated some men may seem today, the bulk of fathers have not had much experience or training in childrearing. It is still not socially condoned for boys to play with dolls, to play house, or to engage flexibly in the role-playing of other domestic functions, which is a central way that children learn these adult roles. Traditional, stereotyped sex roles are still largely encouraged, and children's deviations from these roles is viewed by most adults with concern and discomfort. As Brooks-Gunn and Matthews (1979, p. 19) note, "The stereotypes have not hanged much since the early 1800s, when the poem 'What are little boys made of?' first appeared."

In our present society, when a mother divorces and takes primary custody of her children, she is shown little respect, is overburdened with responsibilities, and is offered little emotional or financial support. Moreover, her parenting skills are looked at critically and she is freely blamed for any difficulties experienced by her children. However, when a father even participates in the day-to-day care of his child, he is praised for going beyond the call of duty. If he is divorced and chooses to function as a single parent and primary caregiver, he is commended, much support is offered by friends and family, and he is generally viewed with respect simply for being a single parent. If his children experience difficulties, understanding and support are given to him, but he is rarely blamed or criticized.

In light of the above, the mediator often faces a dilemma when a father wants equal or primary caregiving responsibility for his children. This request almost always is disputed by the mother, who typically claims that the father does not offer proper care to the children. She may add that he knows nothing about being a father, since he was never around much during the marriage, and that he neglects the children–doesn't bathe them properly, never washes their hair, doesn't supervise their play, doesn't feed them balanced meals, and so on. In response to these allegations, the father typically retorts defensively that he does just fine, and then refuses to deal with specifics.

The mediator is thus put in the position of having to consider the parenting skills of the father. However, if the mediator questions the father about his skills or suggests that he take a parenting class, the father is likely to react defensively and accuse the mediator of bias in believing the mother's story. If, however, the mediator ignores the issue, then the care of the children may be compromised if the father does retain significant caregiving responsibility for the children.

Knowing that fathers with effective caregiving skills are the exception rather than the rule, should the mediator routinely question fathers or steer couples away from agreements that allot significant caregiving time to the father? Should fathers be expected to prove their parenting competence before assuming such responsibilities? How could the mediator effect this without losing impartiality in the negotiations? Should he just ignore the issue entirely and assume that some children will receive less than adequte care—as no doubt occurs at times even with mothers—but that in time, out of necessity, the fathers will learn the necessary skills? Is this too great a sacrifice to expect of the children?

The many issues of ethics, values, and morals raised in this chapter have no easy answers. However, this author hopes that those of us who are responsible for facilitating major decisions that affect the lives of children will ponder these questions well, for we need to raise our moral consciousness and learn how to act more effectively to create happiness, peace, and a sense of well-being for our children.

14

Making Mediation Work:
Recommendations for Mediators, Attorneys, and Judges

Divorce continues to take its toll on our children. For most children of divorce, memories of the emotional pain, the confusion and turmoil, and the parental bitterness haunt them for years after the divorce, and sometimes throughout their lives. For the luckier ones whose parents manage to make their parting relatively peaceful, the pain is less but not gone. When the parents keep their acrimony toward each other in check and maintain their relationships with their children through cooperative co-parenting efforts, the children are better able to adjust to the divorce trauma and accept the new family structures that develop. By maintaining control over decisions about postdivorce childrearing arrangements, parents are able to provide for their children the sense of security and trust that is created when children know their parents are mutually making decisions about their care and well-being.

Throughout this book I have tried to emphasize the inadequacy of the adversarial approach for resolving parenting disputes. As an alternative to the abusive legal tradition, mediation is sensible and effective, yet it cannot perform magic. As we saw in Chapter Eleven, there is a certain population of disputing spouses with whom mediation is ineffective, and there are cases in which a mediated agreement breaks down in the months following its construction. Moreover, there are the various ethical and moral difficulties discussed in Chapter Thirteen, which cast confusion upon mediation practice and confront mediators with conceptual challenges in need of resolution. Clearly, there is a great deal of work ahead in evaluating, clarifying and expanding the mediator's role, conceptual framework, and methodology.

Much research needs to be done in order to answer the wide range of pragmatic questions that arise regarding the efficacy of mediation. These can be summed up as follows: Which mediators, with what kinds of training, working in what kinds of legal and social settings, with what kinds of extended community and professional support systems, using what kinds of methods and techniques, work best for which families, with what age children, in what kinds of family structures, with what kinds of family dynamics, to resolve what specific kinds of disputes?

In future research, perhaps we can avoid the mistakes made by psychotherapy researchers, who tried for scores of years to discover which therapy approach was the most effective by pitting one against the other. After it became apparent that *all* therapy approaches were effective *some* of the time, researchers began to develop an appreciation for the common elements among therapies and for the complexities of the specific factors that can lead to cognitive, emotional, and behavioral change. Conceptually and practically, mediation research should be easier to carry out than psychotherapy research, because of the more circumscribed nature of the mediation task (reaching a workable and lasting agreement), which stands in contrast to the variable processes and goals of psychotherapy. And early evaluation in the development of our approaches can help to curtail the seemingly inevitable theoretical and pragmatic mythologies that tend to develop around new social intervention approaches.

The acutely sensitive, potentially volatile, and extraordinarily significant nature of family relationships in crisis demands respect of intervenors. Ignorance, carelessness, or incompetence on the part of mediators can have devastating consequences for the lives of the family members involved. We must understand that parent-child bonds are precious and must be preserved and nurtured. Mediators who lack appropriate skill and training may not only be ineffective in mediation but may also do psychological and emotional harm to children. Clearly this is not something that we can tolerate. Because of the enormous responsibility one bears in conducting custody mediation, it is essential that the mediator be fully knowledgable, trained, and competent in doing this kind of work.

Mediators who are attorneys need to be aware of the pain experienced by divorcing spouses. These couples must be dealt with sensitively and compassionately. The strategies detailed in this book are not the same as attorneys' strategies which are dispassionate legal maneuvers. The strategies of children and spouses are their ways of coping with the emotional pain of the divorce. As such, they must be understood in terms of their emotional roots, as complex expressions of a stress that can be neither overlooked nor manipulated away. Mediation work by attorneys requires that they maintain the interpersonal sensitivity and emotional understanding required of mental health professionals. Attorneys who want to develop their custody mediation skills should consider taking courses or professional workshops in child development, family dynamics, and clinical interviewing of couples, families, and children. Doing co-mediation work with an experienced custody mediator can provide an excellent opportunity for supervised training and experience.

Mediators who are mental health professionals need also to be well versed in child development and in marital and family dynamics. Moreover, they need to be thoroughly familiar with the legal practices and procedures of family law within their local areas of jurisdiction. In particular, they need to be fully aware of the various legal options locally available to couples who are making postdivorce parenting arrangements. Working together with an experienced attorney who specializes in family law is a useful way for the mental health professional to get access to legal information and advice on the pertinent legal literature.

Both therapists and lawyers who want information on specific training in family mediation can contact the following national organizations dealing with mediation:

Association of Family and Conciliation Courts
2680 Southwest Glen Eagles Road
Lake Oswego, Oregon 97034

Family Mediation Association
9308 Bulls Run Parkway
Bethesda, Maryland 20817

Academy of Family Mediators
Box 246
Claremont, California 91711

American Association for Mediated Divorce
5435 Balboa Boulevard, Suite 208
Encino, California 91316

For a comprehensive current list of mediation centers offering training, and of universities offering graduate degrees in divorce and family mediation, see the excellent article by Brown (1982).

When spouses approach attorneys for assistance in a custody dispute, they are emotionally polarized and may appear angry, spiteful, and vindictive. If the attorney is to be optimally helpful, he or she must understand and pay attention to the hurt and scared feelings that lie beneath the surface. Out of such vulnerable feelings arise the many coping strategies that spouses utilize. Attorneys who respond only to the surface requests for aggressive legal action while ignoring the emotional context in which such requests arise encourage actions that ultimately have destructive consequences for the children.

Once attorneys begin to appreciate the complex and systemic nature of family dynamics, they will see that there are no heroes or villains in family disputes, only participants who have reciprocal roles in the family system. Even though, ethically, attorneys may feel a need to maintain their prescribed role as advocates for their clients, it would behoove them to learn to view the client within the family context. From this perspective, it becomes apparent that the interests of the client can best be served by reducing the destructive effects of divorce on the client's children. And this can best be accomplished by minimizing adversarial efforts and maximizing mediational efforts. Attorneys can accomplish this by repeatedly emphasizing to their clients the serious risks to their children of custody litigation and by informing them of the proven benefits of mediation. If more clients received strong, supportive, and convincing premediation preparation from their attorneys, then more would come to accept mediation as the better alternative and couples would, no doubt, more easily reach lasting agreements. To the degree that their attorneys are supportive and encouraging of mediation, most couples will strive to make it work. And to the degree that it works, attorneys will have more satisfied clients with children who will grow up psychologically healthy in spite of the trauma of their parents' divorce.

While judges are bound to function within the boundaries of, and serve as models for, established legal practices, they paradoxically also have wide discretionary powers in matters of family law. Hence, in a given custody dispute case, they may choose from a range of judicial options, from hearing the case within the traditional adversarial context to ordering that the case be settled in mediation. When a judge is strongly supportive of mediation as the better way to resolve custody and visitation disputes, the attorneys and their clients tend to settle the dispute outside of litigation (King, 1979). Moreover, as attorneys in a community experience a local judge's strong support of mediation, they will more readily advise their clients to seriously consider mediation efforts. Because local court attitudes and decisions set a climate of expectations for attorneys regarding likely case outcomes, judges have the power to gradually influence the attitudes of disputing spouses via their attorneys. After a time, a ripple effect sets in and further shifts the consciousness and actions of divorcing parents within a community toward cooperative and self-determined settlements of their disputes.

Perhaps we can best end this book with a legendary story of Japanese dispute resolution, looking to history for an ideal for the future:

> This is a story about a trial during the Tokugawa period which is suggestive of the Japanese concept of adjudication. One day, so the story goes, a plasterer picked up on the road a purse containing three *ryo.* (A *ryo* is an old Japanese gold coin.) The purse also contained a piece of paper identifying a certain carpenter as its owner. The plasterer took the trouble of locating the carpenter to return the purse. For all his pains the plasterer was told by the carpenter: "Since the purse elected to slip out of my pocket, I don't want such ungrateful money. Go away with the money." The plasterer insisted that the money belonged to the carpenter. Thereupon a brawl started and finally they agreed to take the case to arbitration by the Lord Ooka of Echizen. Having heard the story from both sides, the Lord added one *ryo* to the three *ryo,* split the sum into two, handed two *ryo* to each party, and announced: "My good men, this is my decision. The plasterer could have gained three *ryo* if he had walked away as the carpenter told him to do. By this decision, he will end up with two *ryo,* so he is to lose one *ryo.* The carpenter could have recovered all three *ryo* if he had accepted the plasterer's kindness with a good grace. Instead he refused to accept the purse. By this decision, he is to lose one *ryo.* I also have to contribute one *ryo.* So each of the three is to end up with one *ryo* less" [Tanaka, 1976, pp. 306–307].

Appendix A
California Statutes Regarding Joint Custody

Civil Code

Sec. 4600:

(a) The Legislature finds and declares that it is the public policy of this state to assure minor children of frequent and continuing contact with both parents after the parents have separated or dissolved their marriage, and to encourage parents to share the rights and responsibilities of child rearing in order to effect this policy.

In any proceeding where there is at issue the custody of a minor child, the court may, during the pendency of the proceeding or at any time thereafter, make such order for the custody of the child during minority as may seem necessary or proper. If a child is of sufficient age and capacity to reason so as to form an intelligent preference as to custody, the court shall consider and give due weight to the wishes of the child in making an award of custody or modification thereof. In determining the person or persons to whom custody shall be awarded under paragraph (2) or (3) of subdivision (b), the court shall consider and give due weight to the nomination of a guardian of the person of the child by a parent under Article 1 (commencing with Section 1500) of Chapter 1 of Part 2 of Division 4 of the Probate Code.

(b) Custody should be awarded in the following order of preference according to the best interests of the child:

(1) To both parents jointly pursuant to Section 4600.5 or to either parent. In making an order for custody to either parent, the court shall consider, among other factors, which parent is more likely to allow the child or children frequent and continuing contact with the noncustodial parent, and shall not prefer a parent as custodian because of that parent's sex.

The court, in its discretion, may require the parents to submit to the court a plan for the implementation of the custody order.

(2) If to neither parent, to the person or persons in whose home the child has been living in a wholesome and stable environment.

(3) To any other person or persons deemed by the court to be suitable and able to provide adequate and proper care and guidance for the child.

(c) Before the court makes any order awarding custody to a person or persons other than a parent, without the consent of the parents, it shall make a finding that an award of custody to a parent would be detrimental to the child and the award to a nonparent is required to serve the best interests of the child. Allegations that parental custody would be detrimental to the child, other than a statement of that ultimate fact, shall not appear in the pleadings. The court may, in its discretion, exclude the public from the hearing on this issue.

Sec. 4600.5:

(a) There shall be a presumption, affecting the burden of proof, that joint custody is in the best interests of a minor child where the parents have agreed to an award of joint custody or so agree in open court at a hearing for the purpose of determining the custody of the minor child or children of the marriage.

If the court declines to enter an order awarding joint custody pursuant to this subdivision, the court shall state in its decision the reasons for denial of an award of joint custody.

(b) Upon the application of either parent, joint custody may be awarded in the discretion of the court in other cases. For the purpose of assisting the court in making a determination whether an award of joint custody is appropriate under this subdivision, the court may direct that an investigation be conducted pursuant to the provisions of Section 4602. If the court declines to enter an order awarding joint custody pursuant to this subdivision, the court shall state in its decision the reasons for denial of an award of joint custody.

(c) For the purposes of this section, "joint custody" means an order awarding custody of the minor child or children to both parents and providing that physical custody shall be shared by the parents in such a way as to assure the child or children of frequent and continuing contact with both parents; provided, however, that such order may award joint legal custody without awarding joint physical custody.

(d) Any order for joint custody may be modified or terminated upon the petition of one or both parents or on the court's own motion if it is shown that the best interests of the child require modification or termination of the order. The court shall state in its decision the reasons for modification or termination of the joint custody order if either parent opposes the modification or termination order.

(e) Any order for the custody of the minor child or children of a marriage entered by a court in this state or any other state may, subject to the jurisdictional requirements set forth in Sections 5152 and 5163, be modified at any time to an order of joint custody in accordance with the provisions of this section.

(f) In counties having a conciliation court, the court or the parties may, at any time, pursuant to local rules of court, consult with the conciliation court for the purpose of assisting the parties to formulate a plan for implementation of the custody order or to resolve any controversy which has arisen in the implementation of a plan for custody.

(g) Notwithstanding any other provision of law, access to records and information pertaining to a minor child, including but not limited to medical, dental, and school records, shall not be denied to a parent because such parent is not the child's custodial parent.

Appendix B
California Statutes Regarding Mandatory Mediation

Civil Code

Sec. 4607:

(a) Where it appears on the face of the petition or other application for an order or modification of an order for the custody or visitation of a child or children that either or both such issues are contested, as provided in Section 4600, 4600.1 or 4601, the matter shall be set for mediation of the contested issues prior to or concurrent with the setting of the matter for hearing. The purpose of such mediation proceeding shall be to reduce acrimony which may exist between the parties and to develop an agreement assuring the child or children's close and continuing contact with both parents after the marriage is dissolved. The mediator shall use his or her best efforts to effect a settlement of the custody or visitation dispute.

(b) Each superior court shall make available a mediator. Such mediator may be a member of the professional staff of a family conciliation court, probation department, or mental health services agency, or may be any other person or agency designated by the court. In order to provide mediation services, the court shall not be required to institute a family conciliation court. The mediator shall meet the minimum qualifications required of a counselor of conciliation as provided in Section 1745 of the Code of Civil Procedure.

(c) Mediation proceedings shall be held in private and shall be confidential, and all communications, verbal or written, from the parties to the mediator made in a proceeding pursuant to this section shall be deemed to be official information within the meaning of Section 1040 of the Evidence Code.

(d) The mediator shall have the authority to exclude counsel from participation in the mediation proceedings where, in the discretion of the mediator, exclusion of counsel is deemed by the mediator to be appropriate or necessary. The mediator shall have the duty to assess the needs and interests of the child or children involved in the controversy and shall be entitled to interview the child or children when the mediator deems such interview appropriate or necessary.

(e) The mediator may, consistent with local court rules, render a recommendation to the court as to the custody or visitation of the child or children. The mediator may, in cases where the parties have not reached agreement as a result of the mediation proceeding, recommend to the court that an investigation be conducted pursuant to Section 4602, or that other action be taken to assist the parties to effect a resolution of the controversy prior to any hearing on the issues. The mediator may, in appropriate cases, recommend that mutual restraining orders be issued, pending determination of the controversy, to protect the well-being of the children involved in the controversy. Any agreement reached by the parties as a result of mediation shall be reported to the court and to counsel for the parties by the mediator on the day set for mediation or any time thereafter designated by the court.

(f) The provisions of this section shall become operative on January 1, 1981.

Appendix C

California Statutes Regarding Family Conciliation Courts

Code of Civil Procedure

Article 2. Family Conciliation Courts

Sec. 1740:

Each superior court shall exercise the jurisdiction conferred by this chapter, and while sitting in the exercise of such jurisdiction shall be known and referred to as the "family conciliation court."

Sec. 1741:

In counties having more than one judge of the superior court, the presiding judge of such court shall annually, in the month of January, designate at least one judge to hear all cases under this chapter. The judge or judges so designated shall hold as many sessions of the family conciliation court in each week as are necessary for the prompt disposition of the business before the court.

Sec. 1742:

The judge of the family conciliation court may transfer any case before the family conciliation court pursuant to this chapter to the department of the presiding judge of the superior court for assignment for trial or other proceedings by another judge of the court, whenever in the opinion of the judge of the family conciliation court such transfer is necessary to expedite the business of the family conciliation court or to insure the prompt consideration of the case. When any case is so transferred, the judge to whom it is transferred shall act as the judge of the family conciliation court in the matter.

Sec. 1743:

The presiding judge of the superior court may appoint a judge of the superior court other than the judge of the family conciliation court to act as judge of the family conciliation court during any period when the judge of the family conciliation court is on vacation, absent, or for any reason unable to perform his duties. Any judge so appointed shall have all of the powers and authority of a judge of the family conciliation court in cases under this chapter.

Sec. 1744:

In each county in which a family conciliation court is established, or in which counties have by contract established joint family conciliation court services, the superior court or the superior courts in contracting counties jointly may appoint one supervising counselor of conciliation and one secretary to assist the family conciliation court in disposing of its business and carrying out its functions.

The supervising counselor of conciliation so appointed shall have the power to:

(a) Hold conciliation conferences with parties to, and hearings in proceedings under this chapter and make recommendations concerning such proceedings to the judge of the family conciliation court.

(b) Provide such supervision in connection with the exercise of his jurisdiction as the judge of the family conciliation court may direct.

(c) Cause such reports to be made, such statistics to be compiled and such records to be kept as the judge of the family conciliation court may direct.

(d) Hold such hearings in all family conciliation court cases as may be required by the judge of the family conciliation court, and make such investigations as may be required by the court to carry out the intent of this chapter.

(e) Make recommendations relating to preage marriages.

(f) Make investigations, reports and recommendations as provided in Section 281 of the Welfare and Institutions Code under the authority provided the probation officer in such code.

(g) Act as domestic relations cases investigator.

(h) Conduct mediation of child custody and visitation disputes.

The superior court, or contracting superior courts, may also appoint, with the consent of the board of supervisors, such associate counselors of conciliation and other office assistants as may be necessary to assist the family conciliation court in disposing of its business. Such associate counselors shall carry out their duties under the supervision of the supervising counselor of conciliation and shall have the powers of the supervising counselor of conciliation. Office assistants shall work under the supervision and direction of the supervising counselor of conciliation.

The classification and salaries of persons appointed under this section shall be determined by the board of supervisors of the county which by contract has the responsibility to administer funds of the joint family conciliation court service, or by the board of supervisors of the county in which a noncontracting family conciliation court operates.

Sec. 1745:

(a) Any person employed as a supervising counselor of conciliation or as an associate counselor of conciliation shall have the following minimum qualifications:

(1) A master's degree in psychology, social work, marriage, family and child counseling, or other behavioral science substantially related to marriage and family interpersonal relationships.

(2) At least two years' experience in counseling or psychotherapy, or both, preferably in a setting related to the areas of responsibility of the family conciliation court and with the ethnic population to be served.

(3) Knowledge of the court system of California and the procedures used in family law cases.

(4) Knowledge of other resources in the community to which clients can be referred for assistance.

(5) Knowledge of adult psychopathology and the psychology of families.

(6) Knowledge of child development, clinical issues relating to children, the effects of divorce on children, and child custody research sufficient to enable a counselor to assess the mental health needs of children.

(b) The family conciliation court may substitute additional experience for a portion of the education, or additional education for a portion of the experience, required under subdivision (a).

(c) The provisions of this section shall be met by all counselors of conciliation not later than January 1, 1984, provided that this section shall not apply to any supervising counselor of conciliation who is in office on the effective date of this section.

Sec. 1746:

The probation officer in every county shall give such assistance to the family conciliation court as the court may request to carry out the purposes of this chapter, and to that end the probation officer shall, upon request, make investigations and reports as requested, and in cases pursuant to this chapter, shall exercise all the powers and perform all the duties granted or imposed by the laws of this state relating to probation or to probation officers.

Sec. 1747:

Notwithstanding the provisions of Section 124, all superior court hearings or conferences in proceedings under this chapter shall be held in private and the court shall exclude all persons except the officers of the court, the parties, their counsel and witnesses. Conferences may be held with each party and his counsel separately and in the discretion of the judge, commissioner or counselor conducting the conference or hearing, counsel for one party may be excluded when the adverse party is present. All communications, verbal or written, from parties to the judge, commissioner or counselor in a proceeding under this chapter shall be deemed to be official information within the meaning of Section 1040 of the Evidence Code.

The files of the family conciliation court shall be closed. The petition, supporting affidavit, conciliation agreement and any court order made in the matter may be opened to inspection by any party of his counsel upon the written authority of the judge of the family conciliation court.

Sec. 1748:

Upon order of the judge of the family conciliation court, the supervising counselor of conciliation may destroy any record, paper, or document filed or kept in the office of the supervising counselor of conciliation which is more than two years old, except records of child custody or visitation mediation, which may be destroyed when the minor or minors involved are 18 years of age. In his discretion the judge of the family conciliation court may order the microfilming of any such record, paper, or document.

Sec. 1749:

(a) Any county may contract with any other county or counties to provide joint family conciliation court services.

(b) Any agreement between two or more counties for the operation of a joint family conciliation court service may provide that the treasurer of one participating county shall be the custodian of moneys made available for the purposes of such joint services, and that the treasurer may make payments from such moneys upon audit of the appropriate auditing officer or body of the county for which he is treasurer.

(c) Any agreement between two or more counties for the

operation of a joint family conciliation court service may also provide:

(1) For the joint provision or operation of services and facilities or for the provision or operation of services and facilities by one participating county under contract for the other participating counties.

(2) For appointments of members of the staff of the family conciliation court including the supervising counselor.

(3) That, for specified purposes, the members of the staff of the family conciliation court including the supervising counselor, but excluding the judges of the family conciliation court and other court personnel, shall be considered to be employees of one participating county.

(4) For such other matters as are necessary or proper to effectuate the purposes of the Family Conciliation Court Law.

(d) The provisions of this chapter relating to family conciliation court services provided by a single county shall be equally applicable to counties which contract, pursuant to this section, to provide joint family conciliation court services.

Article 3. Proceedings for Conciliation

Sec. 1760:

Whenever any controversy exists between spouses, or between parents regardless of their marital status when such controversy relates to child custody or visitation, which may, unless a reconciliation is achieved, result in the dissolution or annulment of the marriage or in the disruption of the household, and there is any minor child of the spouses or parents or of either of them whose welfare might be affected thereby, the family conciliation court shall have jurisdiction over the controversy, and over the parties thereto and all persons having any relation to the controversy as further provided in this chapter.

The family conciliation court shall also have jurisdiction over the controversy, whether or not there is any minor child of the parties or either of them, where such controversy involves domestic violence.

Sec. 1761:

Prior to the filing of any proceeding for determination of custody or visitation rights, dissolution of marriage, legal separation, or judgment of nullity of a voidable marriage, either spouse or parent, or both, may file in the family conciliation court a petition invoking the jurisdiction of the court for the purpose of preserving the marriage by effecting a reconciliation between the parties, or for amicable settlement of the controversy between the spouses or parents, so as to avoid further litigation over the issue involved.

Sec. 1762:

The petition shall be captioned substantially as follows:

In the Superior Court of the State of California
in and for the County of ______________

<table>
<tr><td>Upon the petition of
____
(Petitioner)
And concerning
__________________ and
____
__________, Respondents</td><td>Petition for
Conciliation
(Under the Family
Conciliation
Court Law)</td></tr>
</table>

To the Family Conciliation Court:

Sec. 1763:

The petition shall:

(a) Allege that a controversy exists between the spouses or parents and request the aid of the court to effect a reconciliation or an amicable settlement of the controversy.

(b) State the name and age of each minor child whose welfare may be affected by the controversy.

(c) State the name and age of the petitioner, or the names and addresses of the petitioners.

(d) If the petition is presented by one spouse or parent only, the name of the other spouse or parent as a respondent, and state the address of that spouse or parent.

(e) Name as a respondent any other person who has any relation to the controversy, and state the address of the person, if known to the petitioner.

(f) If the petition arises out of an instance of domestic violence, so state generally and without specific allegations as to the incident.

(g) State such other information as the court may by rule require.

Sec. 1764:

The clerk of the court shall provide, at the expense of the county, blank forms for petitions for filing pursuant to this chapter. The probation officers of the county and the attaches and employees of the family conciliation court shall assist any person in the preparation and presentation of any such petition, when any person requests such assistance. All public officers in each county shall refer to the family conciliation court all petitions and complaints made to them in respect to controversies within the jurisdiction of the family conciliation court. The jurisdiction of the family conciliation court in respect to controversies arising out of an instance of domestic violence shall not be exclusive, but shall be coextensive with any other remedies either civil or criminal in nature that may be available.

Sec. 1765:

No fee shall be charged by any officer for filing the petition.

Sec. 1766:

The court shall fix a reasonable time and place for hearing on the petition, and shall cause such notice of the filing of the petition and of the time and place of the hearing as it deems necessary to be given to the respondents. The court may, when it deems it necessary, issue a citation to any respondent requiring him to appear at the time and place stated in the citation, and may require the attendance of witnesses as in other civil cases.

Sec. 1767:

For the purpose of conducting hearings pursuant to this chapter, the family conciliation court may be convened at any time and place within the county, and the hearing may be had in chambers or otherwise, except that the time and place for hearing shall not be different from the time and place provided by law for the trial of civil actions if any party, prior to the hearing, objects to any different time or place.

Sec. 1768:

The hearing shall be conducted informally as a conference or a series of conferences to effect a reconciliation of the spouses or an amicable adjustment or settlement of the issues in controversy. To facilitate and promote the purposes of this act the court may, with the consent of both parties to the proceeding, recommend or invoke the aid of medical or other specialists or scientific experts, or of the pastor or director of any religious denomination to which the parties may belong. Such aid, however, shall not be at the expense of the court or of the county unless the board of supervisors of the county specifically provides and authorizes such aid.

Sec. 1769:

(a) At or after the hearing, the court may make such orders in respect to the conduct of the spouses or parents and the subject matter of the controversy as the court deems necessary to preserve the marriage or to implement the reconciliation of the spouses, but in no event shall such orders be effective for more than 30 days from the hearing of the petition, unless the parties mutually consent to a continuation of such time.

(b) Any reconciliation agreement between the parties may be reduced to writing and, with the consent of the parties, a court order may be made requiring the parties to comply fully therewith.

(c) During the pendency of any proceeding under this chapter, the superior court may order the husband or wife, or father or mother, as the case may be, to pay any amount that is necessary for the support and maintenance of the wife or husband and for the support, maintenance and education of the minor children, as the case may be. In determining the amount, the superior court may take into consideration the recommendations of a financial referee when such referee is available to the court. An order made pursuant to this subdivision shall not prejudice the rights of the parties or children with respect to any subsequent order which may be made. Any such order may be modified or revoked at any time except as to any amount that may have accrued prior to the date of filing of the notice of motion or order to show cause to modify or revoke.

Sec. 1770:

During a period beginning upon the filing of the petition for conciliation and continuing until 30 days after the hearing of the petition for conciliation, neither spouse shall file any petition for dissolution of marriage, legal separation, or judgment of nullity of a voidable marriage.

If, however, after the expiration of such period, the controversy between the spouses, or the parents, has not been terminated, either spouse may institute proceedings for dissolution of marriage, legal separation, or a judgment of nullity of a voidable marriage, or a proceeding to determine custody or visitation of the minor child or children. The pendency of a proceeding for dissolution of marriage, legal separation, or declaration of nullity, or a proceeding to determine custody or visitation of the minor child or children, shall not operate as a bar to the instituting of proceedings for conciliation under this chapter.

Sec. 1771:

Whenever any petition for dissolution of marriage, legal separation, or declaration of nullity of a voidable marriage is filed in the superior court, and it appears to the court at any time during the pendency of the proceedings that there is any minor child of the spouses, or of either of them, whose welfare may be adversely affected by the dissolution of the marriage or the disruption of the household or a controversy involving child custody, and that there appears to be some reasonable possibility of a reconciliation being effected, the case may be transferred to the family conciliation court for proceedings for reconciliation of the spouses or amicable settlement of issues in controversy in accordance with the provisions of this chapter.

Sec. 1772:

Whenever application is made to the family conciliation court for conciliation proceedings in respect to a controversy between spouses, or a contested proceeding for dissolution of marriage, legal separation, or judgment of nullity of a voidable marriage, but there is no minor child whose welfare may be affected by the results of the controversy, and it appears to the court that reconciliation of the spouses or amicable adjustment of the controversy can probably be achieved, and that the work of the court in cases involving children will not be seriously impeded by acceptance of the case, the court may accept and dispose of the case in the same manner as similar cases involving the welfare of children are disposed of. In the event of such application and acceptance, the court shall have the same jurisdiction over the controversy and the parties thereto or having any relation thereto that it has under this chapter in similar cases involving the welfare of children.

Government Code

Sec. 26840.3:

(a) The superior court in any county may, for the support of the family conciliation court or for conciliation and mediation services provided pursuant to Section 4607 of the Civil Code, upon action of the board of supervisors to provide all space costs and indirect overhead costs from other sources, increase:

(1) The fee for filing a petition, except a joint petition filed pursuant to Section 4551 of the Civil Code, for dissolution of a marriage, legal separation, or nullity of a marriage, and the fee for a response to such a petition, by an amount not to exceed fifteen dollars ($15).

(2) The fee for issuing a marriage license, by an amount not to exceed five dollars ($5).

(3) The fee for issuing a marriage certificate pursuant to Section 4213 of the Civil Code, by an amount not to exceed five dollars ($5).

(b) The funds shall be paid to the county treasury and an amount equal thereto shall be used exclusively to pay the costs of maintaining the family conciliation court or conciliation and mediation services provided pursuant to Section 4607 of the Civil Code.

Appendix D
Confidentiality Forms

Form used in Private Mediation

AGREEMENT RE: CONFIDENTIALITY OF MEDIATION SERVICES

IT IS HEREBY STIPULATED AND AGREED by and between ____________ and ____________ AS FOLLOWS:

1. We are making this agreement because we have not agreed with each other on the custody and/or visitation privileges regarding our child(ren). We both would like to make decisions which are in the best interests of our child(ren), and we both feel that it would be best if we could settle these differences without a court fight.

2. In order to facilitate our making good decisions for our child(ren) we have agreed to hire a mediator, who, as we understand it, will not make our decisions for us, but will simply help us make our own decisions, together.

3. We recognize that in order to reach good decisions about this matter, we need to be able to talk in a frank, open,

and honest atmosphere. In order to further the presence of this atmosphere, we agree that the mediation services of Dr. Donald T. Saposnek, his records, and all disclosures made in connection with mediation services rendered by him shall be deemed to be of a privileged, confidential nature and therefore will not be revealed to anyone. All communications between the parties and Dr. Saposnek and between the children of the parties and Dr. Saposnek shall be protected from disclosure by Dr. Saposnek as provided for in Section 1014 of the Evidence Code of the State of California, and no party to this agreement shall waive such privilege, regardless of whether disclosures are made in the presence of both parties. The privilege shall not be waived without the express written consent of both parties and Dr. Donald T. Saposnek.

4. In the absence of such written consent, neither party shall subpoena the records of Dr. Donald T. Saposnek or seek to take testimony from him in connection with the above or any other proceeding, or act in any other way to divulge the records or communications to third parties.

5. No change may be made in this stipulation without the written approval of Dr. Saposnek.

6. Either party or Dr. Saposnek may at any time file this stipulation in the court records of the above proceeding.

7. Dr. Saposnek's mediation fees shall be paid at the end of each mediation session. We agree that we will each pay one-half of the fee for each session, unless we agree to a different arrangement for fee payment.

Dated:_______________ ________________________
Mother

Dated:_______________ ________________________
Father

Dated:_______________ ________________________
Donald T. Saposnek, Ph.D.

Form used by court-appointed mediators for mandatory mediation

FAMILY MEDIATION SERVICE

AGREEMENT REGARDING CONFIDENTIALITY OF MEDIATION SERVICES

IT IS HEREBY STIPULATED AND AGREED by and between ____________ and ____________ AS FOLLOWS:

1. In entering mediation, we recognize that in order to reach good decisions about this matter, we need to be able to talk in a frank, open, and honest atmosphere. In order to further the presence of this atmosphere, we agree that the mediation services of our mediator, his/her records, and all disclosures made in connection with mediation services rendered by him/her shall be deemed to be of a privileged, confidential nature and therefore will not be revealed to anyone. All communications between the parties and our mediator and between the children of the parties and our mediator shall be protected from disclosure by our mediator as provided for in Section 1014 of the Evidence Code of the State of California, and no party to this agreement shall waive such privilege, regardless of whether disclosures are made in the presence of both parties. The privilege shall not be waived without the express written consent of both parties and our mediator.

2. In the absence of such written consent, neither party shall subpoena the records of our mediator or seek to take testimony from him/her in connection with the above or any other proceeding, or act in any other way to divulge the records or communications to third parties.

3. No change may be made in this stipulation without the written approval of our mediator.

4. Either party or our mediator may at any time file this stipulation in the court records of the above proceeding.

Dated: ________________ ______________________________
Mother

Dated: ________________ ______________________________
Father

Dated: ________________ ______________________________
Mediator

Appendix E
Sample Mediation Agreements

Sample Agreement A

1. Both parents agree to share joint legal custody of their children, Brandon and Lilia.
2. The children will share time with their parents according to the following schedule:
   (a) Brandon will be with Mother on Monday and Tuesday, and Friday, Saturday, and Sunday of the first week, and on Tuesday, Wednesday, and Thursday of the second week, with this pattern repeating on a biweekly basis. Brandon will be with Father on the other days.
   (b) Lilia will be with Mother on Friday, Saturday, and Sunday of the first week, and on Wednesday of the second week, with this pattern repeating on a biweekly basis. Lilia will be with Father on the other days.
   (c) This plan will begin January 1, 1983, and will continue until March 1, 1983, at which time Mother and Father will evaluate the progress and negotiate a modification, if necessary.

3. During the transfer times within the above plan, Father will pick up the children from their grandmother's house at the start of the children's time with him, and he will return the children to Mother's house at the end of the children's time with him.
4. Both children will spend alternate holidays with each parent throughout the year, with details to be arranged between the parents.
5. Both parents agree to inform each other of the location and duration of any special trips taken with the children.
6. Both parents agree to consult directly with each other rather than through either of the children, in the event of an issue arising regarding the children.
7. Both parents agree to allow both children to have totally open access by phone to either parent at any time.
8. In the event of any future dispute regarding the children which the parents are unable to resolve between themselves, both parents agree to seek mediation before legal action.

________________	________________	__________
Mother	Father	Date

____

Mediator

Sample Agreement B

1. Both parents agree to share joint legal custody of Lynette.
2. Lynette will share time with her parents according to the following schedule, until December 1, 1982:
   (a) Lynette will be with Mother from Tuesdays at 8 A.M. to Saturdays at 2 P.M.
   (b) Lynette will be with Father from Saturdays at 2 P.M. to Tuesdays at 8 A.M.
   (c) Details of transfer times will be arranged between the parents.
3. Beginning December 1, 1982, Lynette will stay at Mother's house four days and four nights, and at Father's house three

days and three nights, with details to be arranged between the parents to fit with their schedules at that time.

4. By March 1983, both parents agree to have worked out their schedules so that they have reached their goal of equalizing the time that Lynette spends with each of them.
5. The sharing of time with Lynette during holidays will be arranged between the parents.
6. Both parents agree to minimize the number of primary caretakers that care for Lynette.
7. Both parents agree to call each other any time there is any special concern regarding Lynette that needs sharing with the other parent.
8. During the summer before Lynette enters kindergarten, both parents will reevaluate the time-sharing plan either between themselves or together with a mediator if necessary.
9. In the event of any future dispute regarding Lynette which the parents are unable to resolve between themselves, both parents agree to seek mediation before legal action.

________________ ________________ __________

Mother Father Date

____

Mediator

Sample Agreement C

1. Both parents agree that Mother shall retain sole legal custody of their children, Scott and Jason.
2. During the school year, the children will reside at Mother's house and be with Father every other weekend, from Friday after school until Sunday at 8 P.M. Also, the children will be with Father on alternate Saturday afternoons, from 1 P.M. until 5 P.M.
3. During the summers and holidays, Father agrees to make direct plans with the children on an event-by-event basis. The children will make every effort possible to spend a

significant amount of available time with Father, and Mother agrees to not interfere with these plans, either by making counter-plans or by discouraging the plans already made.

4. Mother agrees to send certain children's clothing (with an itemized list) to Father's house which will remain at Father's house after the children return to Mother's house, for the children to use upon their subsequent stays at Father's house.
5. Both parents agree to place any written communications to each other that pertain to an issue of dispute between them in a sealed envelope, before transferring the note to the other parent.
6. Both parents agree to ask the children about where they would like to keep any gifts they receive, and the children's desires will be respected.
7. Both parents agree to inform each other whenever either of the children has any illness or doctor's appointments.
8. Mother agrees to sign and file a permission slip for Father to receive any information about the educational and medical status and condition of the children at any time he wishes.
9. Father agrees to issue health insurance identification cards to each of the children.
10. Mother agrees to indicate in writing that Father is designated "next of kin" on the children's school records.
11. Father agrees to have the children in bed by 10 P.M. on the nights that they are with him.
12. Both parents agree to refrain from bad-mouthing each other and each other's extended family members in the presence of the children.
13. Both parents agree to discuss small issues that may come up regarding the children between themselves. These discussions will take place when transferring the children. If one parent feels the need for more lengthy discussion, it will take place during a designated phone call. If this still is not satisfactory, then a face-to-face meeting on neutral ground, away from the children, will be arranged by the parents to resolve the matter.

14. In the event of any future dispute regarding the children that the parents are unable to resolve between themselves, both parents agree to seek mediation before legal action.

____________________	____________________	___________
Mother	Father	Date

____

Mediator

Sample Agreement D

1. Both parents agree to share joint legal custody of their children, Danielle and Nathan.
2. The children will share time with their parents according to the following schedule, during the school year:
   (a) Danielle's primary residence will be at Mother's house.
   (b) Nathan's primary residence will be at Father's house.
   (c) Both children together will spend alternate weekends with each parent.
   (d) Fridays between 6 P.M. and 6:15 P.M., the parent who is to have both children for the weekend will pick up the second child at the other parent's house.
   (e) Sundays between 8 P.M. and 8:15 P.M., the parent who does not have the children for the weekend will pick up the child whose primary residence is with that parent from the other parent's house.
   (f) Wednesdays between 6 P.M. and 6:30 P.M., Father will bring Nathan to Mother's house and will pick up Danielle.
   (g) Thursdays between 7:30 A.M. and 7:45 A.M., Mother will bring Nathan to Father's house. Father will be responsible for caretaking of Danielle until 5:15 P.M. on Thursdays.
   (h) Thursdays between 5 P.M. and 5:15 P.M., Mother will pick up Danielle from Father's house.

3. Time in the summers will be shared as follows:
   (a) During the months of June and September, the regular school-year schedule will be followed.
   (b) Both children will spend the month of July with Mother, and the month of August with Father.
   (c) During July and August, the children will spend the equivalent of four twenty-four-hour periods with the parent with whom they are not staying. Details for this will be arranged between the parents.
4. If either child goes to summer camp (not to exceed two weeks), the time will be divided and reduced equally from each parent's equivalent time with the child.
5. Holidays will be shared according to the following schedule:
   (a) The children will be with Mother during Thanksgiving vacation from Wednesday after school until Friday evening at 6:30 P.M., at which time Father will pick them up; on Christmas Eve day until 11 P.M., at which time Father will pick them up; on New Year's Day; on Mother's Day; on Mother's birthday; and on Memorial Day weekend.
   (b) The children will be with Father on Halloween; during Thanksgiving vacation from Friday evening at 6:30 P.M. until Sunday at 5 P.M.; on Easter Day; on Father's Day; on Father's birthday; on the Fourth of July; and on Labor Day weekend.
   (c) Except for Father's Day, Mother's Day, and Father's and Mother's respective birthdays, the above holiday time-sharing schedule will alternate yearly.
   (d) The children's birthdays will be celebrated with each parent on the weekend before or after the specific day of birth.
6. If either parent is unavailable to care for either child during his or her regular time with the child, both parents agree to request first that the other parent caretake, before making other childcare arrangements. It is agreed that the requested parent has the option of turning down the request, without needing to give any reason, and without being under any obligation.

7. Both parents agree to negotiate with each other any occasional changes in the above schedule for any unanticipated special events that may come up. It is understood that such opportunities would be for the benefit of the children.
8. Both parents agree to refrain from being under the influence of alcohol or drugs while with the children, and especially while driving them in any motor vehicle. This also holds true for any other caretakers with whom they may be.
9. Both parents agree to keep both children restrained in seat belts while driving them in any motor vehicle.
10. In the event that a special school activity arises to which parents are invited, both parents agree to inform each other of the event and to discuss and decide between them which parent will go to the particular event with the child(ren).
11. If either parent anticipates a move out of the area, both parents agree to discuss with each other the consequences of the move well in advance. If either parent feels the need for assistance with such discussions, both parents agree to seek a mediator.
12. In the event of any future dispute regarding the children that the parents are unable to resolve between themselves, both parents agree to seek mediation before legal action.

__________________ __________________ __________

Mother Father Date

____

Mediator

References

Appleton, W., and Appleton, J. *How Not to Split Up*. New York: Berkeley Books, 1981.

Aries, P. *Centuries of Childhood: A Social History of Family Life*. New York: Knopf, 1962.

Aronson, E. *The Social Animal*. (3rd ed.) San Francisco: W. H. Freeman, 1980.

Bahr, S. J. "An Evaluation of Court Mediation: A Comparison in Divorce Cases with Children." *Journal of Family Issues*, 1981, *2*, 39-60.

Bateson, G., Jackson, D. D., Haley, J., and Weakland, J. "Toward a Theory of Schizophrenia." *Behavioral Science*, 1956, *1*, 251-264.

Bell, R. Q. "A Reinterpretation of the Direction of Effects in Studies of Socialization." *Psychological Review*, 1968, *75*, 81-95.

Bohannan, P. (Ed.). *Divorce and After: An Analysis of the Emotional and Social Problems of Divorce*. Garden City, N.Y.: Doubleday, 1970.

Brooks-Gunn, J., and Matthews, W. S. *He and She: How Chil-*

dren Develop Their Sex-Role Identity. Englewood Cliffs, N.J.: Prentice-Hall, 1979.

Brown, D. G. "Divorce and Family Mediation: History, Review, Future Directions." *Conciliation Courts Review,* 1982, *20* (2), 1-44.

Budman, S. H. (Ed.). *Forms of Brief Therapy.* New York: Guilford Press, 1981.

Butcher, J. N., and Koss, M. P. "Research on Brief and Crisis-Oriented Psychotherapies." In S. Garfield and A. Bergin (Eds.), *Handbook of Psychotherapy and Behavior Change: An Empirical Analysis.* (2nd ed.) New York: Wiley, 1978.

Clingempeel, W. G., and Reppucci, N. D. "Joint Custody After Divorce: Major Issues and Goals for Research." *Psychological Bulletin,* 1982, *91* (1), 102-127.

Committee on the Family of the Group for the Advancement of Psychiatry. *New Trends in Child Custody Determinations.* Law and Business, Inc./Harcourt Brace Jovanovich, 1980.

Conway, F., and Siegelman, J. *Snapping: America's Epidemic of Sudden Personality Change.* New York: Delta, 1978.

Coogler, O. J. *Structured Mediation in Divorce Settlement.* Lexington, Mass.: Lexington Books, 1978.

Derdeyn, A. P. "A Consideration of Legal Issues in Child Custody Contests: Implications for Change." *Archives of General Psychiatry,* 1976, *33,* 165-171.

Derdeyn, A. P. "Child Custody Contests in Historical Perspective." In S. Chess and A. Thomas (Eds.), *Annual Progress in Child Psychiatry and Child Development.* New York: Brunner/Mazel, 1977.

Deutsch, M. *The Resolution of Conflict: Constructive and Destructive Processes.* New Haven, Conn.: Yale University Press, 1973.

Erickson, M. H., and Rossi, E. *Hypnotherapy: An Exploratory Casebook.* New York: Irvington, 1979.

Fainer, R., and Wasser, D. M. "Child Custody and Visitation Disputes: An Overview." *Los Angeles Lawyer,* July 1978.

Federico, J. "The Marital Termination Period of the Divorce Adjustment Process." *Journal of Divorce,* 1979, *3* (2), 93-106.

Felder, R. L. *Divorce: The Way Things Are, Not the Way Things Should Be.* New York: World, 1971.

Festinger, L. *A Theory of Cognitive Dissonance.* Stanford, Calif.: Stanford University Press, 1957.

Fisch, R., Weakland, J. H., and Segal, L. *The Tactics of Change: Doing Therapy Briefly.* San Francisco: Jossey-Bass, 1982.

Folberg, J. "The Changing Family–Implications for the Law." *Conciliation Courts Review,* 1981, *19,* 1-6.

Folberg, J. Personal communication, September 17, 1982.

Foster, H. H., and Freed, D. J. "Joint Custody: Legislative Reform." *Trial,* 1980, *16,* 22-27.

Frank, J. D. "Therapeutic Components of Psychotherapy: A 25-Year Progress Report of Research." *Journal of Nervous and Mental Disease,* 1974, *159,* 325-342.

Frank, J. D. "Expectation and Therapeutic Outcome–The Placebo Effect and the Role Induction Interview." In J. D. Frank, R. Hoehn-Saric, S. D. Imber, B. L. Liberman, and A. R. Stone, *Effective Ingredients of Successful Psychotherapy.* New York: Brunner/Mazel, 1978.

Goffman, E. *The Presentation of Self in Everyday Life.* New York: Doubleday, 1959.

Goldstein, J., Freud, A., and Solnit, A. J. *Beyond the Best Interests of the Child.* New York: Free Press, 1973.

Haley, J. *Uncommon Therapy: The Psychiatric Techniques of Milton H. Erickson, M.D.* New York: Norton, 1973.

Haley, J. *Problem-Solving Therapy: New Strategies for Effective Family Therapy.* San Francisco: Jossey-Bass, 1976.

Haley, J. Remarks at conference on family therapy. Berkeley, Calif.: May 1979.

Haynes, J. M. *Divorce Mediation: A Practical Guide for Therapists and Counselors.* New York: Springer, 1981.

Hetherington, E. M. "Effects of Father Absence on Personality Development in Adolescent Daughters." *Developmental Psychology,* 1972, *7,* 313-326.

Hetherington, E. M. "Children of Divorce." Talk presented at University of California, Santa Cruz, May 9, 1979.

Hetherington, E. M. "Children and Divorce." In R. W. Henderson (Ed.), *Parent-Child Interaction: Theory, Research, and Prospects.* New York: Academic Press, 1981.

Hetherington, E. M., Cox, M., and Cox, R. "The Aftermath of Divorce." In J. H. Stevens, Jr., and M. Matthews (Eds.), *Mother-Child, Father-Child Relations.* Washington, D.C.: National Association for the Education of Young Children, 1978.

Hetherington, E. M., Cox, M., and Cox, R. "Family Interaction and the Social, Emotional, and Cognitive Development of Children Following Divorce." In V. Vaughn and T. B. Brazelton (Eds.), *The Family: Setting Priorities.* New York: Science and Medicine Publishing Company, 1979.

Hetherington, E. M., and Parke, R. D. (Eds.). *Contemporary Readings in Child Psychology.* (2nd ed.) New York: McGraw-Hill, 1981.

Ilfeld, F. W., Ilfeld, H. Z., and Alexander, J. R. "Does Joint Custody Work? A First Look at Outcome Data of Relitigation." *American Journal of Psychiatry,* 1982, *139,* 62-66.

In re *Marriage of Duke,* January 17, 1980, California Court of Appeal, 4 Civil 18262, Div. 1, 101 CA3d 152, 161 CR 444.

Irving, H. H. *Divorce Mediation: The Rational Alternative.* Toronto: Personal Library, 1980.

Kantor, D., and Lehr, W. *Inside the Family: Toward a Theory of Family Process.* San Francisco: Jossey-Bass, 1975.

Kellam, S. G., Ensminger, M. A., and Turner, J. T. "Family Structure and the Mental Health of Children." *Archives of General Psychiatry,* 1977, *34,* 1012-1022.

Kent, J. *Commentaries on American Law.* Vol. II. New York: O. Halsted, 1826.

Kessler, S. *The American Way of Divorce: Prescriptions for Change.* Chicago: Nelson-Hall, 1975.

King, D. B. "Child Custody—A Legal Problem?" *California State Bar Journal,* 1979, *54* (3), 156-161.

Kressel, K., Jaffe, N., Tuchman, B., Watson, C., and Deutsch, M. "A Typology of Divorcing Couples: Implications for Mediation and the Divorce Process." *Family Process,* 1980, *19* (2), 101-116.

Kurdek, L. A. "An Integrative Perspective on Children's Divorce Adjustment." *American Psychologist,* 1981, *36,* 856-866.

Lasch, C. *The Culture of Narcissism.* New York: Norton, 1978.

Lerner, R. M., and Spanier, G. B. (Eds.). *Child Influences on Marital and Family Interaction: A Life-Span Perspective.* New York: Academic Press, 1978.

Leve, R. *Childhood: The Study of Development.* New York: Random House, 1980.

Lindsley, B. F. "Custody Proceedings: Battlefield or Peace Conference." *Bulletin of the American Academy of Psychiatry and the Law,* 1976, *4,* 127-131.

Maccoby, E. E., and Jacklin, C. N. *The Psychology of Sex Differences.* Stanford, Calif.: Stanford University Press, 1974.

MacGowan, E. "Custody and Visitation." In *Representing Parents and Children in Custody Proceedings.* CAL-CEB (California–Continuing Education of the Bar) Program Booklet. Berkeley: Regents of the University of California, Feb./Mar. 1981.

McIsaac, H. "Mandatory Conciliation Custody/Visitation Matters: California's Bold Stroke." *Conciliation Courts Review,* 1981, *19* (2), 73-81.

McKinney's Consolidated Laws of New York. Vol. 29: *Judiciary Law.* St. Paul, Minn.: McKinney, 1975.

Madanes, C. *Strategic Family Therapy.* San Francisco: Jossey-Bass, 1981.

Milne, A. "Custody of Children in a Divorce Process: A Family Self-Determination Model." *Conciliation Courts Review,* 1978, *16,* 1-10.

Minuchin, S. *Families and Family Therapy.* Cambridge, Mass.: Harvard University Press, 1974.

Minuchin, S., and Fishman, H. C. *Family Therapy Techniques.* Cambridge, Mass.: Harvard University Press, 1981.

Mnookin, R. H., and Kornhauser, L. "Bargaining in the Shadow of the Law: The Case of Divorce." *Yale Law Journal,* 1979, *88,* 950-997.

Neal, J. H. "Children's Understanding of Their Parents and Their Parents' Divorce: A Systems Perspective." Paper presented at the 59th annual meeting of the American Orthopsychiatric Association, San Francisco, March 29-April 3, 1982.

Nehls, N., and Morgenbesser, M. "Joint Custody: An Exploration of the Issues." *Family Process,* 1980, *19,* 117-125.

Oster, A. M. "Custody Proceedings: A Study of Vague and Indefinite Standards." *Journal of Family Law,* 1965, *5,* 21–38.

Pearson, J., and Thoennes, N. "Divorce Mediation: Strengths and Weaknesses over Time." Paper presented at the International Society on Family Law Fourth World Conference, Cambridge, Mass., June 11–16, 1982a.

Pearson, J., and Thoennes, N. "Mediation and Divorce: The Benefits Outweigh the Costs." *Family Advocate,* 1982b, *4,* 26–32.

Pederson, F. A., Rubenstein, J., and Yarrow, L. J. "Infant Development in Father-Absent Families." *Journal of Genetic Psychology,* 1979, *135,* 51–62.

Poll, E. "The Evolution of Joint Custody." *Conciliation Courts Review,* 1981, *19,* 53–59.

Ramos, S. *The Complete Book of Child Custody.* New York: Putnam's, 1979.

Ricci, I. *Mom's House, Dad's House.* New York: Macmillan, 1980.

Roman, M., and Haddad, W. *The Disposable Parent: The Case for Joint Custody.* New York: Holt, Rinehart and Winston, 1978.

Rutter, M. "Protective Factors in Children's Responses to Stress and Disadvantage." In M. W. Kent and J. E. Rolf (Eds.), *Primary Prevention of Psychopathology.* Vol. 3: *Promoting Social Competence and Coping in Children.* Hanover, N.J.: University Press of New England, 1978.

Saposnek, D. T. "Aikido: A Model for Brief Strategic Therapy." *Family Process,* 1980, *19,* 227–238.

Saposnek, D. T. "Short-Term Psychotherapy." In N. Endler and J. McV. Hunt (Eds.), *Personality and the Behavioral Disorders.* (2nd ed.) New York: Wiley, in press.

Saposnek, D. T., Hamburg, J., Delano, C., and Michaelsen, H. "Child Custody Disputes: Outcomes of Mandatory Mediation, Evaluations, and Implications for Social Policy." Paper presented at 60th annual conference of the American Orthopsychiatric Association, Boston, Mass., April 4–8, 1983.

Selvini Palazzolli, M., Boscolo, L., Cecchin, G., and Prata, G.

Paradox and Counterparadox. New York: Jason Aronson, 1978.

Strupp, H. H., Hadley, S. W., and Gomes-Schwarz, B. *Psychotherapy for Better or Worse: The Problem of Negative Effects.* New York: Jason Aronson, 1977.

Tanaka, H. *The Japanese Legal System.* Tokyo: University of Tokyo Press, 1976.

Thomas, A., and Chess, S. *Temperament and Development.* New York: Brunner/Mazel, 1977.

Toffler, A. *The Third Wave.* New York: William Morrow, 1980.

Visher, E. B., and Visher, J. S. *Stepfamilies: A Guide to Working with Stepparents and Stepchildren.* New York: Brunner/Mazel, 1979.

Wallerstein, J. S. "The Effect of Divorce on the Child." Paper presented at the California Chapter of the Association of Family Conciliation Courts Conference on Custody and Visitation for Judges and Mediators, San Francisco, June 1981.

Wallerstein, J. S., and Kelly, J. B. *Surviving the Breakup: How Children and Parents Cope with Divorce.* New York: Basic Books, 1980.

Watzlawick, P. *How Real is Real?* New York: Vintage Books, 1976.

Watzlawick, P. *The Language of Change: Elements of Therapeutic Communication.* New York: Basic Books, 1978.

Watzlawick, P., and Weakland, J. (Eds.). *The Interactional View.* New York: Norton, 1977.

Watzlawick, P., Weakland, J., and Fisch, R. *Change: Principles of Problem Formation and Problem Resolution.* New York: Norton, 1974.

Weiss, R. S. *Marital Separation.* New York: Basic Books, 1975.

Whitaker, C. Remarks during workshop on family therapy. Watsonville, Calif., May 7, 1982.

Wright, D. C. "The New Joint Custody: What it Does and How it Works." *Alameda County Bar Association Bulletin,* 1981, *11* (9), 5–7.

Zeig, J. (Ed.). *A Teaching Seminar with Milton H. Erickson.* New York: Brunner/Mazel, 1980.

Index